D0569760

Quotable
Quotes

THE COOK

Quotable Quotes

THE COOK

Magpie Books

LONDON

Constable & Robinson Ltd
3 The Lanchesters
162 Fulham Palace Road
London W6 9ER
www.constablerobinson.com

This edition published by Magpie Books,
an imprint of Constable & Robinson Ltd 2004

ISBN 1 84529 052 6

Compiled and designed by Tony and Penny Mills

A copy of the British Library Cataloguing in Publications Data
is available from the British Library

Printed and bound in the EU

Contents

MENU

Cooks Praised and Blamed

*A*SKILLED COOK HAS *always been as much of a status symbol as a luxury car or a well turned-out coach and four, and, for many people, given more pleasure and satisfaction. From Roman times until today a cook has been worth his or her weight in gold and just as desirable.*

The discovery of a new dish confers more happiness upon humanity than the discovery of a new star.

JEAN ANTHELME BRILLAT-SAVARIN
(1755–1826)

❖

England can boast of a Spenser, Shakespeare, Milton, and many other illustrious poets, clearly indicating that the national character of Britons is not deficient in imagination; but we have not had one single masculine inventive genius of the kitchen.

Reminiscences of Captain Gronow
1862

❖

A cook today costs as much as a Triumph, a fish as much as a cook, and no human being fetches more than the slave who knows best the art of ruining his master.

PLINY THE ELDER
(AD 23–79)

❖

The Spirit of each dish, and Zest of all,
Is what ingenious Cooks the Relish call;
For though the market sends in loads of food,
They are all tasteless till that makes them good.

Art of Cookery
KING
(18th Century)

❖

The cook was a good cook, as cooks go:
and as cooks go, she went.

'Reginald on Besetting Sins'
Reginald
H.H. MUNRO ('SAKI')
(1870–1916)

8

It has been asserted, that English cookery is, nationally speaking, far from being the best in the world. More than this, we have been frequently told by brilliant foreign writers, half philosophers, half chefs, that we are the worst cooks on the face of the earth.

Book of Household Management
MRS BEETON
(1836–65)

We may live without poetry, music and art;
We may live without conscience, and live
     without heart;
We may live without friends; we may live
     without books;
But civilised man cannot live without
     cooks.

Lucile
EDWARD ROBERT BULWER LYTTON
1ST EARL OF LYTTON
(1831–91)

The English ideal of cooking is the best in the world; it is the aristocratic ideal and consists in the desire to give to each article of food its own especial flavor, whereas French cooking is apt to obliterate all distinctions with a democratic sauce.

My Life and Loves
FRANK HARRIS
(1856–1931)

❖

So much is the blind Folly of this Age, that they would rather be imposed on by a French Booby, than Give Encouragement to a good English Cook!

The Art of Cookery Made Plain and Easy
HANNAH GLASSE
1747

❖

She transferred her attention to the dinner menu, which the boy had thoughtfully brought in as an alternative to the more solid literary fare. 'Rabbit curry' met her eye, and the lines of disapproval deepened on her already puckered brow.

The cook was a great believer in the influence of environment, and nourished an obstinate conviction that if you brought rabbit and curry-powder together in one dish a rabbit curry would be the result.

From 'The Jesting of Arlington Stringham'
Chronicles of Clovis
H.H. MUNRO ('SAKI')
(1870–1916)

What does cookery mean? It means the knowledge of Medea and of Circe, and of Calypso, and Sheba.

It means knowledge of all herbs, and fruits, and balms and spices, and of all that is healing and sweet in grapes and savoury in meat.

It means carefulness, and inventiveness, watchfulness, willingness, and readiness of appliances.

It means the economy of your great-grandmother and the science of modern chemistry, and French art, and Arabian hospitality.

It means, in fine, that you are to see imperatively that everyone has something nice to eat.

JOHN RUSKIN
(1819–1900)

A rich man who does not hire the best of cooks will miss one of life's greatest pleasures.

ANTONIN CARÊME
(1783–1834)

Heaven sends us good meat, but the Devil sends cooks.

DAVID GARRICK
(1717–79)

We could not have had a better dinner, had there been a Synod of cooks.

The Life of Samuel Johnson
JAMES BOSWELL
(1740–95)

❖

He cooked a fish so exquisitely, that it returned him admiring and grateful looks from the frying pan.

Coquus Gloriosus
PHILEMON
(361–262 BC)

Too many cooks
spoil the broth.

PROVERB

'But what,' said Bella, as she watched the carving of the fowls, 'makes them pink inside, I wonder, Pa! Is it the breed?'

'No, I don't think it's the breed, my dear,' returned Pa. 'I rather think it's because they are not done.'

'They ought to be,' said Bella.

'Yes, I am aware they ought to be, my dear,' rejoined her father, 'but they – ain't.'

Our Mutual Friend
CHARLES DICKENS
(1812–70)

A master cook! Why he is the man of men;
For a professor; he designs, he draws,
He paints, he carves, he builds, he fortifies,
Makes citadels of curious fowl...

BEN JONSON
(1572–1637)

❖

Perhaps had it not been for the influx among us of French and Italian experts we should not have progressed much beyond the pancake and oatmeal period.

Old Cookery Books and Ancient Cuisine
W. CAREW HAZLITT,
1886

❖

Our neighbours in France, are so justly famous for their skill in the affairs of the Kitchen, that the adage says,

as many Frenchmen, as many cooks.

The Cook's Oracle
WILLIAM KITCHINER
1822

Iam not one of those fellows who are content to suppose that they learnt their art by wearing an apron for a couple of years. My study of the art has not been superficial; it has been the work of my life; and I have learnt the use and appliances of every herb that grows – for kitchen purposes. But I especially shine in getting up funeral dinners. When the mourners have returned from the doleful ceremony, it is I who introduces to the mitigated affliction department. While they are yet in their mourning attire, I lift the lids of my kettles, and straightway the weepers begin to laugh. They

sit down with their senses so enchanted, that every guest fancies himself at a wedding.

Report of Cyrus's Chef
HEGESIPPUS
(d.180)

❖

You are more the child of our own age than you are the son of your father.

To his chef Antonin Carême
PRINCE CHARLES MAURICE TALLEYRAND
(1754–1826)

❖

Many very indifferent cooks pique themselves on never doing anything by rule, and the consequence of their throwing together at random … the ingredients which ought to be proportioned with exceeding exactness is repeated failure in all they attempt to do.

Modern Cookery for Private Families
ELIZA ACTON
1845

'Alice,' said her father, 'I can't compliment your cook upon her soup.'

'You don't encourage her, papa, by eating it often enough. And then you only told me at two o'clock today.'

'If a cook can't make soup between two and seven, she can't make it in a week.'

Can You Forgive Her?
ANTHONY TROLLOPE
(1815–82)

❖

We have some good families in England by the name of Cook or Coke. I know not what they may think; but we may depend on it, they originally sprang from real and professional cooks; and they need not be ashamed of their extraction, any more than the Butlers, Parkers, etc.

Forme of Cury
DOCTOR PEGGE
1780

❖

The drawback of English cooking is that England has scarcely any cooks.

My Life and Loves
FRANK HARRIS
(1856–1931)

❖

If your Employers are hasty, and have scolded without reason – bear it patiently – they will soon see their error, and be happy to make you amends – muttering on leaving the room – or slamming the door after you, is as bad as an impertinent reply – it is, in fact, showing that you would be impertinent if you dared.

Advice to Young Cooks in *The Cook's Oracle*
WILLIAM KITCHINER
1822

Then there was a cook, the most useful slave that could be, and began to be much esteemed and valued, and, all bedabbled with broth and bedaubed with soot, was welcomed out of the kitchen into the schools; and that which before was accounted as a vile slavery was honoured as an art whose chiefest care is only to search out everywhere the provocatives of appetite, and study in all places for dainties to satisfy a most profound gluttony.

LIVY
(59 BC–AD 17)

'I'd as soon be called on to choose a Prime Minister for the country, as I would a cook for a club.'

'Of course you would,' said Mr Vavasor. 'There may be as many as a dozen cooks about London to be looked up, but there are never more than two possible Prime Ministers about. And as one of them must be going out when the other is coming in, I don't see that there can be any difficulty. Moreover, nowadays, people do their politics for themselves, but they expect to have their dinners cooked for them.'

Can You Forgive Her?
ANTHONY TROLLOPE
(1815–82)

❖

To young people who love cookery; you must have courage, determination and, above all, belief in all you do. Have faith in your ability, your honesty, and you will succeed.

Advice to Young Chefs
ANTONIN CARÊME
(1783–1834)

❖

Banquets and Feasts

*S*INCE THE DAWN OF HISTORY *a great banquet has been one of the greatest pleasures the world affords. Good company, rich food, an ancient hall: who could ask for more?*

Your Mother sends you the cook Pythegnos, for he is acquainted with all the sacrificial rituals of your ancestors, as well as those of the mysteries and the feasts of Dionysus. He is well acquainted with the rites proper for the Olympic Games.

Letter to her Son, Alexander the Great
OLYMPIA
(C. 380 BC)

❖

The true essentials of a feast are only fun and feed.

OLIVER WENDELL-HOLMES
(1809–94)

❖

The usual allowance at a Turtle Feast is Six Pounds live weight per Head – at the Spanish Dinner, at the City of London Tavern, in August 1808, four hundred guests attended and two thousand five hundred pounds [more than a ton] of turtle were consumed.

Bell's Weekly Messenger
7th August 1808

Every decoration was added to the different dishes that the cook's imagination suggested to gratify the eye. The frequent use of gold and silver, the splendid representation of armorial cognizances, and the grand devices in pastry and sugar which they termed sotelties, must have given a magnificence to the ancient English table of which we at present have no idea.

Antiquitates Culinariae
REV. R. WARNER
1791

THE SWAN

Take three pounds of beef, beat fine in a mortar,
Put it into the swan – that is when you've caught her.
Some pepper, salt, mace; some nutmeg, and onion,
Will heighten the flavour in gourmand's opinion.
Then tie it up tight, with a small piece of tape,
That the gravy and other things may not escape.
A meal paste, rather stiff, should be laid on the breast,
And some whited brown paper should cover the rest.

24

Fifteen minutes at least, ere the swan you get down,
Pull the paste off the bird, that the breast may get
brown.

The present of a Norwich cygnet was always accompanied by
the above traditional recipe recorded c.1800

The peacock was skinned, stuffed with spices and roasted ... a cloth continually wetted was kept round the bird's head to save it from the action of the fire ... allowed to cool, and then the skin was neatly sewn on again, the tail feathers spread out, the comb gilt, and a piece of cloth dipped in spirits of wine placed in its mouth, to be set on fire while it was being served up at table...

After all this expenditure of art ... its flesh was tough and tasteless.

Good Cheer
F. W. HACKWOOD
1911

25

When I make a feast, I would my friends
should praise it, not the cooks.

SIR JOHN HARINGTON
(1561–1612)

LORD MAYOR'S DINNER AT GUILDHALL

Nov. 10th, 1828
and we can vouch for its accuracy, viz.:—

200 tureens of turtle, 60 dishes of fowls, 35 roasted capons, 35 roasted pullets, 30 pigeon pies, 10 sirloins of beef, 50 hams (ornamented), 40 tongues, 2 barons of beef, 10 rounds of beef, 50 raised French pies, 60 dishes mince-pies, 40 marrow-puddings, 25 tourtes of preserves, 25 apple and damson tarts, 90 marbree jellies, 50 blanc-manges, 10 chantilly baskets, 4 fruit-baskets, 36 dishes shell-fish, 4 ditto prawns, 4 lobster salads, 60 dishes of vegetables, 60 salads.

Remove — 50 roasted turkeys, 30 leverets, 50 pheasants, 2 dishes pea-fowl, 24 geese, 30 dishes of partridges.

Dessert — 200lb. of pine-apples, 100 dishes of hot-house grapes, 200 ice-creams, 60 dishes of apples, 60 dishes of pears, 50 Savoy cakes (ornamented), 30 dishes of walnuts, 75 ditto dried fruit and preserves, 55 ditto rout cakes, 20 ditto filberts, 20 ditto preserved ginger, 4 ditto brandy-cherries.

Quoted in *Tales of the Table,*
Kitchen, and Larder
DICK HUMELBERGIUS SECUNDUS
1829

Of all the things I ever swallow
Good, well dressed turtle beats them hollow
It almost makes me wish, I vow,
To have two stomachs, like a cow.

'In Praise of Turtle'
THOMAS HOOD
(1799–1845)

The old bad habit of eating and drinking to excess was still rampant in the eighties at city dinners. I remember how astonished I was at my first Lord Mayor's Banquet in 1883.

...The first thing that struck me was the extraordinary gluttony displayed by seven out of ten of the city magnates. Till that night I had thought that as a matter of courtesy every man in public suppressed any signs of greed he might feel, but here greed was flaunted. The man next to me ate like an ogre. I took a spoonful or two of turtle soup and left the two or three floating morsels of green meat. When he had finished his first plateful, which was emptied to the last drop in double quick time, my neighbor, while waiting

for a second helping, turned to me. 'That's why I
like this table,' he began, openly licking his lips.
'You can have as many helpings as you want.'

> *My Life and Loves*
> FRANK HARRIS
> (1856–1931)

❖

S uch is the variety of dishes [served at Roman
banquets] that it must be injurious to any man.
You have on one plate a mixture of boiled and
roast together, with thrushes and crustacea, the
most delicious juices turn to bile and phlegm
distress the stomach. See the pallour of each guest
as he rises from so doubtful a mixture of dishes.

> HORACE
> (65 BC–AD 8)

❖

Then receive him as best such an advent beomes,
With a legion of cooks, and an army of slaves.

> *The Irish Avatar*
> LORD BYRON
> (1788–1824)

There is to be a wedding this morning at the corner house in the terrace. The pastry-cook's people have been there half-a-dozen times already; all day yesterday there was a great stir and bustle, and they were up this morning as soon as it was light.

...and then surely there never was anything like the breakfast table, glittering with plate and china, and set out with flowers and sweets, and long-necked bottles, in the most sumptuous and dazzling manner. In the centre, too, is the mighty charm, the cake, glistening with frosted sugar, and garnished beautifully.

Sketches By Boz
CHARLES DICKENS
(1812–70)

FOR A GRAND DINNER

Make the likeness of a ship and cover it with paste [marzipan or fruit paste], with flags and streamers and guns, and with such holes and trains of powder that they might all take fire. Place on a charger ...

In another charger [place] a castle with battlements, portcullises, gates and drawbridges made of paste, with guns ...

At each end place pies ... in one of which there be live frogs, in the other live birds ...

[Present for] the admiration of the beholders. Fire the guns of the castle; then fire the guns on one side of the ship as in a battle.

All dangers being over, by this time they will desire to see what is in the pies; lifting off the lid of one pie, out skip some frogs, which makes the ladies skip and shriek; next the other pie, whence come out the birds, who by a natural instinct flying at the light, will put out the candles.

These were formerly the delights of the nobility, before good housekeeping had left England.

The Accomplish't Cook, or
The Art and Mystery of Cookery
ROBERT MAY
1671

The fire, with well-dried logs supplied,
Went roaring up the chimney wide;
The huge hall-table's oaken face,
Scrubb'd till it shone, the day to grace,
Bore then, upon its massive board,
No mark to part the squire and lord.
Then was brought in the lusty brawn,
By old blue-coated serving-man;
Then the grim boar's head frown'd on high,
Crested with bays and rosemary.
Well can the green-garb'd ranger tell
How, when, and where the monster fell;
What dogs before his death he tore,

32

And all the baiting of the boar;
While round the merry wassel bowl,
Garnish'd with ribbons, blithe did trowl.
There the huge sirloin reek'd; hard by
Plum-porridge stood, and Christmas pie;
Nor fail'd old Scotland to produce,
At such high tide, her savoury goose.

SIR WALTER SCOTT
(1771–1832)

Servilius Rullus was the first Roman to serve up a whole wild boar at a table – a luxury which has today become a commonplace, because today we serve up at the table two or three boars at a time, and they are just for the first course alone.

PLINY THE ELDER
(AD 23–79)

❖

FEAST FOR THE ARCHBISHOP OF YORK 1469

Sixty-two cooks were employed to prepare the feast ... besides great beef and mutton, oxene, porcele, antelopes, boars' heads, venison, and roe, there were game birds and tame birds of every kind; swans and egrets, ganets and gulls, heron and peacock, pheasants, partridges, plover, wood-cock, goodwitts, redshanks ... bittern and curlew,

34

quails, pigeons, chyckens and capons, larks, dotterelles and martynets ... Soups and pottage, sweet dishes and fruits ... Besides the four hundred tarts, there were served on this occasion five thousand dishes of jelly, four thousand cold custards, and two thousand hot custards. There were a thousand servers or waiters employed, and the sixty-two cooks had at their command 515 kitchen assistants. Such was the luxury and magnificence of an English prelate.

The Noble Boke of Cookery (Begun 1467)
quoted in *Good Cheer*
F . W. HACKWOOD
1911

❖

One day, when he was supping alone, a single course had been prepared for him. He called his slave and asked why nothing more costly had been prepared. 'What sayest thou?' said Lucullus, 'Did'st thou not know that today Lucullus sups with Lucullus?'

PLUTARCH
(c.46–c.120)

The present king [William IV] has dined in his palace during the first three months of his reign, upwards of 21,000 persons including domestics; but what is very extraordinary, the kitchen bills for the same period are less in amount than those of the corresponding quarter in the reign of George IV. His Majesty does not employ in the department of the cuisine at any one of his palaces, *one single French cook.*

Cheltenham Chronicle
1830

A sucking pig, like a young child, must not be left for an instant.

The Cook's Oracle
WILLIAM KITCHINER
1822

When I went to work for Prince Talleyrand I noticed at once that the great showpieces of the first courses of his formal dinners were outshone by the elegance of his bronzes, his glass and his plate. I resolved that I would rebuild all the old methods, even though their rules had been laid down by the greatest masters of the kitchen.

ANTONIN CARÊME

(1783–1834)

❖

Under the most favourable circumstances a Roman dinner must have been a sloppy affair, even to nicely circumspect feeders. Consumed hastily, in an hour of vexations and untoward incidents, it must have been less advantageous to the eater than his tailor.

A Book about the Table

J.C. JEAFFRESON

1875

After their convivial banquets, among the wealthy classes, when they have finished supper, a man carries round in a coffin the image of a dead body carved in wood, made as like as possible in colour and workmanship, and in size generally about six feet in length; and showing this to each of the company, he says: 'Look upon this, then drink and enjoy yourself; for when you are dead you will be like this.'

HERODOTUS
(c.485–425 BC)

The ushers of Louis XIV solemnly summoned the guard when the table was to be laid, and a detachment of men under arms were at once spectators and guardians of the dressing of the table. They stood by while the appointed officers touched the royal napkin, spoon, knife, fork and tooth-picks with a piece of bread which they subsequently swallowed. This was the trial against poisoning.

Table Traits
JOHN DORAN
1854

November had come; the crops were in, and barn, buttery, and bin were overflowing with the harvest that rewarded the summer's hard work. The big kitchen was a jolly place just now, for in the great fireplace roared a cheerful fire; on the walls hung garlands of dried apples, onions, and corn; up aloft from the beams shone crook-necked squashes, juicy hams, and dried venison—for in those days deer still haunted the deep forests, and hunters flourished. Savory smells were in the air; on the crane hung steaming kettles, and down among the red embers copper saucepans simmered, all suggestive of some approaching feast.

An Old-Fashioned Thanksgiving
LOUISA MAY ALCOTT
(1832–88)

THE GOOD TABLE

Plenty to look at, plenty to eat, and plenty to leave.

LANCASHIRE MOTTO

❖

The 'sit-down supper' was excellent; there were four barley-sugar temples on the table, which would have looked beautiful if they had not melted away when the supper began; and a water-mill, whose only fault was that instead of going round, it ran over the table-cloth. Then there were fowls, and tongue, and trifle, and

sweets, and lobster salad, and potted beef – and everything. And ... the greengrocer ran about till he thought his seven and sixpence was very hardly earned; and the young ladies didn't eat much for fear it shouldn't look romantic, and the married ladies eat as much as possible, for fear they shouldn't have enough; and a great deal of wine was drunk, and everybody talked and laughed considerably.

'The Bloomsbury Christening'
Sketches By Boz
CHARLES DICKENS
(1812–70)

❖

Strange to see how a good dinner and feasting reconciles everybody.

Diary, 9 November 1665
SAMUEL PEPYS
(1633–1703)

The Dinner – Preparations

*O*RGANISING A GOOD meal can be enough to test the mettle of a general. Between collecting the ingredients, cooking everything just so, laying in wine and negotiating the prejudices of your guests every dinner has all the makings of a disaster – or a triumph.

Their table was a board to tempt even ghosts
To pass the Styx for more substantial feasts.
I will not dwell upon ragouts or roasts,
Albeit all human history attests
That happiness for man – the hungry sinner! –
Since Eve ate apples, much depends on dinner.

The mind is lost in mighty contemplation
Of intellect expended on two courses;
And indigestion's grand multiplication
Requires arithmetic beyond my forces.
Who would suppose, from Adam's simple ration,
That cookery could have call'd forth such
    resources,
As form a science and a nomenclature
From out the commonest demands of nature?

LORD BYRON
(1788–1824)

❖

However hard you try to prepare – to buy and check all you need for a dinner party; once you put on the vegetables you'll find you're out of salt.

TONY SMYTHE
2004

Invite a lord to dine, and let him have
The nicest dish his appetite can crave;
Still if it be on oaken table set,
His lordship will grow sick, and cannot eat.
Something's amiss he knows not what to think;
Either your ven'son's rank, or sauces stink.
Order some other table to be brought,
Something at great expense, and latest wrought;
Beneath whose orb large yawning panthers lie,
Carv'd in rich pedestals of ivory!
He finds no more of that offensive smell;
The meat recovers, and my lord grows well.

ROBERT BURTON
(1577–1640)

'Mrs Goodenough's respects to Mr Sheep-shanks, and hopes he is in good health. She would be very glad if he would favour her with his company to tea on Monday. My daughter, in Combermere, has sent me a couple of guinea fowls, and Mrs Goodenough hopes Mr Sheep-shanks will stay and take a bit of supper.'

No need for the dates of the days of the month. The good ladies would have thought that the world was coming to an end if the invitation had been sent out a week before the party therein named. But not even guinea fowls for supper could tempt Mr Sheepshanks. He remembered the made-wines he had tasted in former days at Hollingford parties, and shuddered.

Wives and Daughters
ELIZABETH GASKELL
1854

❖

I have no credit with either butcher or poulterer, but if you can put up with turtle and turbot I shall be happy to see you.

LORD ALVANLEY
(1789–1849)

LARGE DINNER FOR TWELVE

Men of rank and fortune who keep a regular house steward or *maitre d'hotel* have this trouble taken off their hands, for a confidential servant, or a French *chef de cuisine* arranges with the master of the establishment or the lady of the house what is to be the menu or bill of fare.

A Book About Dinners,
Wines and Desserts
A.V. KIRWAN
1864

THE HIRED CHEF FIXES THE MENU

He produced from a pocket-book a pink paper and a blue paper, on which he had written two bills of fare...

'Madame will see that the dinners are quite simple,' said M. Cavalcadour [the chef].

'Oh, quite!' said Rosa, dreadfully puzzled.

'Which would Madame like?'

'Which would we like, mamma?' Rosa asked; adding, as if after a little thought, 'I think, sir, we should prefer the blue one.'

At which Mrs. Gashleigh nodded as knowingly
as she could; though pink or blue, I defy anybody
to know what these cooks mean by their jargon.

A Little Dinner At Timmins's.
WILLIAM MAKEPEACE THACKERAY
(1811–63)

A dinner invitation, once accepted, is a sacred
obligation. If you die before the dinner takes
place, your executor must attend the dinner.

Society As I have Found It
WARD MCALLISTER
1890

Besides understanding the management of the Spit, – the Stewpan, –
and the Rolling Pin, a Complete Cook
must know how to go to Market.

The Cook's Oracle
WILLIAM KITCHINER
1822

At this hour stir and bustle pervaded the
interior of Winterborne's domicile from cellar
to apple-loft … Being a bachelor of rather retiring
habits the whole of the preparations devolved upon
himself and his trusty man and familiar Robert
Creedle…

Winterborne was standing in front of the
brick oven in his shirt-sleeves, tossing in thorn-

sprays, and stirring about the blazing mass with a long-handled, three-pronged Beelzeebub kind of fork, the heat shining out upon his streaming face and making his eyes like furnaces; the thorns crackling and sputtering; while Creedle, having ranged the pastry dishes in a row on the table till the oven should be ready, was pressing out the crust of a final apple-pie with a rolling-pin. A great pot boiled on the fire; and through the open door of the back-kitchen a boy was seen seated on the fender, emptying the snuffers and scouring the candle-sticks, a row of the latter standing upside down on the hob to melt out the grease.

The Woodlanders
THOMAS HARDY
(1840–1928)

Try to imagine working in a palatial kitchen before a grand dinner. There are twenty chefs, each rushing furiously hither and thither in the great bowl of heat. Consider the vast furnace of roaring charcoal for the cooking of the entrées; another equally large and fierce for preparing the soups, the sauces, the ragouts, the frying and keeping warm the bains-maries. Another fire before which four spits are turning, one of which bears a sirloin of thirty kilos, another a joint of veal weighing between fifteen and twenty kilos; the other two loaded with poultry and game. In this unbearable inferno everyone works with

enormous speed, and not a sound is heard; only I speak and, at the murmur of my quiet voice, everyone obeys.

ANTONIN CARÊME
(1783–1834)

The glare of a scorching fire, and the smoke so baneful to the eyes and the complexion, are continual and inevitable dangers; – and a Cook must live in the midst of them, as a Soldier on the field of battle surrounded by bullets, bombs, and ... rockets.

Almanach des Gourmands
GRIMOD DE LA REYNIÈRE
1805

Poor Dinner-giving Snobs! you don't know what small thanks you get for all your pains and money! How we Dining-out Snobs sneer at your cookery, and pooh-pooh your old hock, and are incredulous about your four-and-six-penny champagne, and know that the side-dishes of to-day are *rechauffés* from the dinner of yesterday, and mark how certain dishes are whisked off the table untasted, so that they may figure at the banquet tomorrow.

The Book of Snobs
By One of Themselves
WILLIAM MAKEPEACE THACKERAY
(1811–63)

❖

The business of chopping so many herbs for the various stuffings was found to be aching work for women; and ... Loveday called in a friendly dragoon of John's regiment who was passing by, and he, being a muscular man, willingly chopped all the afternoon for a quart of strong, judiciously administered, and all other victuals found, taking off his jacket and gloves, rolling up his shirt-sleeves and unfastening his stock in an honourable and energetic way.

All windfalls and maggot-cored codlins were excluded from the apple pies; and as there was no known dish large enough for the purpose, the puddings were stirred up in the milking-pail, and boiled in the three-legged bell-metal crock, of great weight and antiquity, which every travelling tinker for the previous thirty years had tapped with his stick, coveted, made a bid for, and often attempted to steal.

The Trumpet Major
THOMAS HARDY
(1840–1928)

The half-hour before dinner has always been considered as the great ordeal through which the mistress, in giving a dinner-party, will either pass with flying colours, or, lose many of her laurels. The anxiety to receive her guests,— her hope that all will be present in due time, — her trust in the skill of her cook, and the attention of the other domestics, all tend to make these few minutes a trying time …

How sad it is to sit and pine,
The long half-hour before we dine!
Upon our watches oft to look,
Then wonder at the clock and cook, …

54

And strive to laugh in spite of Fate!
But laughter forced soon quits the room,
And leaves it in its former gloom.
But lo! the dinner now appears,
The object of our hopes and fears,
The end of all our pain!

> *Book of Household Management*
> MRS BEETON
> (1836–65)

But hark! a sound is stealing on my ear –
  A soft and silvery sound – I know it well
Its tinkling tells me that the time is near
  Precious to me – it's the Dinner Bell.

> C.S. CALVERLEY
> (1831–84)

Dinner Is Served

*J*UST AS A NOVELIST HOPES *to grab his readers' attention with his first paragraph so it is imperative that a dinner should commence with an inviting aroma and flavour — enough to stimulate the taste buds, but not so much as to damage the appetite — and a mixture of guests promising an evening of good fellowship.*

The first bite
is with the eye.

SAYING

❖

I have always been punctual at the hour of
Dinner, for I knew, that all those whom I kept
waiting at that provoking interval, would employ
those unpleasant moments to sum up all my faults.

BOILEAU
(1636–1711)

❖

The best way for an epicure to appreciate his meal is for him to have it
served to him by his cook himself.

ANTONIN CARÊME
(1783–1834)

❖

He who does not mind his belly
will not mind anything.

SAMUEL JOHNSON
(1709–84)

O hour of all hours, the most blest upon
    earth,
Blest hour of our dinners!
The sermon he heard when to church he last
    went;
The money he borrow'd, the money he spent;
All of these things a man, I believe, may forget,
And not be the worse for forgetting; but yet
Never, never, oh, never! earth's luckiest sinner
Hath unpunish'd forgotten the hour of his
    dinner!

From 'The Dinner Hour'
EDWARD ROBERT BULWER-LYTTON,
1ST EARL OF LYTTON
(1831–91)

❖

The gourmand either is, or ought to be, *par excellence*, a punctual man...Any other business may be put off for a few hours without much inconvenience; but when there is a piece of roast meat, a goose, turkey, sucking-pig, or what not, upon the spit, a pie in the oven, a saucepan on the range, there is only a set time for them to remain there; once this precious moment elapsed, the substance, whatever it may be, must lose of its flavour, and become rigid and dry – there is no other remedy.

Apician Morsels
Tales of the Table, Kitchen, and Larder
DICK HUMELBERGIUS SECUNDUS
1829

Ten folio volumes would not contain the Receipts of all the Soups that have been invented in the Grand School of Good Eating, – the Parisian Kitchen.

Almanach des Gourmands
GRIMOD DE LA REYNIÈRE
1805

The most consummate cook is alas seldom noticed by the master, or heard of by the guests who, while they are devouring his Turtle and drinking his wine, care very little who dressed the one or sent the other.

Almanach des Gourmands
GRIMOD DE LA REYNIÈRE
1803

We hope … that it will not be said, in future, that an Englishman only knows how to make soup in his stomach, – by swilling down a large quantity of Ale, or Porter, to quench the thirst occasioned by the Meat he eats.

The Cook's Oracle
WILLIAM KITCHINER
1822

'Now, gentlemen,' said Mr Jorrocks, casting his eye up the table, as soon as they had all got squeezed and wedged round it, and the dishes were uncovered, 'you see your dinner, eat whatever you like except the windmill [table decoration] – hope you'll be able to satisfy nature with what's on – would have had more but Mrs J. is so werry fine, she won't stand two joints of the same sort on the table.'

Jorrocks' Jaunts and Jollities
R.S. SURTEES
(1803–1864)

He is a fellow, now, that would send up his plate twice for soup.

Speaking contemptuously of someone
BEAU BRUMMELL
(1778–1840)

'Soup?' says Mr. Osborne, clutching the ladle, fixing his eyes on her, in a sepulchral tone; and having helped her and the rest, did not speak for a while.

'Take Miss Sedley's plate away,' at last he said. 'She can't eat the soup – no more can I.

'It's beastly. Take away the soup, Hicks, and to-morrow turn the cook out of the house, Jane.'

Vanity Fair
WILLIAM MAKEPEACE THACKERAY
1847

Do not throw yourself out of a good place for a slight affront. Come when you are called, and do what you are bid. Saucy answers are highly aggravating and answer no good purpose.

Advice for Young Cooks in *The Cook's Oracle*
WILLIAM KITCHINER
1822

This soup [turtle] is, without contradiction, the most lengthened in its details of any that are known; the composition of its seasoning claims an able hand and a strong memory. The palate of the cook who executes it should be very fine; none of the ingredients should predominate, not even the cayenne or allspice, which the English cooks inconsiderately employ.

ANTONIN CARÊME
(1783–1834)

❖

The potage was little better than bread soaked in dish-washings, luke warm; the ragouts looked as if they had been once eaten and half digested; the fricossées were involved in a nasty yellow poultice; and the rotis were scorched and stinking; the dessert consisted of faded fruit and iced froth; the table beer was sour, the water foul, and the wine vapid; but there was a parade of plate and china, and a powdered lackey stood behind every chair, except those of the master and mistress of the house, who were served by two valets dressed like gentlemen.

TOBIAS SMOLLETT
(1721–71)

There were two soups – at least two plated tureens, one containing pea-soup, the other mutton-broth. Mr Jorrocks said he didn't like the latter, it always reminded him of 'a cold in the 'ead'. The pea-soup he thought werry like 'oss-gruel: – that he kept to himself.

Handley Cross
R.S. SURTEES
(1803–1864)

Real turtle soup is seldom made in private houses, unless of the very highest distinction. It is generally obtained ready prepared from the Waterloo Hotel at Liverpool, and from some of the great taverns in the City in Bishopsgate or Aldersgate Street, or from Gunter's at the West end, who has jars ready prepared, from the West Indies and Brazil.

A Book About Dinners,
Wines and Desserts
A. V. KIRWAN
1864

The hostess is smiling resolutely through all the courses, smiling through her agony; though her heart is in the kitchen, and she is speculating with terror lest there be any disaster there. If the soufflé should collapse, or if Wiggins does not send the ices in time – she feels as if she would commit suicide – that smiling, jolly woman!

The Book of Snobs
By One of Themselves
WILLIAM MAKEPEACE THACKERAY
(1811–63)

A guest, whoever or whatever he may be, ought, on his arrival, to be civil; polite, during the first service; gallant, in the second; tender at the dessert; and discreet, on going away.

Tales of the Table, Kitchen, and Larder
DICK HUMELBERGIUS SECUNDUS
1829

It is said, there are seven chances against even the most simple dish being presented to the Mouth in absolute perfection; for instance a leg of mutton.

1st.– The Mutton must be *good*,
2d.– Must have been kept a *good* time,
3d.– Must be roasted at a *good* fire,
4th.– By a *good* cook,
5th.– Who must be in a *good* temper,
6th.– With all this… you must have *good* luck, and
7th.– *Good* appetite. – The Meat, and the mouths which are to eat it, must be ready at the same moment.

> *The Cook's Oracle*
> WILLIAM KITCHINER
> 1822

❖

I shall strongly recommend to all cooks of either sex, to keep their Stomachs free from strong liquors till after dinner, and their Noses from snuff.

> *Professed Cook*
> CLERMONT
> 1776

❖

Well! thanks be to Heaven,
The summons is given;
It's only gone seven
   And it should have been six;
There's fine overdoing
In roasting and stewing
And victuals past chewing
   To rags and to sticks!

How dreadfully chilly!
I shake willy-nilly;
That John is so silly
   And never will learn!
This plate is a cold one,
That cloth is an old one,
I wish they had told one
   The lamp would not burn.

Now then for some blunder,
For nerve to sink under;
I never shall wonder
   Whatever goes ill;
That fish is a riddle!
It's broke in the middle,
A turbot! a fiddle!
   It's only a brill!

It's quite over-boil'd too,
The butter is oil'd too,
The soup is all spoil'd too,
   It's nothing but slop.
The smelts looking flabby,
The soles are as dabby,
It all is so shabby
   That Cook shall
      not stop!

As sure as the morning,
She gets a month's warning,
My orders for scorning—
   There's nothing to eat!
I hear such a rushing,
I feel such a flushing,
I know I am blushing
   As red as a beet!

How very unpleasant!
Lord! there is the pheasant!
Not wanted at present,
   I'm born to be vexed!
The beef without mustard!
My fate's to be fluster'd,
And there comes the custard
   To eat with the hare!

This cooking? —it's messing!
The spinach wants pressing,
And salads in dressing
   Are best with good eggs.
And John—yes, already
Has had something heady,
That makes him unsteady
   In keeping his legs.

How shall I get through it?
I never can do it,
I'm quite looking to it
   To sink by and by.
Oh! would I were dead now,
Or up in my bed now,
To cover my head now,
   And have a good cry!

THOMAS HOOD
(1799–1845)

The Fish Course

*F*ROM A WHOLE TURBOT, *on fine china garnished with shrimp sauce, to fish and chips, seasoned with vinegar and salt and served in yesterday's newspaper; there's nothing like a well-cooked fish.*

Icalled for a dish of fish, which we had for dinner, this being the first day of Lent; and I do intend to try whether I can keep it or no.

Diary, 27 February 1671

Notwithstanding my resolution, yet for the want of other victuals I did eat flesh this Lent, but am resolved to eat as little as I can.

Diary, 28 February 1671
SAMUEL PEPYS

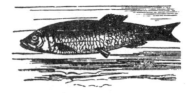

A woman should never be seen eating or drinking, unless it be lobster salad and Champagne, the only true feminine & becoming viands.

LORD BYRON
(1788–1824)

Soup and fish explain half
the emotions of life.

SYDNEY SMITH
(1771–1845)

A red herring is wholesome in a frosty morning; it is the most precious fish merchandise, because it can be carried through all Europe. No where are they so well cured as at Yarmouth. The poorer sort make it three parts of their sustenance. It is every man's money, from the King to the peasant. A red herring drawn on the ground will lead hounds a false scent. A broiled herring is good for the rheumatism. The fishery is a great nursery for seamen and brings more ships to Yarmouth than assembled at Troy to fetch back Helen.

Lenten Stuffe,
or the Praise of the Red Herring
THOMAS NASHE
(1567–1601)

What could be more ridiculous and absurd than, for instance, to see served pike or carp à la Chambord, the garniture of which were composed of larded sweetbreads, young pigeons, cocks' combs, and kidneys? But such was, however, the practice of men highest in reputation [the Prince Regent].

ANTONIN CARÊME
(1783–1834)

Govern a small family as you would cook a small fish, very gently.

CHINESE PROVERB

The fish swim in the dining hall. They are seized under the table to reappear above a moment later, for a mullet is not considered to be fresh unless it has perished in the hands of a guest.

Naturales Quaestiones
SENECA
(c.55 BC–c.AD 40)

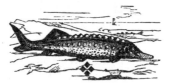

As for caviar, or their eggs being powdered, let Turks, Grecians, Venetians and Spaniards celebrate them ever so much, yet the Italian proverb will ever be true;

Chi mangia di Caviale
Mangia moschi,
Merdi e sale.
[Who eats caviar
eats fly dung and salt]

Health's Improvement
THOMAS MOUFFET
1655

The Fish Course

A fisherman of Yarmouth, having drawn so many herrings he knew not what to do with them all, hung the residue, that he could not sell nor spend in the sooty roof of his shed a-drying... The weather was cold and good fires he kept, and what with his firing and smoking, or smokey firing, in that his narrow lobby, his herrings, which were white as whale-bone when he hung them up, now looked as red as lobster. It was four or five days before either he or his wife espied it; they fell down on their knees and blessed themselves, and cried: 'A miracle, a miracle!' And with the proclaiming it among their neighbours they could not be content, but to the court the fisherman would, and presented it to the King...

Lenten Stuffe, or the Praise of the Red Herring
THOMAS NASHE
(1567–1601)

It wasn't the trout, that gave me the gout;
It was ruby port, of the very best sort.

Waveney Weekly
1882

*Un bon Coulis d'Ecrévisses est le Paradis sur la terre, et
digne de la table des Dieux.*

A good shrimp sauce is heaven on Earth and
worthy of the table of the Gods.

UN DES GRANDS HOMMES
DE BOUCHE DE FRANCE
c. 1780

HERRINGS

Be not sparing,
Leave off swearing.
Buy my herring
Fresh from Malahide,
Better never was tried.
Come, eat them with pure fresh butter and
    mustard,
Their bellies are soft, and as white as a custard.
Come, sixpence a dozen, to get me some bread,
Or, like my own herrings, I soon shall be dead.

From *Market Women's Cries*
JONATHAN SWIFT
(1667–1745)

❖

Philoxenes of Cyther…On being informed by his physician that he was going to die of indigestion, on account of the quantity he was consuming of a delicious fish, "Be it so," he calmly observed; "but before I die, let me finish the remainder."

Book of Household Management
MRS BEETON
(1836–65)

I love no roast but a nut-brown toast, and a
    crab laid in the fire;
A little bread shall do me stead! much
    bread I do not desire.

WILLIAM STEVENSON
(1530?–75)

Oysters are more beautiful than any religion.
There's nothing in Christianity or Buddhism
that quite matches the sympathetic unselfishness
of an oyster.

Chronicles of Clovis
H.H. MUNRO ('SAKI')
(1870–1916)

The Fish Course

This Bouillabaisse a noble dish is —
    A sort of soup, or broth, or brew,
Or hotchpotch of all sorts of fishes,
    That Greenwich never could out do:
Green herbs, red peppers, mussels, saffron
    Soles, onions, garlic, roach and dace:
All these you eat at Terré's tavern
    In that one dish of Bouillabaisse.

Indeed a rich and savoury stew 'tis;
    And true philosophers, methinks,
Who love all sorts of natural beauties,
    Should love good victuals and good drinks.
And Cordelier or Benedictine
    Might gladly, sure, his lot embrace,
Nor find a fast-day too afflicting,
    Which served him up a Bouillabaisse.

From 'The Ballad of Bouillabaisse'
WILLIAM MAKEPEACE THACKERAY
(1811–63)

FLOUNDER-SOUCHY

It has an almost angelic delicacy of flavour; it is as fresh as the recollections of childhood – it wants a Correggio's pencil to describe it with sufficient tenderness.

'Greenwich Whitebait'
WILLIAM MAKEPEACE THACKERAY
(1811–63)

De Green's boy entered with two dishes of fish. On removing the large plated covers, six pieces of skate and a large haddock made their appearance. Mr Jorrocks's countenance fell five-and-twenty per cent, as he would say. He very soon dispatched one of the six pieces of skate, and was just done in time to come in for the tail of the haddock…

'The Duke'll come on badly for fish, I'm thinkin',

...'Nothin' left for Manners, I mean', said Mr Jorrocks, pointing to the empty dish.

Handley Cross
R.S. SURTEES
(1803–64)

The man to whom the order for the oysters had been sent had not been told to open them. It is a very difficult thing to open an oyster with a limp knife or a two-pronged fork.

Pickwick Papers
CHARLES DICKENS
(1812–70)

It [skate] is very good when in good season, but no fish so bad when it is otherwise.

The Cook's Oracle
WILLIAM KITCHINER
1822

❖

The oysters, stewed and pickled, leaped from their capacious reservoirs, and slid by scores into the mouths of the assembly. The sharpest pickles vanished, whole cucumbers at once, like sugar-plums, and no man winked his eye. Great heaps of indigestible matter melted away as ice before the sun. It was a solemn and awful thing to see.

Martin Chuzzlewit
CHARLES DICKENS
(1812–70)

❖

At present, the interior of the kitchen was visible by its own huge fires – a sort of Pandemonium, where men and women, half undressed, were busied in baking, broiling, roasting oysters, and preparing devils on the gridiron; the mistress of the place, with her shoes slip-shod, and her hair straggling like that of Megaera from under a round-eared cap, toiling, scolding, receiving orders, giving them, and obeying them all at once, seemed the presiding enchantress of that gloomy and fiery region.

Guy Mannering
SIR WALTER SCOTT
(1771–1832)

Poultry and Game Birds

*T*HERE ARE FEW MORE *rewarding pleasures for a cook than opening the oven door and seeing a whole bird sizzling in the roasting pan, and then, as the smell slowly slowly drifts through the house, watching as the guests begin to lick their lips in anticipation of delights to come.*

Well-fattened and tender, a fowl is to the cook what the canvas is to the painter; for do we not see it served boiled, roasted, fried, fricasseed, hashed, hot, cold, whole, dismembered, boned, broiled, stuffed, on dishes, and in pies,— always handy and ever acceptable?

> Jean Anthelme Brillat-Savarin quoted in
> *Book of Household Management*
> MRS BEETON
> (1836–65)

❖

It is my wish that there be in my kingdom no peasant so poor that he cannot have a chicken in his pot every Sunday for his dinner.

> *History of Henry the Great*
> HARDOUIN DE PÉRÉFIXE
> (1681)

❖

God didn't give us fingers so that we had to use a fork to eat a drumstick.

> OLD SAYING

Provide a large pair of spectacles of the highest magnifying power; they will make a lark as big as a fowl, a goose as big as a swan, a leg of mutton as large as a hindquarter of beef.

Life of Col. Hanger
18th Century

Fried pork sausages are a very savoury, and favourite accompaniment to either roasted, or boiled Poultry. A Turkey, thus garnished, is called 'An Alderman in Chains'.

The Cook's Oracle
WILLIAM KITCHINER
1822

Many thanks, my dear sir, for your kind present of game ... If there is a pure and elevated pleasure in this world, it is that of roast pheasant and bread-sauce; barn-door fowls for dissenters, but for the real churchman, the thirty-nine times articled clerk, the pheasant! the pheasant!

Letter
SYDNEY SMITH
(1771–1845)

❖

He [the fourth Lord Holland] was entertaining a schoolboy who had come to spend a whole holiday at Holland House, and in the openness of his heart, he told the urchin that he might have whatever he liked for dinner. 'Young in years, but in sage counsels old,' ... the Westminster boy demanded, not sausages and strawberry cream, but a roast duck with green peas, and an apricot tart. The delighted host brushed away a tear of sensibility and said 'My boy, if in all the important questions of your life you decide as wisely as you have decided now, you will be a great and a good man.'

G.W.E. RUSSELL
(1853–1919)

The most delicate morsel of a roast duck is the wing. The best part of a boiled fowl is the thigh, particularly if it be fat, plump, and white. For some years past, the ladies have become very fond of the rumps of fowls; and, if it be a partridge, the stomach.

Tales of the Table,
Kitchen, and Larder
DICK HUMELBERGIUS SECUNDUS
1829

❖

Though Quakers scowl, though Baptists howl,
    Though Plymouth Brethren rage,
We churchmen gay will wallow today
    In apple sauce, onions and sage

Ply knife and fork, and draw the cork,
    And have the bottle handy
For each slice of goose will introduce
    A thimbleful of brandy.

Hymn on Michaelmas Day
quoted by
LORD MACAULAY
(1800–59)

For people who are fond of goose (and who is not?) a greater treat could not be devised. There was no taking the edge of the appetite off with soup or fish, or patties, or cutlets, or side dishes of any sort; but they sat down to dine off the one thing they expected. This, too, was done in the fairest, most equitable way imaginable; for instead of a favoured few getting the breast and tit-bits, leaving nothing but gristly drumsticks for late comers, each man had his own half goose, and could take whatever part he liked first, without eating in haste or fear that the next favoured cut would be gone ere he could get at it again.

R.S. SURTEES
(1803–64)

I dined on Saturday at Lord Essex's in Belgrave Square. But never was there such a take-in. I had been given to understand that his Lordship's cuisine was superintended by the first French artists, and that I should find there all the luxuries of the *Almanach des Gourmands*. What a mistake! His Lordship is luxurious indeed, but in quite a different way. He is a true Englishman. Not a dish on his table but what Sir Roger de Coverley ... might have set before his guests. A huge haunch of venison on the sideboard; a

magnificent piece of beef at the bottom of the table; and before my Lord himself smoked, not a dindon aux truffes, but a fat roasted goose stuffed with sage and onions.

LORD MACAULAY
(1800–59)

Sir Isaac Newton, in his preoccupation, could not always remember whether he had dined or not. A friend once played a joke upon him by eating a chicken which was waiting for the philosopher and leaving the bones on the plate. When Newton came into the room he was quite unconscious of the fact he had not dined, much to his friend's amusement.

Good Cheer
F. W. HACKWOOD
1911

Turkeys, carp, hops, and beer
Came into England all in one year.

OLD SAYING
The year is said to be 1520

❖

At last the dishes were set on, and grace was said. It was succeeded by a breathless pause as Mrs Cratchit, looking slowly all along the carving-knife, prepared to plunge it in the breast; but when she did, and when the long-

expected gush of stuffing issued forth, one murmur of delight arose all round the board, and even Tiny Tim, excited by the two young Crachits, beat on the table with the handle of his knife, and feebly cried Hurrah!

There never was such a goose. Bob said that he didn't believe there ever was such a goose cooked.

A Christmas Carol
CHARLES DICKENS
(1812–70)

❖

Of the huntsmen of France it is said, that when they are out shooting in September, they take with them both pepper and salt. If they kill a very fat bird, they pluck and season it, and, after carrying it some time in their caps, eat it. This, they declare, is the best way of serving it up.

Book of Household Management
MRS BEETON
(1836–65)

❖

The Meat Course

NOTHING CAN MATCH the sight and taste of good beef, marbled with rich seams of fat, unless it is a leg of Welsh mutton served with fresh mint sauce or perhaps a slice of pork crowned with golden, crispy crackling. Avoid this chapter if you are dieting.

Of all the fowls of the air, commend me to the shin of beef –

> for there's marrow for the master, –
> meat for the mistress, –
> gristles for the servants, –
> and bones for the dogs.

OLD PROVERB

❖

No other animal [referring to the pig] can offer raw material more suitable to the talents of a cook. All other flesh has its own individual essence; that of the pig presents us with the possibility of almost fifty different flavours.

PLINY
(AD 62–113)

❖

Raw flesh has but one inconvenience, – from its viscousness it attaches itself to the teeth.

JEAN ANTHELME BRILLAT-SAVARIN
(1755–1826)

It has been all but universally admitted, that the beef of France is greatly inferior in quality to that of England, owing to inferiority of pasturage.

Book of Household Management
MRS BEETON
(1836–65)

Much has been said and written about the benefits to be derived by the lower classes from the use of good wholesome meats which come from the Antipodes preserved in tins ... Last week a supper was given to the members of the Belvedere Working Men's Club, East Street, Walworth, and the meats served were exclusively tinned meats. The bill of fare included rich kidney and ox-tail soups, stewed kidneys, Irish stew, mutton, beef 'boiled and corned' and kangaroo and bacon – the last being considered a great delicacy by the Australians which were all very toothsome and were eaten with great relish by the thirty or forty working men present.

Knife and Fork
18th May 1872

Beef, mutton, and pork, shred pies of the best,
Pig, veal, goose, and capon, and turkey well
    dress'd,
Cheese, apples, and nuts, jolly carols to hear,
As then in the country is counted good cheer.

Five Hundred Points of Good Husbandry
THOMAS TUSSER
(c.1520–c.80)

A Good Cook, is as anxiously attentive to the appearance and Colour of her Roasts, as a Court Beauty is to her Complexion at a Birthday Ball.

The Cook's Oracle
WILLIAM KITCHINER
1822

❖

B eef makes the best stock; veal stock has less colour and taste; whilst mutton sometimes gives it a tallowy smell, far from agreeable, unless the meat has been previously roasted or broiled.

Book of Household Management
MRS BEETON
(1836–65)

❖

M adam, I have been looking for a person who disliked gravy all my life; let us swear eternal friendship.

SYDNEY SMITH
(1771–1845)

❖

When mighty roast beef was the Englishman's
food
It ennobled our hearts and enriched our
blood;
Our soldiers were brave and our courtiers
were good,
  Oh! the roast beef of Old England
  And oh! for Old England's roast beef.

Ascribed to
HENRY FIELDING
(1707–54)

A well-cooked filet mignon has more to tell
about the truth and meaning of life than a
dozen French existentialists could ever do.

KATHERINE MILNE
2002

To my mind a fine well cooked haunch of venison – such as is served during the season every Tuesday and Thursday at the Albion Hotel opposite Drury Lane Theatre is the finest dinner obtainable.

A Man about Town
1850

A dainty bit from the king's [of Persia] was a present meet for a lover to make to his lady; and a wooer who brought a rump steak of horse-flesh in his hand, straight from the regal table, was scarcely a man to be refused anything.

Table Traits
DR DORAN
1854

The Meat Course

At noon, had Sir W. Pen and his son William to my house to dinner—I having some venison given me a day or two ago, and so I had a shoulder roasted, another baked, and the umbles baked in a pie, and all very well done.

Diary, 5th July 1662
SAMUEL PEPYS

The curates had good appetites, and though the beef was tough, they ate a great deal of it. They swallowed, too, a tolerable allowance of the 'flat beer', while a dish of Yorkshire pudding and two tureens of vegetables disappeared like leaves before locusts. The cheese, too, received distinguished marks of their attention; and a 'spice-cake', which followed by way of dessert, vanished like a vision and was no more found.

The Professor
CHARLOTTE BRONTË
(1816–55)

Wh[hen] we [the German troops] are camp-aigning, and get hungry, we knock over the first animal we find, cut off a steak, powder it with salt, which we always have in the sabre-tasche, put it under the saddle, gallop over it for half a mile, and then dine like princes.

A CROAT CAPTAIN
reported by
JEAN ANTHELME BRILLAT-SAVARIN
1815

The labouring classes seldom purchase what are called the coarsest pieces of meat because they do not know how to dress them.

The Cook's Oracle
WILLIAM KITCHINER
1822

Gently stir and blow the fire,
Lay the mutton down to roast,
Dress it quickly, I desire,
In the dripping put a toast,
That I hunger may remove —
Mutton is the meat I love.

On the dresser see it lie;
Oh! the charming white and red;
Finer meat ne'er met the eye,
On the sweetest grass it fed:
Let the jack go swiftly round,
Let me have it nicely brown'd.

On the table spread the cloth,
Let the knives be sharp and clean,
Pickles get and salad both,
Let them each be fresh and green.
With small beer, good ale and wine,
Oh ye gods! how shall I dine!

Receipt to Roast Mutton
SYDNEY SMITH
(1771–1845)

❖

GOODLY TERMS OF CARVING

Breke that dere
thye that pegyon
lyft that swanne
sauce that capon
frusshe that chekyn
unbrace that malarde
unlace that cony
dysplaye that crane
dysfygure that pecocke
tuske that barbell
alaye that fesande
tayme that crabbe
mynce that plover

wynge that quayle
rere that goose
breke that egryt
spoyle that henne
strynge that lampraye
splatte that pyke
dysmembre that heron
splaye that breme
unjoynt that bittern
culpon that troute
wynge that partryche
barbe that lopster
undertraunch ye
purpoise [porpoise]

The Boke of Kervynge
Wynkyn de Worde
(?d.1535)

Bad carving used to spoil three things on the part of the carver, good joints, good temper and a good digestion ... and to short men it was a positive infliction, for I need scarcely say, that

under no circumstances whatever could a man be
permitted to stand up to carve.

The Habits of Good Society
ANON
1859

❖

If the dish be pleasant, either fleshe or fishe,
Ten hands at once swarm in the dishe;
And if it be fleshe ten knives shalt thou see,
Mangling the flesh, and in the platter flee.
To put there thy handes, in peril without fail
Without a gauntlet, or else a glove of mail.

Eclogues
ALEXANDER BARCLAY
(?1475–1552)

❖

Who would make hay of his
food, and pitch it into his
mouth with a fork.

Mediaeval Manuscript
c.1400

The baron of beef. – This noble joint, which consisted of two sirloins not cut asunder, was a favourite dish of our ancestors.

Book of Household Management
MRS BEETON
(1836–65)

Common cooks sometimes stew meat in a mixture of butter and water, *and call it braising.*

Modern Cookery for Private Families
ELIZA ACTON
1845

❖

The English system of cooking it would be impertinent for me to describe; but still when I think of that huge round of parboiled ox flesh, with sodden dumplings, floating in a saline, greasy mixture, surrounded by carrots looking red with disgust, and turnips pale with dismay, I cannot help a sort of inward shudder, and making comparisons unfavourable to English gastronomy.

The Memoirs of a Stomach,
Written by Himself, that All who Eat may Read
SYDNEY WHITING
1853

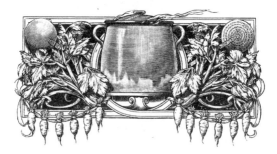

Wild boar's head, would elevate the plainest dinner into dignity.

The Original
THOMAS WALKER
(1784–1836)

❖

There is no flavour comparable, I will contend, to that of the crisp, tawny, well-watched, not over-roasted crackling, as it is well called – the very teeth are invited to their share of the pleasure at this banquet in overcoming the coy, brittle resistance – with the adhesive oleaginous – O call it not fat! but an undefinable sweetness growing up to it – the tender blossoming of fat – the cream and quintessence of the child pig.

Essays of Elia
CHARLES LAMB
(1775–1834)

❖

Fair fa' your honest sonsie face,
Great cheifatin o' the puddin' race!
Aboon them a' ye tak' your place,
  Painch, tripe, or thirm;
Weel are ye wordy of a grace
  As lang's my arm.

From 'To a Haggis'
ROBERT BURNS
(1759–96)

❖

Elizabeth Tudor her breakfast would make
On a pot of strong beer and a pound of
    beefsteak
Ere six the morning was told by the chimes —
Oh, the days of Queen Bess, they were merry
    old times.

      . . .

'Unsheath me, mine host, thy Toledo so
    bright:
Delicious Sir Loin! I dub thee a knight;
Be thine at our banquets of honour the post —
While the Queen rules the realm, Sir Loin
    rules the roast!'

OLD BALLAD

I think that the end of meat rationing was the single greatest factor contributing to the length and happiness of my marriage. Young people today don't realise the misery of placing a slab of whale meat artistically garnished with a leaf of parsley before a young husband when he came home tired out from work. Steak and roast chicken with all the trimmings are the road to a man's heart.

ANNETTE MILLET (WI MEMBER)
1991

❖

As soon as the slightest trace of putrescence is detected, it [meat] has reached its highest degree of tenderness, and should be dressed immediately.

Book of Household Management
MRS BEETON
(1836–65)

❖

No Forsyte has given a dinner without providing a saddle of mutton. There is something
in its succulent solidity which makes it suitable to
people 'of a certain position'. It is nourishing and –
tasty; the sort of thing a man remembers eating. It
has a past and a future, like a deposit paid into a
bank.

The Forsyte Saga
JOHN GALSWORTHY
(1867–1903)

I was a bit worried when I first realised that I spent longer looking in the windows of the butcher and planning my supper than I did in studying the information available on page 3 of *The Sun*. Now I think it's probably a change for the better.

SEAN BROWN
1999

❖

Caledonia's greatest and most characteristic triumph in culinary science is the haggis, which is made in this wise. One of the stomachs of a sheep ... is cut off from the others and thoroughly cleaned to whiteness. It is a bag with a small mouth. The heart, lungs, and the liver of the sheep are minced small and put into the bag, mixed with minced suet, onions, salt, pepper, and some toasted oatmeal. The orifice is then closed and the bag with its contents boiled.

Properly made, it is excellent; badly prepared it is nauseous.

Good Cheer
FREDERICK W. HACKWOOD
1911

Of birth renowned, entitled well to boast,
And reared with care, the little pig is dead:
We sorrow, but we scent the savoury roast,
And mix a bumper while our tears we shed.
We loved him, silky-soft, and plump, and
    fine,
And now that he has felt the crisping fire
We wait his soul and body to enshrine,
A morsel for an epicure's desire.

From 'Dissertation sur le Cochon'
REV. JOSEPH A. ELY'S TRANS.
c.1854

Some say my roasts are lacking panache
My stews only verge on Okay
But when I serve them bangers and mash
I'm celebrity chef for a day.

P.J.M.

R aw flesh, when seasoned with salt is not disagreeable and easily digested.

JEAN ANTHELME BRILLAT-SAVARIN
(1755–1826)

M r. Crawley said a long grace, and Sir Pitt said amen, and the great silver dish-covers were removed.

'What have we for dinner, Betsy?' said the Baronet.

'Mutton broth, I believe, Sir Pitt," answered Lady Crawley.

'*Mouton aux navets,*' added the butler gravely (pronounce, if you please, moutongonavvy); 'and the soup is *potage de mouton à l'Ecossaise*. The side-dishes contain *pommes de terre au naturel*, and *choufleur a l'eau.*'

'Mutton's mutton,' said the Baronet, 'and a devilish good thing.'

Vanity Fair
WILLIAM MAKEPEACE THACKERAY
(1811–63)

No broth, no ball [normally suet pudding but Yorkshire pudding in the North]; no ball, no meat.

Cranford
MRS GASKELL
(1810–65)

❖

In a leg of beef, two things are distinguished – namely, the parish-priest's piece, and the parish clerk's. The last is the least tender; as, indeed, it ought to be, for there is scarcely any thing so tough as an old humbug of this caste.

Tales of the Table,
Kitchen, and Larder
DICK HUMELBERGIUS SECUNDUS
1829

❖

Vegetables

*F*ORGET THE TEPID, *over-boiled Brussell sprouts of childhood; fresh and well-cooked vegetables, from asparagus to zucchini, are one of the glories of the gourmet's table with an unequalled subtlety of natural flavour. And they're good for you.*

As to the quality of vegetables … freshness is their chief value and excellence, and I should as soon think of roasting an Animal alive, as of boiling a Vegetable after it is dead.

The Cook's Oracle
WILLIAM KITCHINER
1822

❖

Vegetables when not sufficiently cooked are known to be so exceedingly unwholesome and indigestible, that the custom of serving them *crisp*, which means, in reality, only half boiled, should be altogether disregarded.

Modern Cookery for Private Families
ELIZA ACTON
1845

❖

A bean in liberty is better than a comfit or any sweetmeat in prison.

Outlandish Proverbs
GEORGE HERBERT
1593-1633

One of the greatest luxuries in dining is to be able to command plenty of good vegetables well served up. But this is a luxury vainly hoped for at set parties. The vegetables are made to figure in a very secondary way, except, indeed, whilst they are considered as great delicacies, which is generally before they are at their best – excellent potatoes, smoking hot and accompanied by melted butter of the first quality would alone stamp merit on any dinner.

The Art of Dining
Thomas Walker
1835

If you are suffering from thoughts of a melancholy dinner at home, Toranius, you may come and dine with me. You will find no lack of common Cappadocian lettuces and well-flavoured leeks; tuna will lurk under slices of egg; a cauliflower hot enough to burn your fingers, which has only just left the cool garden, will be served fresh and green on a black plate; while sausages will float on snow-white porridge and the pale haricot will contrast with the red streaky bacon. If you wish to know the pleasures of the second course, raisins will be set before you, and pears as good as Syrian, and chestnuts from Naples gave birth, roasted at a slow fire.

MARTIAL
(C.40–C.104)

Infinitely more baneful than anchovy sauce is the bottled 'salad dressing' of commerce, in whatever guise it may appear – that milky, mysterious compound which is set upon certain restaurant and hotel tables, and through the cajoleries of the merchant-grocer or blandishments of the advertiser often even invades otherwise respectable households.

The Pleasures of the Table
GEORGE H. ELLWANGER
1903

Give me the lettuce that has cool'd
   Its heart in the rich earth,
Till every joyous leaf is school'd
   To crispy-crinkled mirth.

The wayward endive's curling head,
   Cool cucumber sliced small,
And let the imperial beetroot spread
   Her purple over all.

From 'A Ballad to a Salad'
WARHAM S. LEGER
(1850–c.1915)

Cabbage, when boiled for eight minutes and served with the smallest suspicion of butter, is the equal of any rumpsteak. Boiled for ten and even a hungry pig will reject it.

Letters of Advice to his Son
REV. J. ARBUTHNOT
1864

Our cooks today prepare all vegetables and fruit that comes from the ground in so delightful a way that nothing could be more delicious than mushrooms, root vegetables and all sorts of herbs. I was deceived at the dinner given by Lentulus, and my greed was punished by an indigestion which lasted for more than ten days. I have no problem in holding back from oysters and lampreys, but was caught out by beetroot and mallow. I shall be wiser a second time.

CICERO
(106–43BC)

In answer to a lady's enquiring
whether he ever ate vegetables
Yes, Madam, I once ate a pea.

BEAU BRUMMELL
(1778–1840)

RECIPE FOR A SALAD

To make this condiment, your poet begs
The pounded yellow of two hard-boiled eggs;
Two large potatoes, pass'd through kitchen sieve,
Smoothness and softness to the salad give:
Of mordent mustard add a single spoon,
Distrust the condiment that bites too soon;
But deem it not, thou man of herbs, a fault.
To add a double quantity of salt:
Four times the spoon with oil of Lucca crown,
And twice with vinegar procured from 'town';
Let onion's atoms lurk within the bowl,
And, scarce suspected, animate the whole;
And, lastly, in the flavour'd compound toss
A magic spoonful of anchovy sauce.
Oh! great and glorious, and herbaceous treat,
'Twould tempt the dying anchorite to eat.
Back to the world he'd turn his weary soul,
And plunge his fingers in the salad-bowl.
Serenely full, the epicure would say,
Fate cannot harm me, I have dined today.

Recipe for Salad
SYDNEY SMITH
(1771–1845)

❖

A cucumber should be well sliced and dressed with pepper and vinegar, and then thrown out as good for nothing.

Quoted by Boswell in *Tour to the Hebrides*
SAMUEL JOHNSON
(1709–84)

In wandering through Covent Garden market, and passing from floral dreams to the vegetables, I often pause befor the peas. Do I yearn for them in their adolescence? do I associate them with the duckling and the lamb? Nay; I await a time when they shall have folded and creased within themselves their perfected saccharine excellence, to be released in the kitchen of the winter.

'A Dissertation on Roast Pig'
CHARLES LAMB
(1775–1834)

ONIONS

Come, follow me by the smell,
Here are delicate onions to sell;
I promise to use you well.
They make the blood warmer,
You'll feed like a farmer;
For this is every cook's opinion,
No savoury dish without an onion;
But, lest your kissing should be spoiled,
Your onions must be thoroughly boiled:

From 'Market Women's Cries'
JONATHAN SWIFT
(1667–1745)

Parsley. – If there be nothing new under the sun, there are, at any rate, different uses found for the same thing; for this pretty aromatic herb was used in ancient times, as we learn from mythological narrative, to adorn the head of a hero, no less than Hercules; and now – was ever fall so great? – we moderns use it in connection with the head of – a calf.

Book of Household Management
MRS BEETON
(1836–65)

It [the potato] must be very nutritious, or it would not sustain the strength of thousands of people whose almost sole food it constitutes.

Modern Cookery for Private Families
ELIZA ACTON
1845

If Vegetables are a minute or two too long over the Fire, – they lose all their Beauty and Flavour.

The Cook's Oracle
WILLIAM KITCHINER
1822

❖

The only people who praise nettle soup are those who have never tried it.

JAMES YOUNG
1982

❖

Abstain from beans.

PYTHAGORAS
(6th century BC)

❖

When the ducks and green peas came, we looked at each other in dismay; we had only two-pronged, black handled forks. It is true, the steel was as bright as silver; but what were we to do? Miss Matty picked up her peas, one by one, on the point of the prongs … Miss Pole sighed over her delicate young peas as she left them on one side of her plate untasted; for they would drop between the prongs. I looked at my host; the peas were going wholesale into his capacious mouth, shovelled up by his large round-ended knife. I saw, I imitated, I survived!

Cranford
MRS GASKELL
(1810–65)

I eat my peas with honey –
I've done it all my life.
It makes the peas taste funny
But it keeps them on the knife.

ANON

I beg of you to make a constant use of them at your own table [properly dressed vegetables], as you will find that they will be much better than partaking of half-raw greens, cabbage, turnip tops, spinach, &c., which are so often served up at tables in this country, and are less inviting in flavour, and, consequently, do not get consumed so much as they ought, which causes more meat to be eaten, and, instead of refreshing the blood, as all vegetables will do in their season only irritate it.

The Modern Housewife
ALEXIS SOYER
1851

I have never read of any Roman supper that seemed to me equal to a dinner of my own vegetables; when everything on the table is the product of my own labor... It is strange what a taste you suddenly have for things you never liked before. The squash has always been to me a dish of contempt; but I eat it now as if it were my best friend. I never cared for the beet or the bean; but I fancy now that I could eat them all, tops and all, so completely have they been transformed by the soil in which they grew.

Summer in a Garden
CHARLES DUDLEY WARNER
(1829–1900)

❖

I have often thought the asparagus a great social indicator of wealth. The working class can't afford them; the middle class can afford them three times in season and chew them right down to the tough bitter ends of the stalk; but the pluticrat delicately removes the tips of the youngest shoots and allows them to dissolve gently in his mouth.

ANTHONY SANDYS
2001

Pastries and Puddings, Pies and Desserts

*W*HAT WOULD CHRISTMAS be without its pudding and mince pies; what a birthday without a cake; what a summer without plum tart and apple pie? Whether savoury or sweet, the delights of the pastry cook and the confectioner are a temptation no diner can resist.

A cook they had with them for the nonce,
To boil the chickens and the marrow bones,
And powder marchant, tart and galingale
Well could he know a draught of London ale.
He could roast, and seeth and broil and fry,
Make mortrewes, and well bake a pie.
For blancmange that made he with the best.

Canterbury Tales
GEOFFREY CHAUCER
(c.1345–1400)

❖

The dessert is said to be to the dinner what
the madrigal is to literature – it is the light
poetry of the kitchen, addressed largely to the
gentler sex.

The Pleasures of the Table
GEORGE H. ELLWANGER
1903

❖

Promises and pie-crust
are made to be broken.

JONATHAN SWIFT
(1667–1745)

Souls of Poets dead and gone,
What Elysium have ye known,
Happy field or mossy cavern,
Choicer than the Mermaid Tavern?
Have ye tippled drink more fine
Than mine host's Canary wine?
Or are fruits of Paradise
Sweeter than those dainty pies?

JOHN KEATS
(1795–1821)

❖

Hallo! A great deal of steam! The pudding was out of the copper! A smell like a washing day! That was the cloth. A smell like an eating-house, and a pastry-cook's next door to that. That was the pudding. In half a minute Mrs Cratchit entered – flushed, but smiling proudly – with the pudding, like a speckled cannon-ball, so hard and firm, blazing in a half-a-quatern of ignited brandy, and bedight with Christmas holly stuck into the top.

Oh! what a wonderful pudding!

A Christmas Carol
CHARLES DICKENS
(1812–70)

A master cook...
Rears bulwark pies; and for his outer works,
He raises ramparts of immortal crusts.

BEN JONSON
(1572–1637)

There are a world of bak'd
meats and pies.

The English Housewife
GERVASE MARKHAM
1649

When an eating house keeper sets down afore his customers and deliberately eats one of his own Weal pies, no man can refuse confidence.

SIMMONS
1858

The Pudding is a dish very difficult to be describ'd, because of the several Sorts there are of it; Flower, Milk, Eggs, Butter, Sugar, Suet, Marrow, Raisins, &c &c. are the most common ingredients of a Pudding. They bake them in an Oven, they boil them with Meat, they make them fifty several ways: Blessed be he that invented pudding, for it is a capital Manna that hits the Palates of all Sorts of People; a Manna, better than that of the Wilderness, because the People are never weary of it. Ah, what an excellent Thing is an English Pudding!

Memoirs and Observations
in his Travels over England
H. MISSON
1719

Yes! How can boy make better end,
    An end more sweet and sudden,
Than smiling, die of Elsie's pie
    After a course of pudding.

Ballads from 'Punch'
WARHAM ST LEGER
1890

Like Albion's rich plum-pudding, famous grown,
The mince-pye reigns in realms beyond his own,
Through foreign latitudes his power extends,
And only terminates where eating ends.

'Ode to the Mince-Pye'
WILLIAM HONE
18th century

The comparative merits of pies and puddings present a problem which it is no easy matter to decide. On the whole, we give the preference to puddings, these affording more scope to the inventive genius of the cook. A plum pudding, for instance, our national dish, is hardly ever boiled enough. A green apricot tart is commonly considered the best tart that is made; but a green apricot pudding is a much better thing. A cherry dumpling is better than a cherry tart. A beefsteak pudding, again, is better than the corresponding pie; but oysters and mushrooms are essential to

its success. A mutton-chop pudding with oysters, but without mushrooms, is excellent.

The Original
THOMAS WALKER
(1784–1836)

These [venison, hare, mutton, or veal pies] are dishes contrived rather to excite appetite, than to satisfy it. Putting meat or poultry into a pie is certainly the worst way of cooking it: – it is often baked to rags: – and very rarely does a savoury pie come to the table that deserves to be introduced to the stomach.

The Cook's Oracle
WILLIAM KITCHINER
1822

❖

He [Lord Alvanley] resided in Park Street, St James's, and his dinners there and at Melton were considered to be the best in England. He never invited more than eight people, and insisted upon having the somewhat expensive luxury of an apricot tart on the sideboard the whole year round.

REES HOWELL GRONOW
(1794–1865)

THE MINCE PIE

Oh, King of cates, whose pastry-bounded reign
Is felt and owned o'er Pastry's wide domain.

DOCTOR PARR
19th century

❖

A man cannot have a pure mind who refuses apple-dumplings.

CHARLES LAMB
(1775–1834)

APPLE PIE

But, oh! be careful of the paste! Let it be not like putty, nor rush to the other extreme and make it so flaky that one holds his breath while eating, for fear of blowing it away. Let it not be plain as bread, nor yet rich like cake. Aim at that glorious medium in which it is tender without being too fugaciously flaky; short without being too short; a mild, sapid, brittle thing, that lies upon the tongue, so as to let the apple strike through and touch the papillae with a more affluent flavour. But this, like all high art, must be a thing of inspiration or instinct.

The Pleasures of the Table
GEORGE H. ELLWANGER
1903

❖

Pie, often foolishly abused, is a good creature at the right time and in angles of thirty or forty degrees, although in semicircles and quadrants it may sometimes prove too much for delicate stomachs.

ARTEMUS WARD
(1834–67)

'I think I want some pies this morning,'
Said Dick, stretching himself and yawning;
So down he threw his slate and books,
And saunter'd to the pastry cook's.

And there he cast his greed eyes,
Round on the jellies and the pies,
So to select with anxious care,
The very nicest that was there.

At last the point was thus decided:
As his opinion was divided
'Twixt pie and jelly, being loth
Either to leave, he took them both.

From 'Greedy Richard'
JANE AND ANN TAYLOR
(1783–1824 and 1782–1866)

Mrs. Crupp then said what she would recommend would be this. A pair of hot roast
fowls – from the pastrycook's; a dish of stewed
beef, with vegetables – from the pastrycook's;

two little corner things, as a raised pie and a dish
of kidneys – from the pastrycook's; a tart, and (if
I liked) a shape of jelly – from the pastrycook's.
This, Mrs. Crupp said, would leave her at full
liberty to concentrate her mind on the potatoes,
and to serve up the cheese and celery as she could
wish to see it done.

David Copperfield
CHARLES DICKENS
(1812–1870)

The tottering wall of jelly would look infinitely more comfortable had it been broken
down and its quivering pieces put into glasses.

Etiquette of Good Society
LADY COLIN CAMPBELL
1898

Those who keep up the old style … In the way of fruits, display oranges in their original golden skin, Ribston pippins in their mournful ones, American apples with their vermillion cheeks, large winter pears in their substantial state, the whole ornamented and crowned with laurel, no doubt to signify their immortality, being present upon almost every table from year to year, especially the unsociable pear, which no teeth can ever injure.

The Modern Housewife
ALEXIS SOYER
1851

There by the bedside, where the faded moon
Made a dim silver twilight, soft he set
A table, and, half-anguish'd, threw thereon
A cloth of woven crimson, gold, and jet.

While he, from forth the closet, brought a heap
Of candied apple, quince, and plum, and gourd;
With jellies smoother than the creamy curd,
And lucent syrups tinct with cinnamon;
Manna and dates, in argosy transferr'd
From Fez; and spiced dainties, every one,
From silken Samarcand to cedar'd Lebanon.

Eve of Saint Agnes
JOHN KEATS
(1795–1821)

EVENING PARTY OR BALL

Flowers and fruits should occupy the middle of
the table, from one end to the other. Bon-
bons, crackers, and ornamented cakes should
spring up on all sides, together with frothy trifles,
quivering jellies, snowy creams, and light
soufflés, all placed in glass dishes.

Etiquette of Good Society
LADY COLIN CAMPBELL
1898

Ah! on Thanksgiving day, when from East and
    from West,
From North and from South, come the
    pilgrim and guest,
When the gray-haired New Englander sees
    round his board
The old broken links of affection restored,
When the care-wearied man seeks his mother
    once more,
And the worn matron smiles where the girl
    smiled before.
What moistens the lip and what brightens the
    eye?
What calls back the past, like the rich
    Pumpkin pie?

JOHN GREENLEAF WHITTIER
(1807–92)

This [trifle] is fit to go to the King's table, if well made, and very excellent.

The Art of Cookery Made Plain and Easy
HANNAH GLASSE
1747

❖

It was Easter week, and Mrs. Tulliver's cheese-cakes were more exquisitely light than usual. 'A puff o' wind 'ud make 'em blow about like feathers,' Kezia the housemaid said, feeling proud to live under a mistress who could make such pastry.

The Mill on the Floss
GEORGE ELIOT
(1819–80)

The Kitchen and
The Housewife

*N*OT ONLY MUST THE *good* housekeeper provide
*delicious meals if she is to keep her family and
home together but she must also make certain she buys
economically, keeps her kitchen tidy and clean, and all
her utensils well scrubbed and in their proper place. Not
a chapter for the faint hearted.*

Ill-cooked, untidy meals, are as great a cause of bad temper as many a moral wrong.

A Woman's Thoughts About Women
DINAH MARIA MULOCK CRAIK
(1826–87)

❖

MRS PEPYS'S NEW OVEN

She [when she first baked pies and tarts] did heat it too hot, and so did a little overbake her things but now knows how to do better another time.

Diary Entry
SAMUEL PEPYS
(1633–1703)

❖

Do everything at the proper time.
Keep everything in its proper place.
Use every thing for its proper purpose.

The Cook's Oracle
WILLIAM KITCHINER
1822

I have always thought that there is no more fruitful source of family discontent than a housewife's badly-cooked dinners and untidy ways. Men are now so well served out of doors, – at their clubs, well-ordered taverns, and dining-houses, that in order to compete with the attractions of these places, a mistress must be thoroughly acquainted with the theory and practice of cookery, as well as be perfectly conversant with all the other arts of making and keeping a comfortable home.

Book of Household Management
MRS BEETON
(1836–65)

A spoilt dinner will spoil a good temper and disarrange a whole household.

SAYING

If you can't stand the heat, get out of the kitchen

HARRY S. TRUMAN
USA President 1945–53

❖

If a hard-working man cannot get a comfortable meal at home, he soon finds the way to the Public House, – the poor Woman contents herself with Tea and Bread and Butter, – and the Children are little better than starved.

The Cook's Oracle
WILLIAM KITCHINER
1822

❖

No, Madame; women can spin very well, – but they cannot make a good book of Cookery.

SAMUEL JOHNSON
(1709–84)

❖

Assuredly, appetising cookery will tend more than any other means to maintain the masculine element in good humour, and thereby foster a spirit of liberality and the condoning of feminine foibles.

The Pleasures of the Table
GEORGE H. ELLWANGER
1903

❖

A small portion of the Time which young Ladies sacrifice to torturing the strings of their Piano-Forte, employed in obtaining domestic accomplishments – might not make them worst wives, or less agreeable Companions to their Husbands.

The Cook's Oracle
WILLIAM KITCHINER
1822

❖

Kissing don't last:
cookery do!

The Ordeal of Richard Feverel
GEORGE MEREDITH
(1828–1909)

There was a young lady of Hitchen
Who would never go down to the kitchen
   Till her father said 'Rose,
    You're a goose to suppose
Affectation's genteel or bewitchin.'

ANON.
1863

It is particularly directed that each kitchen be provided with a furnace sufficiently large to roast two or three oxen.

HUGH DE NEVILL
[directing the construction of the King's kitchen at Clarendon 1206]

THE NEW KITCHENS AT THE REFORM CLUB

The kitchen is as spacious as a ballroom, kept in perfect order, and gleams white as a young bride … in an age of utilitarianism and of the search for the comfortable such as ours, one can learn more here than among the ruins of the Coloseum or the Parthenon.

Courrier de L'Europe
THE VICOMTESSE DE MALLEVILLE
c.1840

Cooking in large kitchens is mediocre at best.

FRIEDRICH NIETZSCHE
(1844–1900)

A MUSICAL TURNSPIT
BELONGING TO THE COUNT DE CASTEL MARIA

The spits of this machine turned 130 roasts at the same time; and the chef was informed, by the progress of the melodies when the moment had arrived for moving each piece of meat.

A Book about the Table
J.C. JEAFFRESON
1875

❖

There is comprehended, under the curs of the coarsest kind, a certain dog in kitchen service excellent, For when any meat is to be roasted they go into a wheel, which they turning about with the weight of their bodies, so diligently look to their business that no drudge or scullion can do the feat more cunningly, whom the popular sort hereupon term turnspits.

Of Englishe Dogges
DR JOHN CAIUS
Translated into English under the above title
by Abraham Fleming
1570

❖

The dinner must be dished at one.
Where's this vexatious turnspit gone?
Unless the skulking cur is caught
The sirloin's spoilt and I'm in fault.

Was ever cur so cursed (he cried);
What star did at my birth preside?
Am I for life by compact bound
To tread the wheels eternal round?

JOHN GAY
(1685–1732)

If you have a lacke of cooks – how to persuade a Goose to roast him-self!!!

Natural Magicke
BAPTISTA DE PORTA
1658

Have the Dust, &c. removed regularly once a fortnight, – and have your Kitchen Chimney swept once a month; – many good Dinners have been spoilt and many houses burnt down by the soot falling.

The Cook's Oracle
WILLIAM KITCHINER
1822

HOW TO ROAST IF YOU CAN'T AFFORD A SPIT

Silas was thinking of his supper. Supper was his favourite meal … whenever he had roast meat, he always chose to have it for supper. This evening, he had ingeniously knotted his string fast round his bit of pork, twisted the string according to rule over his door-key, passed it through the handle, and made it fast on the hanger …

Silas Marner
GEORGE ELIOT
(1819–80)

Housekeeping ain't no joke.

Louisa May Alcott
(1832–88)

❖

Carrie Gore let me in to the Mill kitchen through the meal room and loft over the machinery, and there was Mrs Gore making up the bread into loaves and putting them into the oven …

Mrs Gore had made her some apple hop-abouts,

but forgot to put them in the oven till I reminded her of them. Mrs Gore wanted me to have some gin and when I declined offered me tea as an alternative. I accepted the tea....Oh the dear old Mill kitchen, the low, large room so snug, so irregular and full of odd holes and corners, so cosy and comfy with its low ceiling, horse-hair couch, easy chair by the fire, flowers in the window recess, the door opening into the best room or parlour. Oh these kindly hospitable houses about these hospitable hills. I believe I might wander about these hills all my life and never want a kindly welcome, a meal, or a seat by the fireside.

Diary, 26th October 1870
FRANCIS KILVERT

❖

A surgeon may as well attempt to make an incision with a pair of Shears, or open a vein with an Oyster Knife, as a Cook pretend to dress a Dinner without proper Tools.

Cookery
VERBALL
1759

A HAWKER'S CRY

Buy a fine toasting fork for toast or fine spice-grater – tools for an host; if these in winter be lacking, I say, your guests will pack, your trade decay.

Fancified food such as pork goosified or game in the shape of a crawfish or poultry made to look like hedgehogs – such dishes are... more for show and sport than for belly-Timber, and about which the Good Huswife never troubles her head.

Kitchen
JOAN CROMWELL
1664

❖

He is an ill cook that cannot lick his own fingers.

TRADITIONAL SAYING

The Kitchen and The Housewife

The cook must be cleanly both in body and garments. She must have a quick eye, a curious nose, a perfect taste, and a ready ear; and she must not be butter-fingered, sweet-toothed, nor faint hearted. For the first will let everything fall; the second will consume what it should increase; and the last will lose time with too much niceness.

The English Housewife
1683

Though we don't suppose our cook to be such a naughty Slut, as to wilfully neglect her broth pots, &c. yet we recommend her to wash them immediately.

The Cook's Oracle
WILLIAM KITCHINER
1822

I remember Grannie going down into the kitchen one day and scolding the cook till she could bear it no longer, when she seized the dinner-bell from the shelf and rang it in her ears till she ran out of the kitchen.

Life With Mother
AUGUSTUS HARE
(1834-1903)

In bleak northern farmsteads there was much to be done before November weather should make the roads too heavy for half-fed horses to pull carts through ... There was meat to salt

160

while it could be had; for, in default of turnips and mangoldwurzel, there was a great slaughtering of barren cows as soon as the summer herbage failed; and good housewives stored up their Christmas piece of beef in pickle before Martinmas was over. Corn was to be ground while yet it could be carried to the distant mill; the great racks for oat-cake, that swung at the top of the kitchen, had to be filled. And last of all came the pig-killing, when the second frost set in.

Sylvia's Lovers
ELIZABETH GASKELL
(1810–65)

❖

When my old wife lived, upon
This day she was both pantler, butler, cook,
Both dame and servant, welcomed all,
     served all,
Would sing her song and dance her turn,
     now here.

The Winter's Tale
WILLIAM SHAKESPEARE
(1564–1616)

❖

G reat care should be taken that nothing is thrown away, or suffered to be wasted in the kitchen, which might, by proper management, be turned to a good account.

> *Book of Household Management*
> MRS BEETON
> (1836–65)

❖

C ooks, half stewed, and half roasted, when unable to work any longer, generally retire to some unknown corner, and die in forlorness and want.

> *Blackwood's Edinburgh Magazine,*
> *Vol.VII*

❖

M y cook prepares and sends up dinner. From long practice, she does it a hundred times better than I could do; nay, even takes a pleasure and pride in it, for which I am truly thankful, and sincerely indebted to her, too: for a good cook is a household blessing, and no small contributor to health, temper, and enjoyment. Accordingly, I treat her with a certain respectful awe. But I do not invite her to eat her own dinner, or mingle in the society which to me is its most piquant sauce. She was not born to it, not brought up for it. Good old soul! she would gape at the finest bon-mot, and doze over the most intellectual conversation. She is better left in peace by her kitchen-fire.

A Woman's Thoughts About Women
DINAH MARIA MULOCK CRAIK
(1826–87)

T hen the cook left; also an old servant, though not so old a one as Betty. The cook did not like the trouble of late dinners; and, being a Methodist, she objected on religious grounds to trying any of Mrs Gibson's new recipes for French dishes. It was not scriptural, she said. There was a deal of mention of food in the Bible; but it was of sheep ready dressed, which meant mutton, and of wine, and of bread-and-milk, and figs and raisins, of fatted calves, a good well-browned fillet of veal, and such like; but it had always gone against her conscience to

cook swine-flesh and make raised pork-pies, and now if she was to be set to cook heathen dishes, after the fashion of the Papists, she'd sooner give it up altogether.

Wives and Daughters
ELIZABETH GASKELL
(1810–65)

❖

The wise woman will have many side-lights in her composition; and in the kitchen her sauces will have many shadings.

Let us toast her in a glass of sparkling St Peray, and acknowledge that without her there were no home cuisine and consequently no home life. So closely does the art advocated by the late lamented Mrs Glasse touch upon the fundamental happiness of mankind.

The Pleasures of the Table
GEORGE H. ELLWANGER
1903

❖

Breakfast and Lunch

*O*NE CANNOT READ OF AN old-fashioned breakfast with its sausage, bacon, ham, kidneys, smoked haddock, kippers and eggs, all accompanied by butter-dripping toast; or of a Victorian luncheon with game pie, salmon-trout and grouse without a sense of mouth-watering nostalgia.

Always breakfast as if you did not intend to dine; and dine as if you had not broken your fast.

CODE GOURMAND

❖

THE HUNT BREAKFAST AND SPORTSMEN'S BREAKFAST

Game pie is a standard dish on these occasions cold beef, devilled turkey, broiled ham, French pies, &c. Cherry brandy is at hand for those who choose that as their beverage, and tankards of beer; but huntsmen nowadays, as a rule, take tea and coffee.

Etiquette of Good Society
LADY COLIN CAMPBELL
1898

❖

Only dull people are brilliant at breakfast.

OSCAR WILDE
(1854–1900)

Ravenous, and now very faint, I devoured a spoonful or two of my portion without thinking of its taste; but, the first edge of hunger blunted, I perceived I had got in hand a nauseous mess: burned porridge is almost as bad as rotten potatoes...

Jane Eyre
CHARLOTTE BRONTË
(1816–55)

The following list of hot dishes may perhaps assist our readers in knowing what to provide for the comfortable meal called breakfast. Broiled fish, such as mackerel, whiting, herrings, dried haddocks, &c.; mutton chops and rump-steaks, broiled sheep's kidneys, kidneys à la maître d'hôtel, sausages, plain rashers of bacon, bacon and poached eggs, ham and poached eggs, omelets, plain boiled eggs, oeufs-au-plat, poached eggs on toast, muffins, toast, marmalade, butter, &c. &c.

Book of Household Management
MRS BEETON
(1836–65)

T he more substantial dishes – such as hams, tongues, and pies – are usually placed on a white cloth on the sideboard; and at an ordinary breakfast the gentlemen help themselves and the ladies also.

Etiquette of Good Society
LADY COLIN CAMPBELL
1898

❖

At Brownhill we always get dainty good cheer,
And plenty of bacon each day in the year;
We've a' thing that's nice, and mostly in season,
But why always Bacon – come, tell me a reason?

Epigram at Brownhill Inn
ROBERT BURNS
(1759–96)

W hen you are invited to breakfast, or to dine in town, never take dogs with you. It is only the common people, and *les dames à la mode* who take such liberties… A dog, how wellsoever he may have been brought up, spoils the furniture, and produces no small embarrassment, should he think proper to do his 'little jobs' before you; but his presence is still worse at table, where he is continually among your legs, or eyeing your plate.

Tales of the Table, Kitchen, and Larder
DICK HUMELBERGIUS SECUNDUS
1829

A verage American's simplest and commonest form of breakfast consists of coffee and beefsteak.

A Tramp Abroad
MARK TWAIN
(1835–1910)

A man of taste is seen at once in the array of his breakfast-table ... Chocolate, coffee, tea, cream, eggs, ham, tongue, cold fowl – all these are good, and bespeak good knowledge in him who sets them forth: but the touchstone is fish: anchovy is the first step, prawns and shrimps the second; and I laud him who reaches even to these: potted char and lampreys are the third, and a fine stretch of progression; but lobster is, indeed, matter for a May morning, and demands a rare combination of knowledge and virtue in him who sets it forth.

Crotchet Castle
THOMAS LOVE PEACOCK
(1785–1866)

❖

Luncheon has been defined as an insult to one's breakfast and an outrage to one's dinner.

Etiquette of Good Society
LADY COLIN CAMPBELL
1898

FRANK HARRIS PLANS A SEDUCTION

Laura lunching with me in my rooms in Gray's Inn. The mere thought took my breath, set the pulses in my temples throbbing and parched my mouth. I had already discovered the Café Royal, at that time by far the best restaurant in London.

So now I ordered the best lunch possible: hors d'oeuvres with caviare from Nijni; a tail piece of cold salmon-trout; and a cold grouse, fresh, not high, though as tender as if it had been kept for weeks, and to drink, a glass of Chablis with the fish, two of Haut Brion of 1878 with the grouse, and a bottle of Perrier-Jouet of 1875 to go with the sweet that was indeed a surprise covering fragrant wild strawberries.

My Life and Loves
FRANK HARRIS
(1856–1931)

❖

For an out-door luncheon, the following list of provisions will be found the most suitable:— Cold roast beef, ribs and shoulder of lamb, roast fowls, ducks, ham, pressed tongue; beefsteak, pigeon and grouse pies, game, veal patties, lobsters, cucumbers and lettuces for salad, cheesecakes, jam or marmalade turnovers, stewed fruit in bottles, bottle of cream, college puddings, blancmange in mould, plain biscuits to eat with fruit and cheese, rolls, butter, cream cheese, and fresh fruit. Bottled beer and porter, claret, sherry, champagne, soda-water, lemonade, cherry-brandy.

Etiquette of Good Society
LADY COLIN CAMPBELL
1898

Chacun à Son Goût

*T*HERE HAVE ALWAYS BEEN those who seek out and embrace the strange and exotic: sushi from Japan, or snails from France, for example; on the other hand there are those who love the dishes of their homeland with patriotic fervour – who would you rather dine with?

Our Italian neighbours regale themselves
    with macaroni and parmesan, and eat
    some things, which we call carrion.
The Welshman he loves toasted cheese and
    makes his mouth like a mousetrap.
The Englishman boasts of his roast beef,
    plum pudding and porter.
The Frenchman feeds on his favourite frog
    and soupemaigre.
The Greenlander preys on garbage and
    train oil.

The Cook's Oracle
WILLIAM KITCHINER
1822

❖

Domestic food is wholesome, though 'tis
    homely,
And foreign dainties poisonous,
    though tasteful.

SIR WALTER SCOTT
(1731–1832)

❖

CHOP-HOUSE CORMORANTS

Critique your wine, and analyse your meat,
Yet on plain pudding deign at home to eat.

'Papa doesn't care what he has, if it's only ready. He would take bread and cheese, if cook would only send it in instead of dinner.'

'Bread and cheese! Does Mr Gibson eat cheese?'

'Yes; he's very fond of it,' said Molly innocently. 'I've known him eat toasted cheese when he has been too tired to fancy anything else.'

'Oh ! but, my dear, we must change all that. I shouldn't like to think of your father eating cheese; it's such a strong-smelling, coarse kind of

176

thing. We must get him a cook who can toss him up an omelette, or something elegant. Cheese is only fit for the kitchen.'

Wives and Daughters
ELIZABETH GASKELL
(1810–65)

❖

I hate French cooks, but love their wine;
On fricassee I scorn to dine;
And bad's the best ragout:
Let me of claret have my fill!
Let me have turtle at my will,
In one large mighty stew!

'The Alderman's Wish'
From *The Gentlemen's Magazine*
19th century

❖

Tell me what you eat and
I will tell you what you are.

JEAN ANTHELME BRILLAT-SAVARIN
(1755–1826)

The organ of Taste in these islanders is very different from our delicate palates – and sauce that would excoriate the palate of a Frenchman would be hardly piquante enough to make any impression on that of an Englishman.

A FRENCH CULINARY PROFESSOR
Quoted in *The Cook's Oracle*
WILLIAM KITCHINER
1822

Though they [the English] have sixty religions, they have only one sauce [melted butter].

Attributed to VOLTAIRE
(1694–1778)

❖

Always have lobster sauce with salmon,
And put mint sauce your roasted lamb on.

Roast pork sans apple sauce, passed out,
Is *Hamlet* with the Prince left out.

Nice oyster sauce gives zest to cod,
A fish when fresh to feast a god!

It gives true epicures the vapours
To see boiled mutton minus capers.

ANON

❖

The conversation of the English is at its deepest at table when they carve their huge mountains of roast beef, and with the most serious manner ask us what part we prefer, rare or well done, from the pink middle or the brown outside, fat or lean? But roast beef and mutton are all they have which is worth eating. Heaven defend us from their gravies, which are made of one-third flour and two-thirds butter, or when a change is needed, one-third butter and two-thirds flour.

HEINRICH HEINE
(1797–1856)

Mrs Sedley had prepared a fine curry for her son, just as he liked it, and in the course of dinner a portion of this dish was offered to Rebecca. 'What is it?' said she, turning an appealing look to Mr. Joseph ...

'Mother, it's as good as my own curries in India.'

'Oh, I must try some, if it is an Indian dish,' said Miss Rebecca. 'I am sure everything must be good that comes from there.'

'Give Miss Sharp some curry, my dear,' said Mr. Sedley, laughing ...

'Do you find it as good as everything else from India?' said Mr. Sedley.

'Oh, excellent!' said Rebecca, who was suffering tortures with the cayenne pepper.

'Try a chili with it, Miss Sharp,' said Joseph, really interested.

'A chili,' said Rebecca, gasping. 'Oh yes!' She thought a chili was something cool, as its name imported, and was served with some. 'How fresh and green they look,' she said, and put one into her mouth. It was hotter than the curry; flesh and blood could bear it no longer. She laid down her fork. 'Water, for Heaven's sake, water!' she cried.

Vanity Fair
WILLIAM MAKEPEACE THACKERAY
(1811–63)

❖

What I cook is not fusion food, but what I have tried to do is to capture the colour and minute attention to detail of a Japanese master. I hope every plate that leaves my kitchen, although the ingredients are entirely English, is a minor masterpiece that would not be despised by either Monet or Hokusai.

MICK HUGHES, Head chef
2001

Health Food

*Y*OU ARE WHAT YOU EAT, *says the old maxim, and ever since the first doctor practised his craft we have been told that longevity and good health are determined by a disciplined diet. For those who are too greedy to heed such advice, though, look at Lord Palmerston at eighty, governing Great Britain and confidently chewing through nine courses as a matter of routine...*

182

Cinnamon – I reckon it a great treasure for a student to have by him, in his closet, to take now and then a spoonful.

Haven of Health
COGGAN
1584

❖

Avoid [at breakfast] new bread and spongy rolls; look on muffins and crumpets as inventions of men of worse than sanguinary [bloodyminded] principles, and hot-buttered toast as of equally wicked origin. Dry toast is the safest morning food.

Table Traits with Something on Them
DR JOHN DORAN
1854

❖

Physicians should be good Cooks at least in Theory.

Hypochondriasis
DR MANDEVILLE

❖

Bull's beef ... of a rancke and unpleasant taste [but good enough for] poore hard labourers.

PIGEONS breed an inflamed bloud, and extimulate carnall lust.

HARE'S FLESH ... breedeth melancholy more than any other flesh.

QUAILS have in their flesh much moist and excremental juyce by reason whereof they quickly putrify in the stomacke and make a bad nourishment.

FISH ... residing and corrupting in the body causeth difficulty of breathing, the goute, the stone, the leprosy, the scurvie and other foule and troublesome affects of the skin.

Via Recta ad Vitam Longam
[The Right Road to a Long Life]
TOBIAS VENNER
1638

184

We may therefore look on it as certain, that the truffle is a food healthy as it is agreeable, and that when taken in moderation it passes through the system as a letter does through the post office. Doctor Malonet, used to eat enough to give an elephant the indigestion. He however lived to be eighty-six.

La Physiologie du Goût
JEAN ANTHELME BRILLAT-SAVARIN
(1755–1826)

❖

If you find your cook neglect his business, – that his *ragouts* are too highly spiced or salted, and his cookery has too much of the *haut goût*, – you may be sure his palate has lost its sensibility, – and it is high time to call in the assistance of the Apothecary.

Almanach des Gourmands
GRIMOD DE LA REYNIÈRE
1805

❖

To still a Cocke for a weak body that is consumed [an invalid] take a red Cocke that is not too old and beat him to death...

Booke of Cookrye
A. W.
1591

❖

Food that is not well relished cannot be well digested; and the appetite of the over-worked man of business, or statesman, or of any dweller in towns, whose occupations are exciting and exhausting, is jaded, and requires stimulation. Men and women who are in rude health, and who have plenty of air and exercise, eat the

186

simplest food with relish, and consequently digest it well; but those conditions are out of the reach of many men.

Book of Household Management
MRS BEETON
(1836–65)

❖

A mong the multitude of causes which impair Health, the most general is the improper quality of our Food ... Few persons bestow half so much attention on the preservation of their own Health, – as they daily devote to that of their Dogs and Horses.

The Cook's Oracle
WILLIAM KITCHINER
1822

❖

He that would have a clear Head must have a clean Stomach.

Health
DR CHEYNE
1724

The best Books of Cookery have been written by Physicians.

The Cook's Oracle
WILLIAM KITCHINER
1822

❖

What is one man's meat is another man's poison.

OLD PROVERB

❖

The plenty of good wheaten bread that now is found among all ranks of people in the south, instead of that miserable sort which used in old days to be made of barley or beans, may contribute not a little to the sweetening their blood and correcting their juices; for the inhabitants of mountainous districts, to this day, are still liable to the itch and other cutaneous disorders, from a wretchedness and poverty of diet.

The Natural History of Selborne
GILBERT WHITE
(1720–93)

Louis XVIII's cook remarked that it was the office of the cook to supply His Majesty with pleasant dishes, and it was the duty of the doctor to enable the King to digest them.

Table Traits with Something on Them
DR JOHN DORAN
1854

Let supper little be, and light;
But none makes always the best night –
It gives sweet sleep without a dream,
Leaves morning's mouth sweet, moist,
and clean.

ANCIENT MAXIM

Till hunger pinches never eat,
And then on plain, not spicèd, meat.
Desist before you've eaten your fill;
Drink to dilute, but not to swill.

ANCIENT MAXIM

The things we eat by various juice controul
The narrowness or largeness of our soul.
Onions will make ev'n heirs or widows weep,
The tender lettuce brings on softer sleep;
Eat beef or pie-crust, if you'd serious be;
Your shell-fish raises Venus from the sea.
For Nature, that inclines to ill or good,
Still nourishes our passions by our food.

Apician Morsels
Tales of the Table, Kitchen, and Larder
DICK HUMELBERGIUS SECUNDUS
1829

Health Food

D r. Paris, in his work on Diet, says, 'Foreign spices were not intended by Nature for the inhabitants of temperate climes; they are heating, and highly stimulant.'

Book of Household Management
MRS BEETON
(1836–65)

❖

To miss a meal sometimes is good,
It ventilates and cools the blood,
Gives Nature time to clean her streets
From filth and crudities of meats;
For too much meat the bowels fur,
And fasting's Nature's scavenger.

ANCIENT MAXIM

❖

I have often thought I could feed or starve men into many virtues and vices, and affect them more powerfully with my instruments of cookery than Timotheus could do formerly with his lyre.

SYDNEY SMITH
(1771–1845)

191

Dined with the Prime Minister who was upwards of eighty years of age. He ate for
dinner two plates of turtle soup; he was then
served very amply to a plate of cod and oyster
sauce; he then took a pâté; afterwards he was
helped to two very greasy looking entrées; he then
dispatched a plate of roast mutton; there then
appeared before him the largest, and to my mind
the hardest, slice of ham that ever figured on the
table of a nobleman, yet it disappeared, just in time
to answer the inquiry of his butler, 'Snipe, my lord,
or pheasant?' He instantly replied 'Pheasant', thus
completing his ninth dish of meat at that meal.

Speaker Dennison Describes a Meal with
Lord Palmerston
c.1864

❖

I think I may say that I have discovered
the principle of immortality, and that
the odour of my dishes would recall life
into the nostrils of the very dead.

Coquus Gloriosus
PHILEMON

❖

AUSLÄNDER

AUSLÄNDER

PAUL DOWSWELL

BLOOMSBURY

LONDON BERLIN NEW YORK

Bloomsbury Publishing, London, Berlin and New York

First published in Great Britain in 2009 by Bloomsbury Publishing Plc
36 Soho Square, London, W1D 3QY

Hardback ISBN 978 0 7475 8909 9
1 3 5 7 9 10 8 6 4 2

Export trade paperback ISBN 978 1 4088 0023 2
1 3 5 7 9 10 8 6 4 2

All papers used by Bloomsbury Publishing are natural, recyclable products
made from wood grown in well-managed forests. The manufacturing
processes conform to the environmental regulations of the country of origin.

Typeset by Dorchester Typesetting Group Ltd
Printed in Great Britain by Clays Ltd, St Ives Plc

www.bloomsbury.com

To Ruth and Ilse, who escaped,
and also to Hannah

CHAPTER 1

Warsaw
August 2, 1941

Piotr Bruck shivered in the cold as he waited with twenty or so other naked boys in the long draughty corridor. He carried his clothes in an untidy bundle and hugged them close to his chest to try to keep warm. The late summer day was overcast and the rain had not let up since daybreak. He could see the goose pimples on the scrawny shoulder of the boy in front. That boy was shivering too, maybe from cold, maybe from fear. Two men in starched white coats sat at a table at the front of the line. They were giving each boy a cursory examination with strange-looking instruments. Some boys were sent to the room at the left of the table. Others were curtly dismissed to the room at the right.

Piotr and the other boys had been ordered to be silent and not look around. He willed his eyes to stay firmly fixed forward. So strong was Piotr's fear, he felt almost detached from his body. Every movement he made seemed unnatural, forced. The only thing keeping him in the here and now was a desperate ache in his bladder. Piotr knew there was no point asking for permission to use the lavatory. When the soldiers had descended on the orphanage to hustle the boys from their beds and into a waiting van, he had asked to go. But he got a sharp cuff round the ear for talking out of turn.

The soldiers had first come to the orphanage two

1

weeks ago. They had been back several times since. Sometimes they took boys, sometimes girls. Some of the boys in Piotr's overcrowded dormitory had been glad to see them go: 'More food for us, more room too, what's the problem?' said one. Only a few of the children came back. Those willing to tell what had happened had muttered something about being photographed and measured.

Now, just ahead in the corridor, Piotr could see several soldiers in black uniforms. The sort with lightning insignia on the collars. Some had dogs – fierce Alsatians who strained restlessly at their chain leashes. He had seen men like this before. They had come to his village during the fighting. He had seen first-hand what they were capable of.

There was another man watching them. He wore the same lightning insignia as the soldiers, but his was bold and large on the breast pocket of his white coat. He stood close to Piotr, tall and commanding, arms held behind his back, overseeing this mysterious procedure. When he turned around, Piotr noticed he carried a short leather riding whip. The man's dark hair flopped lankly over the top of his head, but it was shaved at the sides, in the German style, a good seven or eight centimetres above the ears.

Observing the boys through black-rimmed spectacles he would nod or shake his head as his eyes passed along the line. Most of the boys, Piotr noticed, were blond like him, although a few had darker hair.

The man had the self-assured air of a doctor, but what he reminded Piotr of most was a farmer, examining his pigs and wondering which would fetch the best price at the village market. He caught Piotr staring and tutted impatiently through tight, thin lips, signalling for him to look to the front with a brisk, semicircular motion of his index finger.

Now Piotr was only three rows from the table, and could hear snippets of the conversation between the two men there. 'Why was this one brought in?' Then louder to the boy before him. 'To the right, quick, before you feel my boot up your arse.'

Piotr edged forward. He could see the room to the right led directly to another corridor and an open door that led outside. No wonder there was such a draught. Beyond was a covered wagon where he glimpsed sullen young faces and guards with bayonets on their rifles. He felt another sharp slap to the back of his head. 'Eyes forward!' yelled a soldier. Piotr thought he was going to wet himself, he was so terrified.

On the table was a large box file. Stencilled on it in bold black letters were the words:

RACE AND SETTLEMENT MAIN OFFICE

Now Piotr was at the front of the queue praying hard not to be sent to the room on the right. One of the men in the starched white coats was looking directly at him. He smiled and turned to his companion who was reaching for a strange device that reminded Piotr of a pair of spindly pincers. There were several of these on the table. They looked like sinister medical instruments, but their purpose was not to extend or hold open human orifices or surgical incisions. These pincers had centimetre measurements indented along their polished steel edges.

'We hardly need to bother,' he said to his companion. 'He looks just like that boy in the *Hitler-Jugend* poster.'

They set the pincers either side of his ears, taking swift measurements of his face. The man indicated he should go to the room on the left with a smile. Piotr scurried in. There, other boys were dressed and waiting. As his fear subsided, he felt foolish standing there naked, clutching his clothes. There were no soldiers here, just two nurses, one stout and maternal, the other young and petite. Piotr blushed crimson. He saw a door marked *Herren* and dashed inside.

The ache in his bladder gone, Piotr felt light-headed with relief. They had not sent him to the room on the right and the covered wagon. He was here with the nurses. There was a table with biscuits, and tumblers and a jug of water. He found a spot over by the window and hurriedly dressed. He had arrived at the orphanage with only the clothes he stood up in and these were a second set they had given him. He sometimes wondered who his grubby pullover had belonged to and hoped its previous owner had grown out of it rather than died.

Piotr looked around at the other boys here with him. He recognised several faces but there was no one here he would call a friend.

Outside in the corridor he heard the scrape of wood on polished floor. The table was being folded away. The selection was over. The last few boys quickly dressed as the older nurse clapped her hands to call everyone to attention.

'Children,' she said in a rasping German accent, stumbling clumsily round the Polish words. 'Very important gentleman here to talk. Who speak German?'

4

No one came forward.

'Come now,' she smiled. 'Do not be shy.'

Piotr could sense that this woman meant him no harm. He stepped forward, and addressed her in fluent German.

'Well, you are a clever one,' she replied in German, putting a chubby arm around his shoulder. 'Where did you learn to speak like that?'

'My parents, miss,' said Piotr. 'They both speak –' Then he stopped and his voice faltered. 'They both spoke German.'

The nurse hugged him harder as he fought back tears. No one had treated him this kindly at the orphanage.

'Now who are you, mein Junge?' she said. Between sobs he blurted out his name.

'Pull yourself together, young Piotr,' she whispered in German. 'The Doktor is not the most patient fellow.'

The tall, dark-haired man Piotr had seen earlier strolled into the room. He stood close to the nurse and asked her which of the boys spoke German. 'Just give me a moment with this one,' she said. She turned back to Piotr and said gently, 'Now dry those eyes. I want you to tell these children what the Doktor says.'

She pinched his cheek and Piotr stood nervously at the front of the room, waiting for the man to begin talking.

He spoke loudly, in short, clear sentences, allowing Piotr time to translate.

'My name is Doktor Fischer . . . I have something very special to tell you . . . You boys have been chosen as candidates . . . for the honour of being reclaimed by the German National Community . . . You will undergo further examinations . . . to establish your racial value . . .

and whether or not you are worthy of such an honour
. . . Some of you will fail and be sent back to your own
people.'

He paused, looking them over like a stern school –
teacher.

'Those of you who are judged to be *Volksdeutsche* – of
German blood – will be taken to the Fatherland . . . and
found good German homes and German families.'

Piotr felt a glimmer of excitement, but as the other
boys listened their eyes grew wide with shock. The room
fell silent. Doktor Fischer turned on his heels and was
gone. Then there was uproar – crying and angry
shouting. Immediately, the Doktor sprang back into the
room and cracked his whip against the door frame. Two
soldiers stood behind him.

'How dare you react with such ingratitude. You will
assist my staff in this process,' he yelled and the noise
subsided instantly. 'And you will not want to be one of
those left behind.'

Piotr shouted out these final remarks in Polish. He was
too preoccupied trying to translate this stream of words
to notice an angry boy walking purposefully towards
him. The boy punched him hard on the side of the head
and knocked him to the floor. 'Traitor,' he spat, as he was
dragged away by a soldier.

CHAPTER 2

Piotr and the other boys were taken to an airy, spotlessly clean dormitory in the same building. They were issued with towels and soap and allowed a hot soak in a room with a row of baths and large frosted windows. There in the steamy room, Piotr felt trapped in a bubble of his own misery. His head throbbed where he had been hit and he could feel the lumpy bruise, but at least the skin had not broken. Was he right to have volunteered to translate? Surely, the other children had to know what the Doktor was going to say, and the old nurse's Polish was not good enough to tell them properly.

Anger built inside him. He had never thought of himself as entirely 'Polish' and his parents had always felt like outsiders in Poland. He was frightened of these Germans – with their brusque manners and their occasional displays of terrifying violence. But perhaps they were right to be 'reclaiming' him. It was certainly better than being sent back to the terrible orphanage.

Piotr's mood grew worse when, much to his embarrassment, the nurses came round and massaged a strong smelling chemical lotion into his hair. 'It is for head lice,' said the older nurse when Piotr asked. 'All of you from the orphanage are infested.'

Bath time over they were given clean clothes, warm milk and bread, and allowed to lounge on the beds in the dormitory. His new trousers were too short for his legs, but at least they did not carry the musty, stale smell of his old clothes.

Books and magazines had been left for them to read, although most were in German. Piotr read the German armed forces magazine *Signal*. Some of the articles were about German soldiers in France or Holland, dining in the cafés of the Champs-Elysées or going to dances with the local girls. But most of the pieces trumpeted the successes of the German army in Soviet Russia. Some of the other boys came and asked him to tell them what the articles were about. They didn't mind his skill with German now.

They were all summoned again at midday and the stout nurse addressed the boys in halting Polish, telling them that any further attacks on Piotr would be punished severely. 'I know you worried . . .' she said. 'But no boy, NO boy, to hit this boy Piotr who speak German and Polish.' She held up a long bamboo cane and shook it. She seemed too good-natured to carry out the threat, but she was trying her best to protect him. 'Understand?'

Piotr hoped they would heed her words. Alongside the two nurses, there was now only one soldier to oversee them.

They waited there in the dormitory for the rest of the day, and boys were called out one by one. But this time, they returned after half an hour, at least most of them did. When the first came back, they all looked at him expectantly. 'More measuring,' he said with a bewildered shrug.

While they waited, they were given hot food – stew and potatoes and poppy-seed bread pudding. The food was good; it was a banquet compared to the thin soups and stale bread of the orphanage. Piotr began to feel more comfortable and his mood lifted a little.

Not all the children were reassured. The boy next to Piotr had curled himself into a tight ball and was rocking to and fro. Piotr went to sit on the end of his bed. 'I don't think we need to worry,' he said. 'Isn't it good not to feel hungry all the time?'

'I don't care if they feed us golabki and pierogi with golden spoons,' said the boy. 'I don't want to go to Germany. Not with these Nazi *zboks* . . .'

Just then, the young nurse appeared at the door and called Piotr's name. She took him to a small office close to the dormitory, her hand resting lightly on his shoulder. In the room was the man in the white coat who had made the joke about him being like a boy from a Hitler Youth poster. He smiled at Piotr and beckoned him to sit. Talking in German, he explained they were going to make a record of his appearance for a scientific survey. He was not to be frightened, as he had nothing to worry about.

The man was called away by a commanding voice, leaving Piotr alone to take in his surroundings. There was a table set with the strange pincer-like instruments he had noticed earlier and other peculiar things. One was like a long pencil case that opened on a hinge at one of its narrow ends, and contained twenty eyes of various graded colours. They were so lifelike they made him shudder.

Another similar long tin box contained different swatches of hair, arranged left to right, numbered one to thirty, from fairest to darkest. Unlike the eyes, this was real hair and Piotr tried to imagine the heads it came from. The lightest must be a Finn's, he thought – no one else he was aware of had that almost white blondness. He wondered if the darkest was from a Jew – some of his Jewish friends in Poland had very dark hair. A label in dark Gothic script on the lid read:

Kaiser Wilhelm Institute for Anthropology,
Human Heredity and Eugenics

There was also a white cloth pinned up against the wall, in front of which was placed a strange-looking chair with a metal neck brace and three evenly spaced wooden ridges on the seat. As Piotr wondered what this was the man returned.

He apologised for being called away – Piotr was surprised by this courtesy. The Germans he had seen in Poland had treated the people in his village, Wyszkow, with open contempt. Not that the Brucks were considered Poles. They had been 'reclassified' as ethnic Germans soon after the invasion. But day to day, out in the streets, the German soldiers spoke to the locals as they would to dogs or farm animals.

The man smiled again. He took out a printed form from his briefcase and began to make detailed notes. Name, age, family background – all the usual questions. Then he picked up the hair and glass eyes and Piotr's blond hair, eyebrows and blue eyes were matched and categorised.

He asked Piotr to sit directly in the centre of the chair with his neck pressed tight against the cold metal neck brace. It was very uncomfortable, as the central wooden strut ran right down the cleft of his buttocks.

'It's to make you sit up straight for your photograph,' the man laughed, 'and not lounge about like a lazy Pole.'

Piotr didn't think that was funny, but at least he was being friendly.

The man peered into the viewfinder and took photographs of the front and both sides of Piotr's face, the harsh flash temporarily blinding him. Then he asked him to take off his clothes once more. Piotr hurriedly undressed and was alarmed to discover that he was expected to stand before the camera again for three more photographs.

'You need some meat on those bones,' said the man. 'They've not been feeding you enough, these Polacks. Too many Yids to provide for. Depriving good German boys like you of their proper nourishment! We'll be putting a stop to that.'

Piotr dressed, feeling shaky and flustered. Was he meant to say something back? He thought it best to hold his tongue. On a printed form, the man began to record detailed measurements of his skull and the length and width of his mouth, ears and nose. Sometimes he drew pictures of particular features, such as the shape of Piotr's ears, nostrils and eyelids, all the while making little ums, ahs and even one or two very goods of approval. He seemed particularly pleased with the measurement from Piotr's forehead to the back of his head.

'Let's have your hands,' he said, opening a tin box with an ink-stained pad. Palm prints and fingerprints were made on further forms.

The man indicated for Piotr to return to the ordinary chair, then disappeared again, clutching the forms. He returned with Doktor Fischer.

11

This time the Doktor smiled at him. It was a chilly, cold-eyed smile, but Piotr supposed he was trying to be pleasant.

'You, my friend,' said the Doktor in German, 'are a magnificent specimen of Nordic youth. Tell me about your parents. Tell me how you came to be living out here with the Polacks.'

'My father is . . . was . . . from Prussia,' said Piotr nervously. He didn't want to talk about his parents. It was too raw. Too painful. And he didn't know whether what he had to say would land him in trouble.

'His family had farmed there for as long as anyone could remember,' he continued. 'My mother's father, he was from Bavaria and he married a Polish girl.'

The man winced almost imperceptibly, but it was enough to give away his disapproval. Piotr wondered if he was telling too much of his story. But Doktor Fischer was listening intently and scribbling notes on a form. 'Good, good,' he said. 'Tell me everything you know.'

'My mother was born in Poland but the family moved back to Germany during the Great War. My mother is from farming stock too. Both her brothers were killed in the war and when her parents died she inherited the family farm. My father, well neither of my parents really, wanted to go to Poland. They had both grown up in Germany, but the farm was large and with a grand manor house. So they came. I was born a year or so after they arrived.'

'And what in heaven happened to land you in the orphanage?' said the Doktor. 'Aren't you registered as *Volksdeutscher*?'

'We were,' said Piotr. 'As soon as the soldiers arrived,

12

it was obvious by the way they spoke that my parents were Germans and not Poles. We were put on the "German People's List" at once.' He began to feel indignant. 'I told the orphanage this and I asked them who would look after the farm, but they just waved me away.'

'Yes,' said the Doktor, his face turning hard. 'I shall speak to the wretched man who runs that place. I'm sure your records have been lost. We have processed two million Poles of German ancestry in the last two years. I'm not surprised you slipped through the net. Now tell me what happened to your mother and father.' He was beginning to sound irritated.

'My parents were both killed on the night of the Soviet invasion. They were out visiting friends. It was the first night they had decided to go out and leave me alone in the house. My father said, "You're thirteen now, Piotr. We trust you. Besides, you've got Solveig – that's our collie – to look after you."'

Piotr noticed the Doktor had stopped writing and was staring impatiently, straight at him. Clearly this was unnecessary information. He cut short his story. 'They never came back. I was sent to the orphanage in Warsaw a week later.'

The Doktor spoke frankly.

'Some of the soldiers want to keep you here to act as an interpreter, but I think you deserve better than that. I am going to recommend we return you to the Reich and find you a good German family eager to adopt a fine German son. I know of one, and shall contact them at once.'

'What will happen to the farm?' Piotr asked at once.

'Do you have brothers or sisters? Any relations?'

'I have cousins and aunts and uncles on my mother's side, but all in Germany,' said Piotr.

'And do you know them well?'

'No. There was an awful family feud when my mother inherited the farm. The rest of the family stopped speaking to her. I've never met any of them.'

'We shall have to establish who has responsibility for the farm while you are still a minor,' said the Doktor. 'Then, when you are old enough, you will have an estate to take over.'

Piotr felt flabbergasted. All of this was too extraordinary to take in at once. Yesterday he was starving in a wretched orphanage, sleeping in a dormitory four beds deep and twenty beds long. Now he was being offered a completely new life. Piotr didn't like the Doktor's manner, but he did enjoy being told that he was something special. He began to think he would fit in in Germany. Suddenly, he couldn't wait to leave.

For a couple of weeks Piotr was the star pupil at the holding centre. Right from the start he knew he would not be staying long. The rest of them would have to undergo a long process of 'Germanisation', learning the language and having the Slav beaten out of them. With Piotr that would not be necessary.

From the morning of their selection the boys had been forbidden to speak Polish, and some had been whipped with a belt on the buttocks, in front of the others, for continuing to talk in their own language. It would be a difficult few months for them.

'Polish is a tongue fit only for slaves,' Doktor Fischer had announced, towards the end of that first day. 'You are German stock – reclaimed by the National Community – and so you shall speak only German.'

The children were divided into classes according to their ability. Eager student volunteers, fresh off the train from Berlin, began to teach them the German language. Only Piotr was considered fluent enough to require no further instruction.

While the others were in their German classes, he was allowed to sit and read in the dormitory or the garden. Engrossed in *Signal* magazine, Piotr learned that the German army had conquered the eastern region of Poland taken by the Soviets in 1939, and had now occupied the Ukraine. They were already halfway to Moscow. The magazine was full of photographs of cheering peasants carrying crosses and religious icons as they welcomed the smiling soldiers that swept into their villages.

When the other children came out of classes, the younger ones would flock towards him to try out their new words. 'Eins, Zwei, Drei . . . Vier . . . Fünf,' they would parrot, and Piotr would correct their pronunciation.

The boy who had hit him on the first day, Feliks, had lasted only a fortnight. He refused to accept his fate and ran away twice in as many days, only to be dragged back by soldiers to be beaten in front of them all.

'Some of you are like wild dogs who refuse to be tamed,' announced Doktor Fischer, after Feliks's second escape. 'Some of you do not deserve the honour of German citizenship. Feliks Janiczek has been returned to the orphanage.'

Piotr had not liked Feliks, but he couldn't help feeling

15

sorry for him. There was so little to eat. All the children there would surely starve. Piotr thought Feliks stubbornly stupid. He had been offered an opportunity and rejected it. Poland was finished. Germany was the future.

The next day Piotr was called before Doktor Fischer and told that he too would be leaving soon. 'We are sending you home to the Reich. There's a centre at Landsberg for boys like you. The family I have in mind for you, Piotr, is in Berlin, the very heart of things,' he said. 'I am prepared to recommend you personally. I trust you will not disappoint me.'

CHAPTER 3

Between Warsaw and Landsberg
August 24, 1941

Piotr leaned his forehead against the glass window of the train, and watched the flat fields of the North European Plain roll by. He was tired, and occasionally his heavy eyelids would close and his head drop down, waking him with a jolt. The glass steamed up with his breath and he wiped the condensation away with the sleeve of his new pullover.

Travelling with him was Fräulein Spreckels, the pretty nurse from the holding centre. She chided him at once. 'That is not a rag, Piotr. You must learn to take better care of your clothes.'

By the end of the day, the Fräulein had told him, they would be in Landsberg. If all went well, he would be in a new home, a real home, within a week or two.

On the opposite track a packed troop train thundered east, anti-aircraft guns perched on a flatbed carriage in front of the locomotive. Inside the passenger carriages and through the open doors of the cargo trucks, Piotr could see soldiers sleeping, drinking, playing cards. Some were singing, and as they flashed by he could just about hear their voices above the rattle of wheel on rail and the chuff of the steam engines. They seemed in good spirits.

Seeing the guns at the front of the troop train made Piotr worry about whether they too might be attacked by aircraft. He had heard about the damage a plunging dive-bomber could do to a village and knew a train would be terribly vulnerable to marauding aircraft.

'Fräulein Spreckels, why do we have no guns to protect us?'

She laughed. 'Who is going to attack us, Piotr? Our boys destroyed most of the Soviet air force in the first days of the invasion. And the Tommies can't fly this far from England.'

As the train rattled on, the scenery outside the carriage gradually changed. The scattered farms and fields were replaced by streets and closely packed houses. 'Where are we?' asked Piotr.

'We're in the Wartheland,' she answered proudly. 'You are home in Germany now! This is all territory reclaimed from Poland.'

As the train rounded a bend, they could see the spires and towers of the city centre. 'I know this place,' said Piotr. 'I've been here once before. It's Lodz.'

Fräulein Spreckels looked stern. 'It's not Lodz any more, Piotr. It's called Litzmannstadt now.'

The train stopped briefly at the station and she got out to buy bread and ham from a platform vendor. 'You won't go running away from me?' she asked, only partly in jest.

'I want to go to Germany,' said Piotr sincerely. 'Why would I run away?'

Piotr saw that all the signs on the station had been rewritten in German, in a heavy Gothic script. There was nothing here now that sounded Polish. Yet before the invasion, as every schoolboy knew, Lodz had been Poland's second largest city.

He looked at Fräulein Spreckels shivering on the platform as a chill early autumn wind blew down from the
Baltic. Just behind her was the station waiting room. A
notice on the door said:

> *Entrance is*
> *forbidden to*
> *Poles, Jews*
> *and Dogs.*

The Germans had a cruel sense of humour, he thought.
But he was going to be one of them now. He would have
to get used to it.

All his life he had felt out of place in Poland. Even
though he had been born there and spoke Polish like a
native, he had still had to put up with taunts of 'Adolfki'
from the playground bullies. All this would wipe the smiles
off their stupid faces. He was going to Germany to a better
life. They were stuck in Poland. Slaves in their own country.
That cheered him up, although he always felt a little guilty
when he thought things like that.

After twenty minutes the train pulled away. Piotr had
never been further west than Lodz and was full of curiosity
about the places they passed through. When they crossed
into old Germany – the land that had been Germany
before the invasion of 1939 – the change was immediate.
The fields and farms that drifted by looked well kept and
tidy. The villages and towns were unblemished by war.
This was a land of prosperity and plenty.

At Litzmannstadt, Fräulein Spreckels told him, twenty
other boys had joined the train to travel to the *Lebensborn*
hostel at Landsberg. 'Would you like to meet them?'

Piotr shrugged. He was quite happy staring out of the window. He wondered if she was getting bored. She took him to another carriage and introduced herself to the nurses travelling with the new boys and the two soldiers who were guarding them.

'Guten Tag,' Piotr said to a group of them. They all gave slow, stumbling answers. He felt awkward and instinctively began to talk to them in Polish. 'Dzien dobry,' he said – 'Good day.'

One of the soldiers immediately stood up and raised a hand to hit him. Fräulein Spreckels stood between the two of them and angrily told the man to sit down. Then she turned to Piotr. 'Remember you are not to speak Polish,' she said sharply.

Piotr blushed bright red. Then he felt indignant. Of course they needed to learn to speak German if they were going to live there. But, for now, what was wrong with speaking to these boys in Polish? That was what he wanted to say. But then he thought of the dreadful orphanage he had left behind and he made himself hold his tongue.

The threat of violence hung in the air. Some of the boys looked frightened. Some looked defiant, their lips pursed together in a rebellious pout, hard eyes challenging anyone to dare to speak to them. But most of the boys were quietly wary, like Piotr. Any hope of conversation vanished like the steam from the locomotive.

Fräulein Spreckels steered Piotr back to their own carriage, both of them anxious to be away from the brutish soldier. 'Do be careful,' she whispered urgently. 'I know you didn't mean it, but you could get yourself, and the other boys, into a lot of trouble.'

The incident had soured the atmosphere between them and they passed the next few hours in an uncomfortable silence.

CHAPTER 4

As the train rattled on, Piotr thought about the country he was leaving behind. In the two years before his parents had been killed he had seen with his own eyes how life was for ordinary Poles. Because Piotr and his family had been reclassified as Germans when the Nazis seized Poland, they had been treated better than their Polish neighbours. Pan and Pani Bruck had become Herr and Frau Bruck and carried on farming their land and being paid for their produce. The Polish farmers they knew had been rounded up . . . and taken to who knew where. The farmworkers who stayed now worked for new landowners who had arrived from Germany.

Business had boomed for the Brucks, so much so they bought a new car. The memory of it brought tears to Piotr's eyes. His father had been very proud of that car.

Whenever Piotr thought of his parents, a great black pool of water seemed to rush up to swallow him. He pictured his father, tall and taciturn, with a shock of thick black hair. He was a forbidding man and Piotr had feared as well as loved him. But they had never gone hungry and Piotr's father had been a patient teacher, showing him how to milk the cows, fix a temperamental petrol engine, and tell an oak from a larch.

Piotr remembered his mother more tenderly. She had taught him a lot more than the village school. She always took an interest in his stories, his ideas. They would go on long walks through the fields, talking together for hours. Like him, she was tall and blonde. He definitely took after his mother. They would tell him that every time he went into the village shop.

Mesmerised by the endless vista of fields and villages, Piotr's mind continued to wander. For as long as he had been aware of the world beyond his village, everything had seemed to be tottering on the brink of catastrophe. Then that catastrophe had happened.

He got his first inkling of its approach when he was ten and his parents were sitting around the big wireless in the kitchen, huddled next to the oven in the late winter, listening to news of the Nazi seizure of Austria. His mother looked uneasy. 'He's on the warpath now,' she said. 'Who'll get gobbled up next?'

'Who's "he"?' asked Piotr.

'Hitler,' said his mother tersely. 'The Chancellor of Germany. He's a nasty little man. You only have to hear him speak a couple of words to know how full of hate he is.'

This started a dreadful row between his parents. They rarely argued, and Piotr was so upset he fled to his bedroom. It ended in a stand-up shouting match where he could still hear every word. Piotr's father screaming that Hitler, the one they called *der Führer* – the leader – would make Germany a great nation again. His mother, exasperated to the point of tears, replied that the Nazis were malicious bullies. 'Just look what they've done to the Jews in their country,' she said. 'All the beatings out in the streets, those spiteful boycotts of the Jewish shops

23

. . . and they don't stop there. Sometimes there's cold-blooded murder.'

The shouting stopped. Piotr moved to the landing. Now he wanted to know what they were going to say. Herr Bruck began to speak again. 'The Führer's supporters have sometimes been overzealous,' he said slowly. 'But the Jews in Germany were too greedy. They took too many of the best jobs, and they stabbed the country in the back at the end of the last war.'

'Axel, you know that is rubbish,' spat Frau Bruck. She was incensed. 'You talk like a Nazi – as if there's some great Jewish conspiracy – all of them plotting together!'

Herr Bruck stayed silent. The argument was over for now.

This talk about the Jews puzzled Piotr. He knew Jewish children in the village. Some of them played with him, and if they hadn't told him they were Jews when he asked why he never saw them in church, he would never have known. Others, much poorer children, recently arrived from the east, kept themselves to themselves. They wore their sidelocks long, and the men had big bushy beards and long dark coats. Piotr didn't think they looked very threatening. Were they really controlling everything behind the scenes, like some people said, and taking everyone's money? They seemed the poorest people he had ever met.

Over the summer, the newspapers and radio brought more ominous news. The border regions of Czechoslovakia were seized by the Nazis. Six months later they took the whole country. 'We shall be next,' said Frau Bruck.

Piotr's father kept his temper. Over dinner that day

they discussed the likely fate of their own country. Piotr listened, all ears. He was used to grown-up conversations, being an only child living an isolated life with his parents. He didn't understand everything they said, but he sensed unsettling times ahead.

'They're coming. I know they're coming,' said Frau Bruck. Herr Bruck nodded and took his wife's hand.

'Maybe it's for the best, my dear,' he said. 'Forgive me, but this is a backward little country, and the communists here are always trying to betray us to the Soviets. We'd be safer with the Germans here to protect us. If someone is going to swallow us up, from east or west, I'd rather it were our own kin. I don't want the Polish communists linking up with those madmen across the border in Russia. If the communists take over, people like us will be put up against a wall and shot. All the landowners will. The farms will be taken over by the government and collectivised. Then half the population will starve. Just like in the Ukraine.'

Frau Bruck could see some sense in that argument. She feared the Russians even more than the Nazis.

In the summer of 1939, Piotr had started to shoot up, growing six inches in as many months. He begged his mother to buy him some long trousers as he felt so silly in shorts with his long spindly legs. She promised to make him a pair, but she could never settle to the job. The news they heard of the world outside their farm was too disturbing. Everything, it seemed, was building to a terrible crescendo.

CHAPTER 5

Poland
September 1939

The Brucks heard that war had been declared on a beautiful late summer morning. The world learned a new word that day: *Blitzkrieg* – lightning war. Far to the west, the Germans cut through the Polish army, taking less than a week to reach the outskirts of Warsaw where they laid siege to the Polish capital. The reports Piotr heard on the radio were terrifying. Cities in flames, roads so blocked with fleeing civilians that the army were unable to move their troops to the front.

Frau Bruck wept into her apron when she heard how the brave Polish soldiers had been massacred when they charged against German tanks. Herr Bruck received the news stony-faced. It was terrible, he told them, but Piotr could tell he had convinced himself it was for the best.

As Warsaw was besieged, the thing they feared the most finally happened. The Soviets invaded from the east. The Brucks were trapped. To the west was utter chaos. Roads were still blocked with thousand upon thousands of refugees, fleeing with their horses and carts, their livestock, their possessions in prams, wheelbarrows and railway platform trolleys. If there had been petrol for cars, they would have been useless. There were terrible tales, too, of refugees being strafed by German aircraft.

Herr Bruck travelled to the village to buy provisions and was attacked in the street by some of his own neighbours. The Germans were plain and simple murderers, they shouted as they rained down punches on him. Fortunately there were only two of them, and Herr Bruck was a big man. But he decided to stay at the farm after that and Piotr was forbidden to visit the village alone. They lived off their own farm produce and called on friends to deliver the few things they themselves could not supply.

None of them slept soundly after that beating. Whenever their collie, Solveig, barked in the night, or they heard a strange noise, Herr Bruck would be out there with his shotgun.

The weather stayed beautifully sunny – not the usual September rain, which would turn the dirt roads to muddy bogs. The ground baked hard beneath their feet. 'Ideal weather for tanks,' said Herr Bruck with some satisfaction. Had their world not been turned upside down, they would have enjoyed that Indian summer.

Piotr had not forgotten his father's words the previous year about what would happen if Soviet soldiers arrived. When the wind blew in the right direction, they could hear the sound of artillery fire over in the east. The Soviets were drawing closer. Piotr was so consumed by anxiety he now barely slept at night and spent his daytime hours feeling sick, with a tight ball of fear sunk in the pit of his stomach.

There were wild rumours that French troops were pouring across Germany's western border and heading for Berlin. But as the days went by, no such news was broadcast on the radio. Then they heard the Polish army had made a stand west of Warsaw and the Nazis were in retreat. But if that was the case then it meant no one would be there to stop the Russians. Like the story about the French, it was untrue. The Brucks could breathe again.

When the radio announced the siege of Warsaw had ended and Poland surrendered, the family actually cheered. They heard, too, that the Soviets had stopped at the River Bug, a mere twenty kilometres away from their farm. 'We're safe now,' said Herr Bruck as he hugged his wife and son. Piotr noticed there were tears in his eyes. He had never seen his father like that before.

German motorcycle soldiers arrived in the village three days later – machine guns perched on their sidecars. People began to disappear. Any sense of being 'safe' turned sour. There were terrible rumours, too, of piles of bodies in the woods, crawling with flies and maggots.

When Piotr asked about this, his father shook his head. 'The lesser of two evils,' he said. 'The Germans are doing some house cleaning.' This was a phrase, Piotr noticed, he had picked up from a Nazi radio station. 'If they have killed anyone, it's probably the communists. Those traitors don't deserve our pity.'

The schoolteacher and the village priest had vanished. 'They've probably just taken them away for questioning,' said Herr Bruck. 'To make sure they're not communists.'

'But what about the Jewish boys in the village?' said Piotr. His parents fell silent. His mother began to weep. 'We don't know what's happened to them,' said his father quietly. 'I heard many of the Jews have been rounded up and taken to Warsaw. I don't know why they need them all in the same place.'

After an initial tussle with German soldiers, when Piotr's father was nearly shot for demanding they treat his farmworkers with greater respect, the Brucks were quickly recognised as being of German stock. They were even allowed to keep their radio while all their Polish neighbours had theirs confiscated.

In October of that year, the whole of the western part of Poland – Silesia, Pomerania, Lodz – became part of Germany. Herr Bruck cursed his luck. That would have suited him fine. Instead, the Brucks were now in a part of Poland known as the General Government. Poles driven from the German-occupied lands were dumped in Warsaw and any other town or village that would have them. Herr Bruck found himself constantly approached by newcomers asking for work and soon he had more farmhands than he really needed. 'Some of them haven't got the first idea about farming,' he said. 'There's even one who used to be an accountant.' He was immediately put to good use sorting out the family accounts. He worked in the kitchen, grateful to be away from the fields and the cows.

Even stranger things began to happen. In the towns and cities, they heard, all the universities, schools, museums and libraries were closed. Then the Jews that still remained were ordered to wear yellow stars. 'Better the Nazis than the Soviets,' Herr Bruck insisted doggedly. But Piotr could tell his parents were uneasy.

After the upheaval of the first few months, and when the Poles from the west had been found places to live and work, things settled down. Herr Bruck had always struggled to make ends meet on his farm, but now he began to prosper. The grain, milk and meat he produced were bought for a fair price by the German authorities.

When the war started up again in the west, in the

spring of 1940, the Brucks worried some more. What if the Nazis had bitten off more than they could chew? What would stop the Soviets sweeping over the River Bug and swallowing the rest of Poland? Herr Bruck even began to talk of moving back to Germany.

But once again the German army conquered all before it. Norway, Denmark, Belgium, Holland – all swallowed in a month. When fighting started in France, the Germans were at the Channel within a week. And when France fell by the middle of June, the Brucks knew they were going to be spared a Soviet invasion.

So life went on, until the night of 22nd June 1941. Piotr woke before the dawn with the terrible thunder of aircraft flying overhead and the ominous clatter of tank tracks on the roads. Something world-shaking was happening right on his doorstep. He went at once to his parents' room, but their door, usually closed once they had retired, was still open. He peered inside and was alarmed to discover the bed still made up. They were not there. The previous evening they had promised they would be back by eleven o'clock. It was not at all like them to leave him alone all night.

Piotr called Solveig, who was cowering under the kitchen table, and went into the front garden of the farm. Thick fog hung over the fields and the air was utterly still. Usually he would hear the mournful croak of frogs, but this time their calls were drowned by the roar of artillery. He could see the flashes of the guns lighting up the eastern horizon, close to the River Bug.

He wondered if the Soviets had invaded and the Germans were fighting them off. Perhaps his mother and father had been caught up in the fighting? Piotr began to tremble and rushed inside to sit down. He made some coffee and buttered a slice of bread and waited until first light. Maybe there was a logical explanation for his parents' absence. Perhaps they had been held up by all the military traffic.

Dawn came. With Solveig close by his heels, he hurried up the driveway linking the farm to the main road out of Wyszkow. He could see at once that the aircraft, tanks, motorcycles, lorries and field guns were all going east. It looked like the Germans were doing the invading.

A lorry veered close to the roadside, and Piotr hurriedly leaped out of the way, falling into the verge. Soldiers in the lorry looked down and scoffed. Solveig began to bark and Piotr realised this was no place for his dog. 'Home, girl,' he shouted, pointing up the drive. Solveig reluctantly trotted a few paces back but then sat on her haunches and waited.

Piotr turned back to the road. His parents had gone into Wyszkow to have a meal with friends. It seemed to make sense to walk in that direction. He darted across the road in a gap between the traffic and hurried towards the village.

He recognised the car on the side of the road as soon as he saw it, even though it was terribly mangled. The number plate – WZ 1924 – was still there, dangling off the front of the crushed bonnet by a single strand of metal. By the look of the fading tyre tracks on the dirt road, the car had been dragged into the verge.

There were two men by the car, peering into its interior. Piotr knew them. They were two of his father's farmhands. As soon as they saw him, they waved him away. Piotr ignored them and ran forward. 'Go back,' shouted one of the men urgently.

As he came closer, Piotr noticed a trail of dried blood that had seeped out from the passenger door. Through the smashed windscreen he could see, slumped forward . . . a coat? A hat? He recognised these both immediately and looked away before he registered the full horror of the scene. His legs gave beneath him and he fell to the ground retching.

The men came over. One of them put his jacket over Piotr's shoulders and held on to him. When he'd stopped throwing up, they took him back to their home.

Once Piotr had stopped shaking, he asked to go back to the farm. What else could he do? One of the men walked him back, and he tried not to look at the wreck of the car as they passed. When they got to the track down to the farmhouse, a German soldier waved them away. 'But it's my home,' said Piotr. The soldier knocked him to the ground with the flat end of his rifle butt. 'It's the army's now,' he said. 'Now piss off before I shoot you.'

The farmhand held back. To intervene would be to risk his life. But Solveig appeared from nowhere and bounded up to the soldier, snarling angrily. Without a second thought, the man raised his gun and shot her through the head.

Piotr rushed to his dog but the farmhand grabbed his arm. 'Go, go, before he shoots us!' he whispered urgently. Away from the farm they sat by the side of the road and Piotr cried until he had no more tears. Then the two of them walked back to the village.

The farmhands were brothers who lived together in

32

their family cottage. They were kind to Piotr but they could not afford to keep him for long. Within a week, the authorities were informed and Piotr was sent to the orphanage in Warsaw.

On the day he left, the local policeman came to visit. It was a tank that did for his parents, he said. It went straight into the car at speed. They would have been killed instantly. Piotr shook his head in revulsion.

His parents' last moments constantly replayed in his mind on his first night in the orphanage. The roar of the traffic. The sudden realisation that something huge was hurtling towards them out of the gloom. The awful grinding of metal on metal. Piotr sat up suddenly, fighting the urge to be sick. Then a terrible tightness, like a huge lead weight, settled on his chest. He tried not to cry. When other children cried that night, and many did, the others cursed at them to shut up.

In the nights that followed, Piotr lay there wondering what was going to happen to him. The bed had a single threadbare blanket, with no sheets. His pillow was a disgusting pale yellow and on one side there were ancient bloodstains – at least, Piotr assumed they were bloodstains. Some nights, when it was cold and rainy, he had to sleep in his clothes. At first he worried that he must stink. In Wyszkow, he had a bath three or four times a week. Here, the boys had a cold shower every Thursday. But he soon realised it didn't matter. Everyone else in the orphanage smelled the same – that stale dishcloth stench of poverty that he remembered from the poorest boys in the village school.

All of them made do with a single change of clothes. There were no arrangements for laundry. 'You do your own washing here,' said a boy who slept in the next bed.

Piotr did, in the first week he was there. But when it was rainy there was nowhere to air the clothes and by the time they were dry enough to wear they smelled of mildew. Then a pair of socks he put out to dry went missing. He reported the loss to the woman who managed the orphanage clothes store. She grabbed him by the ear and marched him to a tiny room stuffed full of stinking clothes. 'Find a pair in there, and don't ask me again,' she said.

The food they were given was barely enough to keep a sparrow alive. Thin soup twice a day, with stale bread. Sometimes a sickly pink mince, full of gristle and sharp slivers of bone, with boiled potatoes. Often the bread had green mould on it. Piotr picked it off before he ate it. Other boys didn't even notice. The first time he was given mouldy bread he thought to take it back. But the supervisor who gave them their food made a habit of hitting any boy who complained. That was what happened at the orphanage. You caused any trouble or complained about anything, you were hit. The boys learned that fast.

The only thing they didn't hit you for was being horrible to other children. Bullying was something that didn't seem to bother the adults who worked there at all. Bigger children stole food from smaller children. The more timid children, or boys who had lost limbs or an eye, were endlessly teased. Children who sat in the dormitory reading a book would have it snatched from their hands and thrown across the room.

Piotr couldn't believe how, in barely a week, he had gone from the comfort and security of his home and parents, to this squalor and misery. It was like a terrible nightmare. A strange, numb grief settled over him like a cocoon, and he wondered if he would ever smile again.

Warsaw was in ruins. The siege, the street fighting and, most of all, the bombing in 1939, had left livid scars. Now, two years later, a faint smell of brick dust, leaking gas pipes and ruptured sewers still hung over the city and lodged in the back of the throat. Street lights damaged in the fighting stood at strange angles, unlit and awaiting repair. The roads had been cleared, of course, and the trams were running again. German traffic signs and army vehicles were all over the place. Streets had been renamed. Ujazdowski Avenue was now Siegesstrasse – Victory Street. There were no Polish cars. The Poles had to make do with the tram or a horse and cart.

During the day, Piotr would roam the streets. The children in the orphanage were free to come and go as they pleased. No one cared enough about them to tell them otherwise.

He liked Warsaw. He had been here twice before, with his parents. The buildings still fascinated him, especially the Prudential Insurance Agency offices on Napoleon Square, which were sixteen storeys high and the tallest building in Poland. Now it was covered in ugly scars and most of the windows had the glass missing from them.

The people here looked grey, gaunt and downtrodden. Their museums and galleries had been closed, and they were even barred from some of their own parks. Only Germans could enter Lazienki Park. Ujazdowski Park was for the Poles and on a sunny weekend it was as crowded as ever.

But there was something distracted about the Polish people now. They were clinging on to life at their shoddy markets, desperate to trade anything valuable for a little food. More than a few hobbled on crutches; some with missing legs were younger than Piotr. Musicians played at these street markets, sawing at violins, pulling wheezing accordions, grateful for small change.

The German troops were everywhere – those on leave in their soft caps, those stationed there in their helmets and rifles. They treated the locals with casual brutality, especially the Jews, now easily recognised with their yellow star armbands. The soldiers always had a kick up the backside for a Jew. They had to hurry back to their crowded, stinking ghetto at Chlodna Street. Piotr peered through the windows of the tram as it rattled through the ghetto, wondering if it was here that the boys from the village had been sent. Like him they had lost their homes, and perhaps their parents too. And even in his lowest moments, Piotr suspected fate had treated them far worse than him.

CHAPTER 6

Berlin
August 31, 1941

Professor Franz Kaltenbach felt everything was going his way. It was one of those days. Outside his open window, at the Kaiser Wilhelm Institute for Anthropology, Human Heredity and Eugenics in Dahlem-Dorf, Berlin, the sunshine lit the wide leafy avenue and the sky was a deep blue. The smell of fresh cut grass mingled with the scrubbed bleach tang of the laboratories and the smell of formaldehyde from another batch of human material which had arrived from one of the camps that morning.

For most of the year the avenue below his window would be bustling with students on the way to classes and seminars at the various university buildings scattered along Ihnestrasse. But they were on vacation and he was making the most of his empty timetable to catch up on research and consultancy work.

In that week alone he had made four-hundred Reichmarks for advice to the Reich Committee for the Scientific Registration of Serious Hereditarily and Congenitally-Based Illnesses. He hoped the committee would decide that parents of sickly infants should be sterilised.

Then there was his consultant post with the Genealogical Office of the Reich. Since the occupation of Poland, many *Ostarbeiters* – Eastern workers – had begun to work in Germany. Now more of them would be coming from the conquered territories of the Soviet Union. Despite the strict laws and draconian punishments that forbade relationships between eastern sub-humans – the *Üntermensch* – and Germans, they still came before the courts – a sorry parade of farmers' wives pregnant from affairs with Polish agricultural workers, and middle-aged factory managers fooling about with Polish maids.

Kaltenbach had to establish the degree of racial purity in the child. If the Pole had some German blood, then the offspring might be considered acceptable. If the Pole was unadulterated Slav, then the child would be deemed an 'unwanted population addition'. What happened after that – a termination if the child was yet to be born or consignment to the lowest sort of orphanage – was not the Professor's business. In these cases the parents would be punished harshly. The Slav, especially if male, would be executed. The German would be sent to a labour camp.

More agreeable work came with confirming the authenticity of the Ancestral Passports required for membership of the SS – with candidates having to provide evidence of untainted Aryan bloodline back to 1800.

Deciding who was 'racially valuable' or 'racially worthless' was making Kaltenbach a handsome income. It also made a major contribution to the recovery and cleansing of the blood that Reichsführer Himmler had spoken of when he visited the Institute. Professor Kaltenbach took great pride in that.

Life had not always been so good. When, as a young academic completing his PhD, no one would offer him a

38

university teaching post. The thought of having to waste his abilities teaching basic sciences to children in high school, just to make a living, incensed him.

But then Hitler had come to power in 1933 and the Nazi broom had swept through the universities leaving them *judenfrei* – Jew Free. All at once there were plenty of posts to fill. And Kaltenbach was just the sort of fellow Germany's new masters were looking for. A member of the Nazi Party since 1931, he had particularly impressed them with his research into racial blood groups. He was convinced, given time and funding, that he could discover chemical indicators in blood serum that would prove beyond argument the racial origins of a person.

This idea struck a chord with the new regime and money was immediately made available. Permission to marry, membership of the elite SS, even the right to breed for some of the lesser elements in German society, all depended on racial purity. A medical test that would prove beyond argument that a person was tainted with Jewish or Slavic blood would be a great benefit. And so much more convenient than having to demand, obtain and then check documents proving Aryan ancestry. The paperwork alone was a major waste of human effort and the Reich's resources. The fact that such a test would deprive him of much of his profitable consultancy work had occurred to Kaltenbach. But a discovery like that would see him acclaimed as one of Germany's greatest scientists.

His research had proved frustratingly inconclusive and in the late 1930s had been taken over by scientists at the Robert Koch Institute in the centre of Berlin. His rivals were still working on the idea but seemed no nearer a breakthrough. Now the most prestigious work at the Institute had shifted to research into twins and the gypsies, and to his colleague Frau Doktor Karin Magnussen, who was convinced that a more effective test of racial origin lay in a person's eyes, specifically the colouring and markings of the iris.

Kaltenbach's academic career had faltered along with his research. To achieve a directorship or some other senior post, he would need to make a significant discovery. Now he pottered along as an Assistant Director and contented himself with teaching and making a very comfortable living from his work on the committees.

The phone on his desk jingled. It was his friend, Doktor Fischer from the Race and Settlement Main Office. When work permitted, they often sat together on one or other committee.

'Ah, Kaltenbach,' he said, 'I have a most interesting specimen for you. A young lad from Warsaw. Thirteen years old. Classic Nordic features. He's in Landsberg, awaiting a family.'

'It is generous of you to think of me, Fischer,' sighed Kaltenbach, 'but I don't want a Polack. And neither does Frau Kaltenbach. Liese has no patience with them. You should hear the way she talks to the maids at the hostel.'

'Hear me out, my dear Kaltenbach. This one, he's practically German. His mother has some Polish blood. Of course he speaks German like a native. So no tiresome language lessons. And his Arische table results are excellent. The cranial dimensions are practically perfect. I think you should come and have a look at him.'

The line was very noisy. Kaltenbach needed to discuss

this with his wife. 'I'll call you back tomorrow. Where are you? Still out in the General Government? What number? Good. Thank you.'

That night in their apartment, after the girls had been sent to bed, the Kaltenbachs pondered on their opportunity. 'Reichsführer Himmler himself has said we have a duty to reclaim Nordic blood from the east,' said Professor Kaltenbach. 'If only to replace our losses in the recent campaigns.'

Frau Kaltenbach was unconvinced. 'I know you have always objected to me working. But my job at the *Lebensborn* hostel is very important to me. I do not want to give that up to be a nursemaid for a Polack. Besides, we have this apartment to maintain. I know you do well from your consultancies but until you receive a director's salary, you will still need my income. Unless you want us to move to Kreuzberg. Plenty of cheaper apartments there.'

His wife could be sharp. Kaltenbach looked into those resentful, piercing eyes and found it hard to remember what had drawn him to her when they were young. They had met when they were students together, soon after the Great War. His parents had never approved of the match. She was the first in her family to go to university. The Kaltenbachs had been university professors for the past three generations.

'The boy is thirteen,' said Kaltenbach. 'He won't need a nursemaid. Just some guidance along the right path.'

'And what about the girls?' she said, ignoring his reply. 'How will they take to a boy like that?'

'They will understand that "a boy like that" is to be

welcomed into the National Community with open arms. They understand their duties as National Socialists,' said Kaltenbach. 'Of that I have no doubt.'

The girls would take to him in no time, he felt certain. Although recently, Elsbeth, the oldest at twenty, had been something of a disappointment. Announcing she no longer wished to continue working as a nurse, she had returned to live at home. They had found her work at the post office, which Kaltenbach felt was beneath her and them. She had been such an obedient, dutiful daughter before. Perhaps she was having her rebellious adolescence at a later stage than normal. She had even started to go to church again – not something the Party approved of at all. Traudl, a lively thirteen, and Charlotte, a delightful eight-year-old, had yet to dissatisfy him.

'The boy, he's blond, you say?' said Frau Kaltenbach. 'Won't he look a little out of place in this family?'

Professor Kaltenbach was dark, almost swarthy in appearance. His round face was beginning to look slightly podgy in early middle age. Frau Kaltenbach had thick brown hair. The girls were dark too. Nothing wrong with that. Dark hair was a classic trait of the Bavarian or Austrian German. The Führer himself was dark. But Kaltenbach had always envied his fairer, more Nordic-looking countrymen, like Gruppenführer Reinhard – with his blond hair and sharp features. He would be proud to bring up a boy who looked like that.

'But he must be a strapping lad – thirteen you say?' said Frau Kaltenbach. 'If he was a baby, perhaps the girls would be more likely to accept him.'

Her husband reached across the table and placed his hand on hers. 'Liese, having Charlotte nearly killed you.

42

And even if we took the risk of having another child, the probability is almost certainly for another girl. I propose we go and inspect him. Then we shall make our decision.'

Leave of absence was hastily arranged and Franz and Liese Kaltenbach headed east to the *Lebensborn* hostel at Landsberg.

CHAPTER 7

Landsberg
September 2, 1941

Piotr sat alone in a spartan side room of the hostel. Fräulein Spreckels had taken him here from the train station and left him with a friendly pinch on the cheek. For the last week or so he had been waiting. Too restless to settle down for long with a book or magazine, Piotr had been allowed to go for walks around the grounds, and no further.

'I had two of you Polacks bolt on me the other week,' said the matron when he arrived. 'That will NOT be happening again.'

'Frau Matron,' said Piotr indignantly, 'I *want* to go to Germany. Why are you all assuming I'm going to escape?'

Outside, late summer sunshine fell on the beautifully kept grounds of the hostel. Young women wandered in twos and threes with their babies and prams, chatting together. At first, Piotr had wondered what they were doing there. Then one of the nicer nurses had explained that the *Lebensborn* hostels weren't usually for children like him. They were mainly for unmarried young women eager to give a child to the Reich, but anxious to be away from disapproving relatives or gossiping neighbours. Once they had their baby, they would give it up for adoption and go back to their old lives.

The sunshine made Piotr feel lonely. It was five or six

weeks now since his mother and father had been killed. He had stopped thinking about them as if they were still alive. For weeks afterwards he had said to himself 'Dad will be really pleased with me for doing that' or 'I must tell Mum, she'll find this interesting.'

Then the reality of it would hit him like a steam train and he would have to fight back his tears. This was the time when he most wished he had a brother or sister to keep him company. He had never felt more alone in his life. Still, what was it his mum had always told him? 'Try to look on the bright side.' She used to say that whenever he complained about anything.

So he did. Yesterday the matron here had told him about the family from Berlin who were very interested in meeting him.

'They are well-to-do, important people,' she said. 'Professor Kaltenbach is an assistant director at the Kaiser Wilhelm Institute. Frau Kaltenbach runs a *Lebensborn* hostel in Berlin like this one. They have three daughters. So if they take you, they'll make no end of a fuss of you.'

Now he had been called in and told that they were on their way. As he sat there wondering what they would be like, the clock ticked loudly. Where were they? What was happening?

He stared at a calendar on the wall. The picture for August showed an SS soldier in full uniform and knee-high black boots, crouching by a wicker pram. He was smiling benevolently at a tiny blond-haired baby who poked his head curiously over the side. Piotr thought of the soldier who had shooed him away from his family's farm in Wyszkow and shot his dog. He had the same

45

black boots, and the same lightning stripes and death's-head skulls on his uniform.

Piotr got up and turned the calendar over. It *was* September now, after all. This picture showed a proud German mother with five boys – all dressed in the uniform of the *Hitler-Jugend*, all barely a year apart in age.

There was a commotion at the door. In walked a tall, burly man of middle age with a goatee beard – the kind that scientists often had – and wearing an expensive suit. He was followed by a rather frightening-looking woman of medium height and slim build, hair held back in a tight, elaborate plaited arrangement. She wore a matching skirt and jacket and a white blouse, and carried herself with glacial self-assurance.

'Heil Hitler! My name is Professor Kaltenbach,' said the man, saluting and then shaking Piotr's hand vigorously.

Piotr stood and stared. Was he meant to 'Heil' him back?

'And this is Frau Kaltenbach.'

Frau Kaltenbach did not touch him. She kept her distance, gave him the ghost of a smile and stood, hands folded in front of her, to appraise him.

'Guten Tag,' said Piotr. What was he to say to these people? Much to his embarrassment, he was blushing.

'In Germany these days . . .' said Professor Kaltenbach – he was speaking slowly, as if to a foreigner who knew barely a word of his language, or to a dimwit – '. . . we greet each other with "Heil Hitler" and a salute. Like this.' He gave a Nazi salute, with his right arm fully extended. 'That is the German greeting. You try it!'

Piotr gave a half-hearted salute. 'Er, heil.'

'No, no,' bustled Kaltenbach. He was laughing in a good-natured manner. 'You stand erect. Arm thrust out. Heil Hitler!'

Piotr stood up, feeling very foolish. 'Heil Hitler.' He could barely bring himself to say the words. Surely they didn't expect a boy from Poland to go around heiling everyone?

'Now sit down, my young friend. We must get to know each other.'

Piotr was surprised to find he quite liked Kaltenbach. He seemed pompous but jovial. That was a good combination. Pompous and cold. Pompous and quick-tempered. That would be unbearable. Pompous and jovial might be OK.

'Now tell us your name,' said Kaltenbach.

'My name is Piotr Bruck.'

'A good German name. You will need to say and spell it differently of course. From now on you will be *Payterh*. PAY - AY - TAY - AY - ERR. There will be no need to trill the r.

'Tell us what happened to you,' continued the Professor. 'How did you end up in the orphanage in Warsaw?'

Piotr told them how his parents had been killed on the first day of the Soviet invasion, how the Germans had taken over the farm and shot his dog, and how he had been abandoned in the orphanage. It all poured out of him, and even he could barely believe all the awful things that had happened to him in the last couple of months. As he told the story, he got more and more upset. Herr Kaltenbach put a fatherly arm around him. 'You can have a good cry. You are among friends.'

Even Frau Kaltenbach seemed touched. She tapped him primly on the knee. 'You poor boy,' she said, before turning to her husband. 'He speaks good German for a Polack. Almost without a trace of accent.'

Upset though he was, Piotr felt her scorn. He noticed the two of them give each other a little nod.

'So how would you like to come back to Berlin with us?' said Professor Kaltenbach.

Piotr had too many questions buzzing round his head. Too many questions that he knew he would not be able to ask. Like, what will happen to me if I don't want to go? What will happen if Frau Kaltenbach here decides she doesn't want me? What are your daughters like? Are they spiteful and horrible?

Knowing he had no real choice, Piotr sniffed and said yes.

Piotr's bag of possessions was so pitifully small, Frau Kaltenbach could not believe it was all he had. 'I took nothing from home. The soldiers wouldn't let me back in,' explained Piotr when she asked. 'I was given a few clothes at the holding centre. None of them fit very well.'

On the train back to Berlin, Professor Kaltenbach told Piotr what a marvellous city it was. 'We shall take you to the zoo, and the circus, and the Museum of Antiquities . . .'

Piotr told him indignantly that all the museums in Warsaw had been shut. That did not please the Professor. 'Ours is not to question the policy of the General Government. I am sure it has been done for the good of the Reich.'

They reached the outskirts of the capital in little more than two hours, just as the shadows were lengthening in the late afternoon sun. First, there were rows and rows of small houses, each with their own little garden. Then everything grew denser. Great long apartment blocks, six or seven storeys high, backed on to the broad scar of the railway line that ran into the centre. Piotr was so excited to see this great city he began to forget his troubles. For the first time since his parents' death he felt a surge of hope. Maybe the family would be nice? Maybe the girls would be as friendly as their father? Maybe this would all be for the best?

As soon as they emerged from the station, he was impressed by the grandeur of his new home. Everything was untouched by war. How terrible Warsaw looked in comparison.

The Kaltenbachs had left their car close to the station. It was a plush Mercedes-Benz. Herr Kaltenbach announced he was going to take them on a tour of the sights on the way home.

Kaltenbach was very keen to point out that Berlin in wartime was not the place it had been in the 1930s. Some of the statues on the bridges and boulevards had been taken down to save them from bomb damage. Some of the main streets had been covered by camouflage netting, to confuse enemy aircraft looking for recognisable landmarks. But the city was still magnificent. The ornate iron decorations on the bridges, the beautifully sculptured street lamps, the elaborate plaster work of the grand apartment and office doorways, they all spoke silently of confident prosperity.

Piotr had seen big cities before. But there was something about the scale and magnificence of Berlin that put Warsaw and Lodz in the shade. The Professor pointed out the pink palace of the Royal Armoury, the Museum of Antiquities, the Brandenburg Gate, and with the greatest pride, the glittering gold cannons and angel on the Victory Monument. Even though it was piled high with sandbags to protect it, the monument still looked splendid.

The car wheeled down another wide avenue and Herr Kaltenbach announced they were going home to meet the rest of the family. They slowed to a crawl by a grand apartment block with tall, wide windows and a stone and wood facade. The car squeezed through a narrow passageway into a generous courtyard. A few cars, mostly Mercedes and BMWs, were parked here. Kaltenbach led them towards the main entrance – a tall plaster and brickwork arch with an imposing door of carved wood and glass.

The apartment was on the third floor. Piotr was shown into the wood-panelled hall and then a spacious living room where light streamed in through large windows. The place was spotless and sparkling, the wooden tables and bureaux buffed to a gleaming shine.

There were three girls waiting there, each sitting separately on the sofa, armchair and chaise longue that filled the centre of the room. All had their hair in the elaborate braids fashionable in Germany. Piotr guessed they had dressed in their Sunday best. That made him feel welcome. They were making an effort for him!

Kaltenbach stood behind Piotr, placing a hand on either shoulder. 'This is *Peter*,' he announced to the girls, exaggerating the German pronunciation. 'He is coming to live with us. I would like you to treat him like a brother.'

The girls stood to greet him.

Elsbeth, the oldest, was most like her mother, with angular features and slender build. 'He is tall for his age,' she said when they shook hands. It was said as an indifferent observation rather than a compliment. Their eyes met for only a second. She made him feel uneasy.

Traudl was thirteen like him, and a good fifteen centimetres shorter. She gave a beaming smile and a cheerful 'Heil Hitler! Welcome to Berlin!'

Charlotte was eight and obviously embarrassed by the whole business. She smiled shyly but did not speak. Both these girls took after their father – dark and solid, pleasant round faces with smooth creamy skin.

'We are close to Wittenbergplatz U-Bahn here,' said Frau Kaltenbach. 'You can be in the centre of the city in ten minutes.'

'And five minutes from the aquarium,' said Traudl, 'and the zoological gardens!'

'Come and see my doll's house,' said Charlotte, growing a little bolder and taking Peter by the hand.

She led him into her room. The doll's house was there on a low table, a series of miniature worlds – living room, bedroom, kitchen, bathroom. Each was filled with tiny, exquisite ornaments and furnishings.

Peter feigned interest. 'And who lives here?' he said cheerfully.

'No one,' said Charlotte. 'Mummy says I have to keep it tidy and clean in case the Führer comes to visit.'

There was no one inside. No dolls or little toy animals. The living room had bright orange floral wallpaper, its own tapestry rug, a miniature mahogany sideboard. On the dining table sat a lace tablecloth and a tiny bowl of

51

flowers. In pride of place over the mantelpiece, glowering above the little vases and candelabras, was a miniature portrait of Adolf Hitler. Close by the curtains was a row of tiny swastika flags pinned to the wall.

In the miniature kitchen, along with exquisite little pots and pans, and a full set of crockery, was another portrait of the Führer. This time he was with his friend, Germany's Italian ally, Mussolini. It was the kitchen wallpaper though that really caught Peter's eye. The pattern was made up of girls in military uniform, some marching in formation, some dancing with Nazi flags, some camping and cooking around a fire.

She noticed him peering at the kitchen wallpaper. 'Mummy says when I am ten I can join the *Jungmädel* and go on trips and even stay in a tent like all the big girls!'

Herr Kaltenbach appeared at the door. 'Very nice, Charlotte, but we have not even shown Peter his own room yet.'

The apartment was a series of rooms along both sides of a long corridor. Peter's was at the end, and smaller than the others. 'We usually put guests in here,' said Frau Kaltenbach with a sigh. 'But now we shall have to make other arrangements.'

'They can sleep in our living room, dear,' said Herr Kaltenbach, brushing aside her complaint.

Peter had a bed by the side of the wall, a wardrobe, a desk by the window and a little chest of drawers. On the mantelpiece Kaltenbach proudly pointed out two presents, each carefully wrapped in red paper with a white bow. Peter felt embarrassed by their generosity. They were being so kind to him, these Kaltenbachs. It reminded him of what it felt like to feel part of a family again.

Inside one of the presents was a cardboard box containing a beautiful metal model of an open-topped Mercedes car. Included were little plastic models of the Führer, together with assorted bodyguards and functionaries. Hitler, Peter noticed when he picked him up, had an arm that could be raised in a Nazi salute. Lowered by his side it made him look comically stiff and Peter stifled a chuckle.

The other present contained another cardboard box. This one was full of toy parade-ground soldiers. Some were standing rigidly to attention, others marching in the goose-step fashion.

Peter tried to look pleased. He had toy soldiers and cars at home, but over the last year he had come to feel he was a bit too old for them. Still, as his mother sometimes said, 'It's the thought that counts.'

'Thank you, Herr Kaltenbach, and Frau Kaltenbach. They will make a marvellous decoration for my mantelpiece.'

'You must call us Tante and Onkel – Auntie and Uncle,' said the Professor.

'Now, I expect you are hungry?' said Frau Kaltenbach. She didn't wait for an answer. 'Good. Then we shall eat.'

Elsbeth had prepared a stew, and they sat round a large oak table in the dining room. Candles cast a gentle glow over everyone's faces. There was even a little wine for him and Traudl, although Frau Kaltenbach insisted they mixed it with water. 'Straight from France,' said Herr Kaltenbach. He gave a little snort and raised his glass. 'There is an old German saying: *A good German likes no Frenchman – but he likes to drink his wine.'*

He and Peter quickly discovered a mutual fascination for flying machines. Germany led the world, they both said, in the field of aviation. It was a tragedy, they agreed, the *Hindenburg* going up in flames. Kaltenbach had seen the airship with his own eyes, as it flew low over Berlin. Such a magnificent engineering achievement, he told Peter, the size of an ocean liner. He was convinced Jewish saboteurs were to blame for its destruction – probably in the pay of the Americans.

Peter had heard that story too, but he didn't want to talk about it. This German obsession with the Jews irritated him. Instead he asked about the Focke-Wulf Fw 61 helicopter. He had seen pictures of this extraordinary flying machine in the newspapers, with its twin whirling rotor blades instead of wings. 'Yes,' said the Professor, 'we may not have been the first to fly such an aircraft, but we certainly have the best.'

The girls started to talk among themselves.

'I took them all to see it,' said Kaltenbach, lowering his voice conspiratorially. 'Hanna Reitsch . . .'

'The test pilot!' Peter cut in.

Kaltenbach's eyes lit up approvingly. 'You do know about this!' he beamed. 'Yes, we all went to see her fly the Fw 61 at the Deutschlandhalle – you can just about walk there from here. It was an extraordinary sight, hovering in the air like a gigantic dragonfly! And what did the girls do? They sat there with fingers in their ears, complaining about the noise!'

Frau Kaltenbach smiled indulgently. 'Fw 61,' she tutted. 'Only a man could think up such a dreary name.'

Peter and the Professor barely registered her remark.

They were too wrapped up in discussing the design of the helicopter.

'Tomorrow I shall take you shopping,' said Frau Kaltenbach after a while, trying to steer the conversation towards something they would all be interested in. 'We shall buy you some decent clothes.' She had even smiled at Peter once or twice. He asked her about her work, but she brushed his enquiry aside. 'Unlike Onkel Franz, I do not talk about my job at the table.'

Now the younger girls bubbled with conversation. Both were keen collectors for the government appeals for money and materials for the war. 'Frau Drescher never gives more than a couple of pfennigs,' said Traudl.

'Yes,' said Charlotte. 'We should report her for a lack of National Socialist spirit!'

Peter was confused. Were they joking or were they serious? All families had their little jokes, but no one had laughed when she said that.

Then Herr Kaltenbach said, 'Frau Drescher has only a widow's pension. Perhaps we should not be too unkind about her.'

After he had gone to bed, full of fine food and feeling happy, Peter thought of his old home. The furniture was frayed and occasionally stuffing burst from seats or sofas. Flies buzzed around the dingy kitchen. Really, it was quite shabby. He had never thought about his Polish farmhouse like that before and felt a twinge of guilt. The Kaltenbachs' apartment was luxurious. He assured himself his parents would have been delighted with his good fortune.

He was wary of Frau Kaltenbach and her frosty eldest daughter, but the younger girls seemed to like him. And

Professor Kaltenbach was so different from his own father. So friendly, and interested in him, and full of conversation. He thought he was going to fit in here. That night he slept more soundly than he had for months.

CHAPTER 8

Berlin
September 3, 1941

On Peter's first morning in his new home, Frau Kaltenbach took him shopping for new clothes at the KaDeWe – the Kaufhaus des Westens. It was the biggest department store in Europe, she told him proudly, and just five minutes from where they lived. He was impressed by her generosity. 'We can't have anyone thinking you're our poor relation,' she said.

When they were alone in the living room, later that afternoon, Elsbeth said, 'We weren't expecting someone civilised. Some of the girls I was at school with who're back from their duties in the new territories, they say the German Poles are dirty and speak so badly you can't even understand them. And they have the most stupid peasant superstitions. My friends said they couldn't tell the difference between them and the Polacks. But you're not like that, are you.'

She sauntered off, not even noticing he was blushing. It was the first time she had said more than a few words to him. He supposed this was her version of being friendly. He felt quite pleased about this. He was quietly fascinated by Elsbeth. She was certainly very pretty.

Peter settled in quickly. Professor Kaltenbach could not have been more welcoming. 'A boy here, among all these girls!' he said at breakfast, ruffling Peter's hair. 'We can talk about all the things they have no interest in!'

Here at the Kaltenbachs', it felt as though he were on some luxurious school exchange programme where he had been sent to the big city and one of their children had been sent to Wyszkow. He sometimes amused himself by wondering how they would have got on with his parents and whether his dad would have taught them to milk the cows. He was pleased to realise he could think like this and it didn't upset him.

'Are you and Tante Liese going to adopt me?' said Peter to Herr Kaltenbach. He was very unsure what the arrangements were.

'Not yet, Peter. For now, we are merely your guardians. If all goes well, then sometime in the future we will sort out all the paperwork and adopt you.

'Everything has been moving very fast. In your life and in the world. After all, it is only a few weeks since you lost your parents. It's too early to be thinking about adoption. It would be like getting married a couple of months after you'd lost your wife.'

Peter could see the sense in that, although it didn't make him feel any more sure of his future. So he was pleased when Tante Liese announced that he was to be enrolled at once in the local school.

In Poland, when the Germans came, the schools had been closed. Peter's mother, who had been a schoolteacher before she had married, had educated him at home. He was a quick and curious child and had enjoyed their lessons together, but he had missed the company of other children. It was nice to be back in a real school, with blackboards and desks and a playground.

On the first day, much to his embarrassment, the headmaster spoke about him to the whole school in their morning assembly. 'Peter is a racial comrade. He is to be welcomed in the spirit of National Socialist companionship. He is not an *Ausländer* – a foreigner. He is one of your kith and kin.'

That worked well enough, although a few of the children still teased him for his slight Polish accent. But Peter was a tall boy who was good at sport. He wasn't a natural target for bullies.

When they were in class, learning things, almost everything seemed to be about politics. Even the questions in the maths books were about politics:

The iniquitous Treaty of Versailles, imposed by the French and English, enabled international plutocracy to steal Germany's colonies. France herself acquired part of Togoland. If German Togoland covers 56 million square kilometres and contains a population of 800,000 people, estimate the average living space per inhabitant.

Or:

The construction of a lunatic asylum costs six million Reichmarks. How many houses at 15,000 Reichmarks each could have been built for that amount?

Peter was impressed. These questions really made you think. In Poland his maths questions had been really boring: 'If a farmer has five chickens and each lays seven eggs a week, how many eggs will they produce in three weeks?'

Sport occupied a great deal of his time in school. Here in Berlin, being fit and healthy seemed more important than learning. In Poland, when the schools had closed, Peter kept fit with his chores around the farm, and he enjoyed doing team sports again.

At the end of his first week there, Herr Kaltenbach asked him at supper how he was getting on in school. 'I really like it,' Peter replied. 'All the sport is fun, but there's so much of it. I wouldn't mind learning more in class.'

Kaltenbach ruffled his hair. 'Growing lads need a lot of exercise. If you want to learn more than they're teaching you at school, then there's always the library. And I will be happy to talk to you about your work. But I would remind you of the words of our Führer: "Excessive emphasis on purely intellectual development leads to premature onset of sexual imaginings."'

The girls giggled. Elsbeth and Frau Kaltenbach looked faintly dismayed. Peter blushed. He supposed Herr Kaltenbach was teasing.

Frau Kaltenbach rapidly changed the subject. 'Charlotte, you must tell us all the bedtime prayer they taught you at school today.'

Charlotte stood up and raised her right hand in a Nazi salute.

'Führer, my Führer, given to me by God . . . Protect and preserve my life. You saved Germany in time of need . . . ' She stopped and frowned.

'I thank you for . . .' prompted Frau Kaltenbach.

'I thank you for my daily bread,' she rattled on, hurrying to the end. *'Be with me for a long time, do not leave me, Führer, my Führer, my faith, my light, hail to*

60

my Führer!'

They all clapped and Charlotte looked very pleased with herself.

'And how was your hockey match, Traudl?' asked Frau Kaltenbach.

'We won again,' she said with a grin.

'Do you do a lot of sport too?' Peter asked. He was keen to keep the conversation a safe distance away from 'sexual imaginings'.

'Oh yes,' said Traudl and began to count off on her fingers. 'Hockey, netball, swimming – all for the school, and I'm in the diving team! I like most of all to swim. When I'm in the water I just forget about everything, then before I know it I've done forty lengths of the pool. I like to swim every day.'

That was certainly true. Whenever she walked past, Peter noticed a faint, antiseptic whiff of swimming-pool chlorine.

Traudl had recently appeared in the local newspaper with three other girls on the swimming team. Frau Kaltenbach had cut the picture out and pinned it to the kitchen noticeboard. The girls floated in the water, with euphoric smiles, only their heads above the surface and all wearing rubber swimming caps with a swastika at the front.

Peter confessed he was a poor swimmer. He had only ever managed a few strokes in the sea with his father, and that was no place to learn.

'Didn't they take you to the village pool?' said Traudl.

There were no swimming pools in Wyszkow, or anywhere near it. Peter knew that if he told them this there would be sniggers and superior glances. 'Both my

61

parents did not like swimming,' he lied. 'So we never went.'

'Swimming is the best exercise a girl can take,' said Frau Kaltenbach. 'It is the perfect way to prepare the body for motherhood.'

She turned to Elsbeth. 'You should go, too, mein Liebling.'

Elsbeth bristled. 'I get quite enough exercise with my duties at the post office, thank you, Mutter.'

Peter sensed a row brewing. Was Frau Kaltenbach going to chide her about not being married?

As far as he knew there were no men in Elsbeth's life. He wondered why. She certainly turned heads out in the street. She seemed quite detached from the world, though. There was nothing 'come hither' about her.

An awkward silence followed. Peter chirped up. 'Perhaps you could take me to the pool, Traudl? Show me how to swim.'

The idea appealed to her. 'I like to go first thing. Before school. You'll have to get up early . . .'

He promised he would. These little spats made him feel uncomfortable. He wondered why Elsbeth and her mother seemed so quietly hostile to each other, but he didn't feel he could ask Traudl about it.

Several days a week, after school, Peter started going to the *Deutsches Jungvolk* – the junior branch of the *Hitler-Jugend*. The local squad met in their own 'clubhouse' in the basement of a pub. Its location was supposed to be secret, in the tradition of the HJ, but the boys had taken great pride in decorating the room with Nazi posters and flags.

On Peter's first evening he had been taken to a nearby playing field and asked to pass a series of tests, like running 60 metres in twelve seconds or throwing a ball 25 metres. 'Imagine the ball is a grenade,' said the *Deutsches Jungvolk* leader, 'and you are throwing it into the enemy trench.'

The one he liked the most was the 'courage test' where he had to jump from the second floor of a building where, unseen until the very edge, the bigger boys were waiting with a tarpaulin to catch him.

Most of the boys in his squad were younger than Peter. 'When you are fourteen,' said the leader, 'you go up with the big boys of the *Hitler-Jugend*.'

Right from the start Peter felt at home, not least because as soon as he arrived a dark-haired boy close to him in age immediately introduced himself. 'I'm Gerhart Segur,' he said with a big smile. 'When are you fourteen?'

Peter's birthday was in early October. 'Me too,' said Segur. 'We'll go up to the senior HJ together.' Peter took an instant liking to Gerhart Segur. He seemed to have a hint of mischief about him. A lot of the other boys were very serious.

Peter enjoyed the meetings, especially when they made model aeroplanes or tanks from balsa wood while the squad leader read exciting war stories to them.

His days were so busy, Peter barely had a moment to reflect on what had happened to him any more. He liked that. Sometimes, when he thought about his real parents and Charlotte caught him looking sad, she would come to sit on his lap.

'When I'm upset I talk to Clara,' she said, holding up

her porcelain doll.

That put a smile back on Peter's face. When Charlotte wasn't parroting Nazi slogans, she was lovely.

The nights were still hard. Safe beneath the crisp linen sheets that Frau Kaltenbach had the maid change twice a week, Peter's thoughts would usually drift back to the farm. He tried not to think about that final, awful morning; the mounting feeling of dread in his chest as he waited for the dawn and walked along the track to the main road.

In his mind's eye he would close the great front door of the farmhouse behind him and walk through the kitchen garden his mother had tended, the fresh scent of damp earth lingering in his nostrils, the dew glistening on the raspberries, laid out in careful rows along their cane supports. That day he was to help his mother pick them, as he had done ever since he was a little boy.

He wondered whether the farm would ever be his again. Little things bothered him too. Like those raspberries. Had they just withered or been eaten by birds? Or had the German soldiers picked them? Then there were all his mother's jams and pickles. Whole shelves of them, carefully ladled into old jam jars and sealed, labelled and dated ready for the winter. Had the soldiers taken them or would they just be left to go mouldy in the dark?

How could he have known when he left the farm he would never go back? The kitchen stove was still ticking over. His cosy, fusty bed with its soft, old blankets. The copy of Henryk Sienkiewicz's *With Fire and Sword* that his mother had been reading aloud from in the evenings, left open on the sitting-room table. He had enjoyed hearing this story of Poland's struggle against the Russian Empire. The first chapter had stuck in his mind.

The year 1647 was astonishing in that many signs in the heavens and on earth announced misfortune and unusual events. Contemporary chroniclers tell of locusts swarming in springtime, destroying the grain and the grass; this was a forerunner of Tartar raids. In the summer there was a great eclipse of the sun, and soon after a comet appeared in the sky.

None of those portents had happened in 1939 or 1941, although the catastrophe that had overtaken Poland was far greater.

The next day, Traudl took him to the local library to enrol. Peter asked if they had a copy of Sienkiewicz's book. When he mentioned the author's name to the librarian, a dour, pasty woman with an enamel Nazi Party badge pinned to her cardigan, she looked at him with scorn. 'A Polack author?' she snorted, and so loudly that other people using the library all turned around to look. 'You'll be asking for one by a Yid next. Where on earth did you get the idea that we'd have books by Polacks?'

Traudl had immediately come to his aid. 'Peter is a new arrival in Berlin, Frau Knopf. He is still learning the ropes.'

The head librarian came over, increasing Peter's embarrassment. But rather than admonish him further, the man led Peter away to the children's section and picked up *Winnetou, der rote Gentleman.* 'Karl May's cowboys and Indians books will be more suitable,' he said. 'They were a great favourite of the Führer's when he was a young lad.'

Peter took the book home and read about the wise old Apache chief Winnetou and his German 'blood brother' Shatterhand, who could knock out his enemies with a single punch. He was puzzled as to why Hitler would enjoy reading about the natives of North America when he had such open contempt for other un-Germanic people such as the Slavs and Jews.

Another book he had taken out, *Durch die weite Welt* – Into the Modern World – was far more interesting. It portrayed a future of vast passenger aircraft, twin-deck underground trains shaped like bullets, heliports on the flat roofs of tall buildings, and a massive six-lane highway beneath the Tiergarten. He showed it to his Onkel Franz that very evening. Kaltenbach ruffled his hair again. 'All of this,' he said proudly, 'is what awaits us, as soon as the war is won.'

Peter could absolutely believe it. He could never imagine anything like this coming out of Poland. The Germans, he had no doubt, were the most advanced nation on earth. And here he was, right in the middle of it all, lucky enough to be one of them.

CHAPTER 9

Kaiser Wilhelm Institute, Berlin
September 30, 1941

Professor Kaltenbach was especially keen for Peter to attend his opening lecture for the new students at the Institute, on Racial Science and the work of his department. It was one of the big moments in his annual calendar. 'You must come,' he said over breakfast. 'It will be a good introduction to what I do. You may even decide you want to follow this particular path yourself. I will arrange for you to be excused from school.'

When the day came, Peter and Frau Kaltenbach sat at the back of the lecture theatre at the Kaiser Wilhelm Institute. The room buzzed with a low hum of conversation as the audience waited for the Professor to arrive. There was a smattering of ordinary medical students, but most of those present were young men dressed in the black uniform of the SS. They were this year's intake of trainee military doctors, sent for a ten-month course on the intricacies of Racial Science. Seen together, thought Peter, they were an intimidating bunch of stern Aryan *Übermenschen*.

Peter was nervous. He had an awful feeling that Kaltenbach was going to call him to the front during his lecture and parade him as 'a perfect example of the Nordic race'. He had heard the phrase often in the last three weeks and it made him squirm.

Kaltenbach swept in and the room immediately fell

silent. He stood at the lectern and tapped his papers, took a sip of water from the glass that had been left there and then began to speak in a clear, confident voice.

'Gentlemen,' he boomed, 'and ladies.' He nodded indulgently to the small number of female medical students, who had clustered together to the right of the room. 'You are the sentinels of the nation's genetic health, and you must be ever vigilant as it flows through the generations.'

He paused dramatically, to let the significance of his words sink in.

'I offer you a vision of a world free from illness, criminality, asocials, prostitutes, beggars and the work-shy, and the bacillus of world Jewry . . . You are the foot soldiers of this future utopia. Servants to the National Socialist vision.

'But to attain this dream you must discard false notions of humanity.' He paused. They were hanging on his every word. 'I am reminded forcibly of the words of Reichsminister Goebbels as he addressed the Party Congress in 1938.

' *"Our starting point is not the individual, and we do not subscribe to the view that one should feed the hungry and clothe the naked . . . Our objectives are entirely different. They can be put most crisply in the sentence: we must have a healthy people in order to prevail in the world."*

'I am sure I need not remind you of all the racial laws passed by the National Socialists since we came to power. Today marriages likely to produce offspring prejudicial to the purity of German blood are an impossibility in the Reich.'

Kaltenbach went on to outline the role of his department in this great revolution – and how their mission in the world was to unearth the biological foundations of human difference. He said especially that identifying Jews was Racial Science's greatest challenge. He outlined the cutting edge work carried out at the Institute – the blood serum and iris research in racial diagnosis – and how this would sweep away the time-consuming and costly procedures currently in place.

Peter didn't understand most of what he was saying, but he felt proud of Professor Kaltenbach's ability to fascinate his audience. After forty minutes or so, the Professor began to summarise.

'In *Mein Kampf* the Führer wrote *"The nation state must set race in the centre of all life. It must take care to keep it pure. It must put the most modern medical means in the service of this knowledge."*

'We live at a unique time. Never before in human history has a government been so ready to grasp the essential truths of Racial Science. And never before has that science been so ready to serve the interest of the state.

'When our National Socialist future is ensured there is nothing to stop the regeneration of the German people and our creation of a galaxy of genius – *Übermensch* destined to rule the world. Heil Hitler!'

They all rose to salute in response and then began to applaud as Kaltenbach stood back from the stand.

'Thank you, comrades,' he said. 'Do we have any questions?'

A student in a black uniform asked how long it would be before research into racial diagnosis would offer irrefutable evidence of Jewishness. Kaltenbach assured them such a breakthrough would come within a decade.

'We are making great strides in this area,' he said. 'For example, we know that some races – Ashkenazi Jews for one – are more resistant to the tuberculosis virus than others, such as West African bushmen. The answer lies in the presence, or lack of, certain defence enzymes in the blood, and these characteristics, when fully understood, will aid such a diagnosis.'

Another of the young men in the black uniforms said that he had recently returned from the fighting in the Ukraine where he had been serving in the medical corps. When supplies ran low, he reported, it was common practice to use the local population as involuntary blood donors. Could the Professor see any danger in that?

Kaltenbach was noncommittal. 'On this point Racial Science is undecided. For myself, I would say it would be a last resort. Almost like taking blood from a farm animal.'

The audience sniggered.

Another student – one of the young women in white coats who looked very young – wanted to know why it was so necessary to develop these diagnostic tools. 'Surely, if a subject looks Aryan, they are essentially Aryan?'

The audience prickled with hostility. The woman looked flustered.

Peter thought Kaltenbach was gallant in resisting the temptation to humiliate her further. 'A brave question, fräulein. You are plainly new to the subject. Appearance is but one aspect of race. Let me refer you to Baur, Fischer and Lenz's *Foundation of Human Genetics and*

Racial Hygiene. Let me also refer you to the words of my late Swiss associate, Professor August Forel. "The law of heredity winds like a red thread through the family of every criminal, epileptic, eccentric and insane person."

'And as with the criminal or feeble-minded person so it is with race. A German tainted with the genetic inheritance of lesser racial elements will pass on unfavourable characteristics to their offspring. A half or quarter Jew will be scheming and untrustworthy, a Slav will be lazy, and so forth. The Mendelian laws of inheritance that bequeath blond hair or blue eyes to a son or daughter also applies to the characteristics of the lesser races. The sooner our nation's blood is cleansed of these elements the better.'

Frau Kaltenbach applauded resolutely. It was the first time Peter had seen her look on her husband with anything other than a jaundiced eye.

CHAPTER 10

Berlin
October 12, 1941

Anna Reiter looked at herself in the long mirror. She was quite pleased with what she saw. She was always turning heads in the street, always fending off male attention. Sometimes it was flattering, when she liked the young man who was making eyes at her. Sometimes it was irritating, like when spotty HJ youths leered at her. She was tall – taller than most boys her age – and slim too. She wished she was shorter. She stood out too much. Her face was too angular, she was convinced, too sharp and pointy. She wished her face was a little more rounded, like Greta Garbo or that German actress who had gone off to America and everyone said was a Jew-loving traitor – Marlene Dietrich. She'd like a fuller figure too, like Bette Davis. But at least she had a good complexion.

The *Bund Deutscher Mädel* – League of German Maidens – uniform fitted her well, the short fawn *Kletterjacke* climbing jacket tight around her small waist, the blue-black woollen skirt hanging neatly to her knees. She fussed with her neckerchief, adjusting the toggle so it lodged exactly in the V of her jacket, as the BDM manual instructed. She pulled out the collar of her white blouse so it lay flat and even either side of her shoulders, and stood up as straight as she could so her black hair was clear of the back of her collar.

Her grandmother was always complaining about her

hair. 'A bob, it's too modern. You look like a flapper. Why look like a hussy when you could grow it long and have some lovely plaits? That would be much more Germanic.'

Anna was fed up with people chiding her about her hair. That morning, that sullen little BDM brat, Gretchen, who wore a home-made uniform and who always had to march in the middle of the squad so no one would notice, had even said to her, 'You are dark enough to be a Jew. Got Yids in the family, have you?' Some of the other girls had sniggered, and Anna had had to fall back on cheap insults.

'And you are scruffy enough to be an old washer-woman. Can't you afford a proper uniform?'

The girl had sneered, but she blushed too. Those words had wounded her. Anna hated herself for saying that.

Then, at the end of the school day, she had had a tricky conversation with Elke, a girl who had always screamed the loudest at rallies when Hitler drove past in his big Mercedes convertible, and who was always talking about marrying an SS officer. She had sidled up to Anna in the changing room after gym and whispered, 'Why does the Führer wear a swimming costume in the bath?'

Anna had looked at her with a blank face.

'Because he does not like to look down on the unemployed.'

Anna gave a polite smile and tried to muster an air of disapproval. 'Really, Elke. The Führer has made great sacrifices for us. And not taking a wife so he can commit himself totally to the German Nation deserves our respect not our mockery.'

73

Anna felt like a sanctimonious prig. Elke gave a shrug and maybe she went off to the school authorities to report that Anna Reiter had responded with polite disapproval. Or maybe Elke would spend the night too anxious to sleep in case Anna reported her. Pupils in their school had spent a gruelling four weeks' hard labour in a youth disciplinary camp for showing such disrespect.

It was a sad, rotten business, not being able to trust people. Anna had always known that she and her family were different. Finding out who else was like them was a dangerous, treacherous game. The Gestapo, they had heard, sent agent provocateurs to catch people out. It was even whispered someone would tell an anti-Hitler joke, and then report you if you laughed, or even report you if you did not report them for telling the joke. Rumours like this were always going around. It was impossible to tell what was true and what was false.

Anna bore a striking resemblance to her mother, Ula, who was a magazine journalist. Her father, Colonel Otto Reiter, was on the general staff of the Home Army in Bendlerstrasse. Sometimes Anna thought life would be much easier if her family were like the others. Third Reich robots. The Reiters, when they were alone around their dining table, called them 'the hundred-percenters'. The ones who were completely in thrall to the regime. Most of them seemed to be. But you could never tell. The staunchest Nazis might be putting on an act.

Anna also wished she had been born in Sweden, like her cousins Lennart and Tilda. Her mother's sister, Tante Mariel, had married a Swedish diplomat from the Berlin Embassy in 1930 and had gone to live there that very year. Mariel still came to visit, even now, with the war on. She made no secret of her distaste for the Nazi regime and she worried terribly for Ula and her family.

As well she might, thought Anna. Ula and Otto had always had friends who were Jews. But then Herr Pfister, their hateful block warden, had warned them that such friendships were un-Germanic, and would bring them to the attention of the Gestapo. The Reiters were not stupid people. They just became more careful about who they saw and how they saw them.

Anna's mother had told her about her friend Rachel, who had been fired from her magazine in 1938. She had been the best copy editor in the building and they were all sad to see her leave. Rachel had been transported to the east. 'Relocated' or 'reassigned', these were the expressions that were used. Now there were only a few Jews left in Berlin. Sometimes they stayed because the work they did was important. Sometimes they stayed because the Nazis had simply not yet taken them. Recently the Reiters had heard it whispered that the Jews were sent to the east to be killed.

Ula and Otto had discounted such rumours as enemy propaganda when they first heard them. Like the stories the British had concocted during the Great War about how the German army had gathered up the bodies of its fallen soldiers and shipped them back to the Fatherland to make soap, candles and glycerine in macabre *Kadaververwertungsanstalten* – corpse exploitation factories.

When Anna's brother Stefan returned from the Eastern Front on leave, they asked him if there was any truth in these stories. They hoped he would scoff but what he said filled them with revulsion.

CHAPTER 11

October 13, 1941

The day after his fourteenth birthday the *Deutsches Jungvolk* leader approached Peter at their clubhouse and announced that he would be expected to attend a grand parade on 13th October, to mark his coming of age for the senior branch of the *Hitler-Jugend*. When he told the Kaltenbachs about it, the Professor looked at him proudly and declared, 'This is the most sacred moment in the life of any young German.'

Now the moment had arrived and Peter and his comrades were singing at the top of their voices:

The Reich with our Führer supreme at its head
Pursues its relentless crusade without cost
Come follow us, lad, you are German and proud
The drums are beating, the banners unfurled.

The drums were beating, and the trumpeters played a fanfare, their instruments gleaming in the autumn sunshine, black banners with the runic 'Victory' symbol unfurled beneath.

There was something about singing all together, out in the open, which made the boys feel euphoric. Peter had felt something similar in the times he had gone to church at Christmas with his parents. It was a bit like that, but with hundreds of voices rather than a few score in the congregation.

The song over, a great hush descended on the thousand or so boys gathered on the sports field by Potsdamer Strasse. The grandstand beside the field was also packed with parents and relations.

Today, the leader of the HJ, Reichs-jugend-führer Artur Axmann, was doing them the honour of making a speech at their induction ceremony.

At one end of the field a large platform had been erected, and public-address speakers set up on spindly scaffolding. Surrounding the platform were long red and white banners, each embossed with a black swastika. *Hitler-Jugend* flags from all the Berlin troops hung limply alongside.

'Troop, stand easy!' came the grating, metallic command over the speakers. 'The Reichs-jugend-führer will be among us shortly.'

The boys were given permission to sit on the dry grass and talk among themselves. Peter was with Gerhart Segur. 'Shame we couldn't get Adi here,' said Segur. The boys had nicknames for all the Nazi leaders. Their adult supervisors tolerated the practice as long as familiarity didn't spill into disrespect. Adolf Hitler was said to have a particular affection for the youth of Germany, so it seemed right that the boys should call him 'Adi'.

Segur leaned closer and whispered, 'Adi would be much better than Axi. He's a dreary one, for sure.'

Peter hushed him. Their squad leader Walter Hertz, a sharp-eyed boy of sixteen, might overhear. Segur could be indiscreet, and although Peter liked him, he sometimes wondered if his new friend would land him in trouble. Segur didn't take the HJ too seriously, unlike a lot of these boys. But he'd stuck up for Peter when some of the others had tried to bully him. Not that he needed much help. At his second meeting Peter discovered a hidden talent for boxing, which had earned him immediate respect. Any boy who called him 'Polack Pete' got thumped.

Another announcement brought the boys to their feet. 'Atten-SHUN' shouted a Nazi official on the podium. The trumpets blew another fanfare and the drums rolled.

'Eyes RIGHT!'

The boys turned their heads as one. Heralded by the deafening throb of powerful engines, an open-topped Opel Kapitän accompanied by eight motorcycle outriders drove into the stadium. There he was, Axmann himself, standing in the back of the car, right arm extended in the Nazi salute. A blue haze of exhaust fumes pervaded the arena, causing some of the boys to cough. The car and its entourage circled them on the running track that ran round the outer edge of the field and then drew up at the podium.

'He's a fat bastard,' whispered Segur. Axmann was a little heavy around the middle and under his chin, it was true, but Peter thought he looked impressive enough in his Party uniform.

'Silence in the ranks,' shouted Hertz. There might be trouble later.

Peter felt privileged to see Axmann. His photograph often appeared in the HJ magazine and newspapers. And he had seen him in newsreels, usually at similar events to this. It was a thrill to see one of Germany's leaders in the flesh. Here was a man who had been in direct contact with the great Nazi chieftains – Himmler, Göring and Goebbels, even the Führer himself.

Axmann approached the microphones set up on the rostrum and surveyed the crowd. Peter had seen Hitler do this in newsreels, building the tension before a speech.

Eventually he spoke.

'Heil Hitler!'

The whole stadium roared back.

'HEIL HITLER!'

Silence fell. Then there was just a brief whistle of feedback from the loudspeakers.

'Comrades!' began Axmann. 'I come to share great news with you!

'Every one of you represents, for our Fatherland on the march, the symbol of our future. Remember that the earth is in a state of unceasing evolution. Biological and physiological transformations are taking place before our eyes . . .'

He was losing his audience. Boys snatched puzzled looks at one another, as they tried to fathom these phrases, dimly remembered from half-understood Nazi ideology classes.

'. . . These will influence generations to come. The German people are not prepared to yield to these mutations like the lower species, like unthinking beasts! On the contrary, we must master and direct this metamorphosis. We must attain that state of human perfection – the Superman!'

He paused here, obviously expecting applause. The crowd sensed what was expected of them and obliged.

'To achieve this great revolution we must engender a German race that is mentally and physically pure. The young are the future elite of our race. So you must preserve your bodies and your minds from degrading

79

contacts.'

'I'm all for degrading contacts,' whispered Segur, 'especially if they're with our Polish maid!'

Peter tried to keep a straight face. He wished Segur would stop being silly and shut up. He was trying to concentrate on Axmann's speech. Segur was trying hard not to snigger.

'Segur,' whispered the squad leader, 'control yourself.'

'The duty of your teachers is to make you lords and rulers of tomorrow! In return we ask for your faithful submission to the discipline imposed upon you and that you obey the orders given you, whatever they may be! HEIL HITLER!'

A roar of approval greeted the end of the speech. Who would not be seduced by such a prospect of wealth and power?

Now, as they had been trained to do, the boys all stood with their right arms raised and chanted 'SIEG HEIL, SIEG HEIL, SIEG HEIL', like a great wave of sound, always in groups of three, until Axmann gestured for them to stop.

Now came the most important moment of the ceremony, the oath of allegiance.

The loudspeakers boomed out.

'I SWEAR THAT I WILL SERVE THE FÜHRER ADOLF HITLER FAITHFULLY . . .'

The boys all chanted confidently along. They had practised this moment, each of them, in private and in their clubhouses and meeting halls. Peter felt his heart swell with pride.

'I SWEAR THAT I WILL ALWAYS STRIVE FOR THE UNITY AND COMRADESHIP OF GERMAN

YOUTH.

'I SWEAR OBEDIENCE TO THE *HITLER-JUGEND* LEADER AND TO ALL LEADERS OF THE *HITLER-JUGEND*.

'I SWEAR ON OUR HOLY FLAG THAT I WILL ALWAYS BE WORTHY OF IT, SO HELP ME GOD.'

Now he was truly one of them. He belonged in this mighty throng. Peter felt the hairs on the back of his neck prickle. He had never felt anything like this in church.

With the ceremony over, the boys dispersed. Hertz grabbed Peter by the arm. 'Where is Segur?' he said angrily. Peter shook his head. His friend had vanished, probably off to the stand to greet his parents. 'What on earth was happening during the Reichs-jugend-führer's speech?'

Peter was annoyed with Segur, too, but he wasn't going to betray his friend. So he looked the squad leader straight in the eye and with great seriousness said, 'I am sorry, Hertz. I think Segur was overcome with emotion at this great moment in his life.'

Hertz had been some distance from the boys. He would have to give Segur the benefit of the doubt.

'Very well,' he said. 'But you can tell your friend I am watching him. And you. If I have any cause to doubt your National Socialist spirit, I will be happy to report your failings to the Gestapo.'

Peter was about to protest his own innocence, but Hertz had already disappeared into the milling crowd. Peter felt affronted, being challenged like this, but he wasn't going to let it spoil the moment. Peter felt proud to be in the *Hitler-Jugend*. The uniform made him feel like a real soldier. A real grown-up. Now he was a full

81

member he had even been given a ceremonial dagger. He felt the weight of it on his belt. The black textured handle with its swastika emblem balanced perfectly with the shiny steel blade. On the hilt was engraved in Gothic lettering *Treve bis in den Tod* – Faithful unto Death – and on the blade itself *Blut und Ehre* – Blood and Honour. And that blade was sharp.

As he walked towards the stand to join the Kaltenbachs he hoped he would be able to live up to that ideal. They greeted him with affectionate hugs, even Frau Kaltenbach. 'Peter, you look every inch the political soldier,' she told him proudly. Traudl and Charlotte were desperate to see his new dagger, though their mother told them it was not to be taken from its sheath. Only Elsbeth was missing. She was working. Peter felt a twinge of disappointment.

CHAPTER 12

November 1941

Almost every day, the Kaltenbachs would gather round the radio to listen to another special news bulletin. Each one was trailed an hour or two in advance, each one introduced with a grand orchestral fanfare. Each one told of further successes in the east, as three German armies penetrated further and further into Soviet Russia. First it had been Byelorussia and the Ukraine, the great cities of Odessa and Kiev, Smolensk and Novgorod. Then Kursk and Kharkov, and now, unbelievably, German soldiers encircled Leningrad and were almost at the gates of Moscow.

Peter enjoyed seeing the elation and excitement on their faces. 'Has there ever been a more electrifying time to be alive?' said Professor Kaltenbach to them all. 'The Führer said that we had merely to kick down the door,' he mused, 'and the whole rotten structure would come tumbling down. Well, he's been right about everything else so far.'

Traudl and Charlotte tittered with glee. Kaltenbach continued to pontificate. 'If Moscow falls, that will be that. The rest of the Russian *Untermenschen* can just slink off behind the Urals. We'll just have to build a great defensive wall to keep them out!'

The excitement the boys in Peter's HJ squad felt was contagious. Each one now saw himself as a medieval lord in waiting – a soldier-farmer with his own grand estate somewhere in the vastness of Ostland. Each one with an army of Slav serfs to do his bidding.

It was funny, thought Peter, seeing these city boys fantasising about their country estates. He'd like to see them milk a cow or pluck a chicken. But he was seduced by this vision too. He imagined he'd make a far better farmer than all of the rest of them. And he would be decent to his farmhands too. He wouldn't talk to them like dogs.

Peter told his friends he had his own farm back in Poland. He'd be quite happy with that. 'Why be a minnow when you can be a pike?' said Fassbinder. 'In Ostland you could own land that stretches from one end of the horizon to the other.'

A dark-haired boy named Lothar Fleischer was listening in. 'Bruck couldn't look after a bratwurst stall,' he said, 'never mind an estate. You grow up among Polacks, you pick up their lazy ways.'

Segur spoke up at once. 'Peter is our racial comrade, Fleischer,' he said. 'No one else here doubts it.'

Fleischer was defiant. He looked directly at Peter. 'I don't care what they say about you. You're still an *Ausländer*.'

Peter could feel the anger building inside him. Although the other boys rallied round him, Fleischer's friend Mehler was cawing in agreement. A fight was brewing. Walter Hertz, the squad leader, intervened.

'We shall have no more *Ausländer* talk, Fleischer. Peter Bruck is one of us. He is a doer and a helper. He doesn't complain. I am proud to have him in my squad. If you're going to fight, you can do it in the boxing ring.'

The boys drifted off, some of them patting Peter on the

back as they left. Peter could tell that Fleischer's sense of his own superiority rankled with the other boys too. Maybe it was because his father was a senior SS officer over in the General Government – a Hauptsturmführer, Fleischer boasted, in the Race and Settlement Main Office. Peter recognised the name of the organisation at once. They were the ones who had taken him from the orphanage in Warsaw.

Peter had a more immediate ambition than running his own farm. Two weeks earlier his HJ squad had visited Tempelhof Airport and the boys had been taken on a brief two-man glider ride. What a thrill it was, to race along the ground at terrific speed before lifting off into the sky. Sitting behind the pilot, hanging on for dear life, Peter had never felt more alive.

In his fantasies, he wanted to be a *Luftwaffe* pilot. Not the bombers; they dropped bombs on cities and innocent people. That wasn't real fighting. He would pilot a sleek fighter plane, like the Focke-Wulf Fw 190. The 'Butcher Bird' they called it. He saw himself sweeping across the snowy Russian Steppe, coming in low to destroy a Soviet tank formation. There was something glamorous about being a fighter pilot. You spent your life in comfort, on airbases well away from the front line. You were given the most technologically advanced machines known to man, and you took to the skies like a great bird of prey.

Professor Kaltenbach was delighted to hear that Peter wanted to be a pilot. 'I can just see you, in your *Luftwaffe* uniform,' he said. 'Did you know our fighter pilots destroyed four thousand Soviet warplanes in the first week of the war? Four thousand of them!'

Flying sounded like a splendid way to win the war. Much better than being an ordinary soldier tramping through the snow. And, it was well known, girls found pilots irresistible.

That was what Segur told him, with a wink. Peter wasn't terribly interested in girls, although he always pretended he was with Segur. They didn't like getting their hands dirty trying to get a two-cylinder working, they didn't like getting their knees dirty scrambling round an HJ assault course. Girls didn't like fighting, especially not boxing, which they did every week in the HJ. Imagine a girl doing that. Him and Segur, they had this little joke, whenever they trained together in the ring. If the boxing instructor was elsewhere, they would pretend to be girls, and bat away at each other's gloves, screeching timidly, their heads turned away from each other, faces screwed up in mock displeasure.

They were both proud to be in the *Hitler-Jugend*. And they were thrilled by every German victory. But Segur wasn't one of those nutcases who seemed to think the greatest thing they could hope to do was die for the Führer. He wanted to be alive when the war ended. So did Peter. When the other boys complained about being too young to fight, Peter and Segur pretended to agree with them. But when they walked home together, Segur would have that impish look on his face and say, 'The sooner the war's over the better. If we have to fight, then we have to fight. I'm happy about that. But if we don't . . .' He shook his fist triumphantly.

Peter asked him which of the armed services he would join. 'I'm staying well clear of the SS, not that they would have me anyway,' joked Segur.

Segur's brother Kurt was fighting in Russia with the *Wehrmacht* – the German army. 'My brother says that the front line SS divisions, they get all the worst fighting to do.

'They are the best,' he went on. 'I wouldn't like to face them! But they get the toughest jobs and they also have the most casualties. It's the same with all the elite fighting forces.

'On top of that, imagine spending your whole life with a bunch of Jew-haters. Don't get me wrong, I wouldn't stick up for the Yids, but I get bored hearing about them.'

Peter knew he ought to report Segur for even thinking such things, let alone saying them. But he couldn't bring himself to do it. The Nazis always talked of loyalty – but Peter thought you ought to have loyalty to your friends and family as well as the Party and the German nation. He felt strongly about that, though he knew it was some-thing to keep to himself.

In school, and at the HJ meetings, their teachers and instructors often reminded them it was their duty to report anyone – even their parents – if they did not show the correct National Socialist spirit. At school, Ulrich, one of the boys in his class, had immediately raised his hand and said that his father had told the family that Jews were not bad people and that the Nazis were foolish to persecute them.

The teacher had thanked him for the information and instructed the class to applaud his public-spirited action. Ulrich looked quite pleased with himself. But three days later he came to school looking pale and sick. He did not tell anyone what had happened, but it was whispered that his father had been dragged from his home to the Gestapo headquarters in Prinz-Albrecht-Strasse and returned the following morning covered with bruises. Some of the boys said it served him right and the man was lucky not to have been packed off to Sachsenhausen. But most said nothing. There were no more classroom denunciations after that. Instead, the teachers told their pupils to report such disloyalty privately.

Peter had heard of Sachsenhausen. It was an open secret in Berlin. The nearest concentration camp to the capital, it was frequently branded as a threat to parents who complained to the authorities about the amount of time their children had to spend on HJ duties.

Peter told Segur he wanted to join the *Luftwaffe*. 'All the glamour, none of the pain,' he laughed.

'Unless you get shot down,' said Segur.

'There's always a parachute,' said Peter.

'Kurt tells me the Ivans shoot our pilots in midair, as they float down,' said Segur.

'We'll just have to not get shot down then,' said Peter. He was determined not to be put off the idea. Segur was warming to it too.

'How's your navigation?' said his friend. 'Pilots need to be good at calculations and know all about fuel ratios and bomb loads.'

'I'm not so clever with numbers,' said Peter.

'Ah, but all you need is to be good with a slide rule.'

Peter's dad had tried to teach him how to work a slide rule, shortly before he died.

So each night the following week, Segur and Peter met in the library after school and poured over the mathematics textbooks. One evening Segur read out a question at random:

A Stuka on take-off carries twelve dozen bombs, each weighing 10 kilos. The aircraft heads for Warsaw, the centre of International Jewry. It bombs the town. On take off, with all bombs on board and a fuel tank containing 1,500 kilos of fuel, the aircraft weighs eight tonnes. When it returns from the crusade there are still 230 kilos of fuel left. What is the weight of the aircraft when empty?

Peter stopped in his tracks. He didn't like hearing Segur talk about Poland like that.

Segur saw the look on his face. 'Sorry,' he said. 'I don't think of you as a Polack now. I thought you were one of us.'

CHAPTER 13

Peter's HJ squad marched through a blustery autumn afternoon to the local playing field. Today they were to take part in a boxing tournament. The boys had been drawn against each other beforehand and no match was more keenly anticipated than that between Peter Bruck and Lothar Fleischer.

Fleischer's schoolmates sometimes called him 'westisch', because he looked like one of the 'types' shown on the classroom race identification chart. There he was, among the six major categories of Germanic people, alongside the *nordisch*, *fälisch*, *ostbaltisch*, *dinarisch* and *ostisch*. Westisch he was. Dark hair. Thick dark eyebrows on a heavy brow. Oval face. Fleischer liked to think he looked like a boyish version of that American actor Cary Grant. But he kept quiet about it. After all, Grant wasn't German. But what he really wanted to look like was *nordisch* – they all envied the boys who were *nordisch*. That was closest to the Aryan ideal. And no one was envied more than Peter Bruck. Fleischer thought, *How could anyone have all the luck?* He was tall too – Fleischer was just average height. But today they were going to get even.

In the tradition of the *Hitler-Jugend*, the squad linked hands in the centre of the windswept playing field to form a wide circle around the boxers. One of the most senior boys acted as referee. It was a long afternoon, enlivened only by a few cruel mismatches when some of the toughest boys fought the slight and sensitive ones – the ones who usually found refuge from the rougher activities of the HJ in their district choirs and drum and trumpet bands.

Peter and Lothar were scheduled to fight near the end of the tournament and the group was growing restless when they squared up to each other in the fading afternoon light. Peter had been looking forward to this. In the two weeks since their first quarrel Fleischer had kept up a barrage of little digs, determined to never let Peter forget he was a Pole.

Peter had a good eight centimetres in height on Fleischer, but Fleischer had the bulk. He was nearly a year older than Peter – stocky and well developed for his age.

Fleischer started well with a couple of hard punches, but Peter took them in his stride. He had spent his whole life working on the farm – hauling carts full of fodder for the cows, lifting hay bales, scything crops. It made him a formidable opponent. Fleischer landed one or two more blows to Peter's right cheek, but this just spurred him on to fight even harder.

The circle of boys sensed his advantage and cheered wildly. When they grappled together, Peter grabbed Fleischer in an armlock and punched the side of his head until blood splattered over his leather gloves and they were pulled apart. Fleischer slumped to the ground and Peter could not resist another swift kick when the referee's back was turned. That got him back, for every insult and slur.

As the squad cheered him on, Peter was declared the

winner. He felt a savage joy in his victory. Afterwards, it disturbed him that beating another boy like that could bring him so much pleasure. He wondered if this was what soldiers felt like after victorious combat.

After the fight, Fleischer moved away from the main crowd of boys, dabbing at his bloody nose. But Peter could still hear him talking about Poles to his cronies.

'There is a whole gang of them down by Gleisdreieck U-Bahn, clearing up a bomb site,' he sniggered. A few buildings close to that underground station had been destroyed in an RAF raid shortly before Peter arrived in Berlin. 'They say all the cats have vanished round there, because the filthy Poles catch them and skin them for their fur, then eat them. And they go out at night looking for old ladies to kill so they can steal their ration cards.'

If there was any truth in the gossip Fleischer was spouting, then it sounded like they were starving to death. Peter tried to suppress the impulse to go there and see if he could help them. He knew it was against everything he was being taught. He could imagine the sense of betrayal his new family would feel if he was caught. And besides, it could land him in terrible trouble.

Every night these thoughts tormented him. He remembered an incident at school, when he was ten and two older boys were beating one of his friends. Peter knew he should help but he was too frightened. He felt awful about that for months afterwards. As the days went by, that familiar guilty feeling crept back. He had been one of the lucky ones in Germany's New Europe, he told himself. Why should he not help some of those who had not been so fortunate? He made up his mind. He was going to go.

Gleisdreieck was a half-hour walk from Wittenberg-platz and when Peter got there it was a chilly early evening. A thin drizzle was falling. Work was still going on at the bomb site. Gangs of skinny-looking men and boys in filthy rags were lifting rubble into wheelbarrows. They were soaked and some were shivering with cold. Two soldiers with rifles oversaw them, and a German foreman, who shouted at the Poles contemptuously.

Away from the soldiers, on the other side of the block, Peter could see a young lad working alone, using a chisel to remove a broken windowpane. He was barely older than Peter and he looked terribly weary.

Close by was a baker's and Peter bought bread and cheese.

He crouched down by a car parked close by the bomb site and tried to catch the boy's attention. 'Hey! I have food for you!' he called in Polish. The lad looked up, then studiously ignored him. Peter grew bolder. 'Hey, my friend,' he said louder. 'Let me give you something to eat.'

The boy did not look up, but Peter heard him say, 'Fuck off, Adolfki.'

Peter was surprised and a little hurt. These were words he had not heard since he left Poland. They had often been used against him in the street after the Germans invaded. He called back, 'I'm not an Adolfki! I'm a Polish boy like you.'

The boy was beginning to take an interest. 'If they see me talking to you, I'll be beaten,' he said.

Peter crouched down lower so he wouldn't be seen. 'I'll throw the bread over.'

'Thank you,' said the boy. 'Sometimes the German

boys say they'll give us food, and then toss us paper bags with dog shit in them.'

'I'll come back,' said Peter. 'Look out for me. What's your name and when do you finish?'

'I'm Wladek,' said the boy. 'They march us back to the camp at nine o'clock.' He was getting nervous, looking around. It was time to go.

Although it worried him to distraction, Peter felt compelled to return to the bomb site. The whole journey there he would say to himself, 'What will Onkel Franz say if I'm caught?' He felt so grateful to the Kaltenbachs for saving him from the orphanage and he hated the idea of disappointing them. But on the way back from Gleisdreieck he would feel light-headed with relief and at peace with himself. He had done a good deed. He liked that feeling.

He always came in the early evening and the boy would be there, close to the edge of the site. On one evening he saw Wladek with an older youth and they beckoned him over. Peter was surprised at their boldness, but he could not contain his curiosity. He had not had an actual, real conversation with anyone in Polish, since he'd left Warsaw. It would be marvellous to talk to people in the language he grew up with and not have to worry about his accent giving him away.

Before he knew what was happening the older boy had grabbed him and dragged him down to the remains of the basement. He held a trowel to Peter's throat. The edges flashed silver in the street light. They had been sharpened to a vicious point.

'Give me your ration card,' said the older boy.

'Don't hurt him, Antos,' pleaded Wladek. 'You promised you wouldn't hurt him.' He sounded as afraid as Peter felt.

'I don't carry a ration card,' said Peter. He was terrified. Was this boy going to slit his throat?

'Money then. Give us all your money.'

Peter had a few Reichmarks in his pocket. He fetched them out.

'Papers . . . you must have papers?'

'I forgot.'

It was true. Peter was so anxious about coming to give Wladek food he had forgotten his identity papers.

The trowel pressed sharply against the soft skin of his neck.

'Search him,' said Antos to Wladek.

Wladek ran his hands through Peter's pockets. The boy was red with shame and trying his best not to cry. 'I'm sorry,' he said in a trembling voice.

'Shut your face,' said Antos, and cuffed Wladek around the head.

'Now, Adolfki,' said Antos, 'tell me why I shouldn't kill you.'

Peter began to panic. He wondered if he should call out. But by the time the guards had arrived, Antos would have slit his throat.

'Because I can help you, as I have been helping Wladek,' said Peter.

Wladek tugged at his sleeve. 'When they find him down here, they'll have us all killed.' He was just as terrified as Peter.

'You speak good Polish for an Adolfki,' said Antos. 'Go. Go quickly. And come back tomorrow with food, or

I'll hurt your friend here.'

'Hey, Adolfki,' said Antos, as Peter climbed the stairs. 'Enjoy the war, because the peace will be terrible.'

As he sat on the U-bahn home, Peter trembled with fear and anger. How could Wladek betray him like that? Perhaps the older boy had forced him into it? And would he really harm Wladek if he, Peter, didn't come back? No, he decided, he must be bluffing.

That evening he was desperate to tell the Kaltenbachs what had happened, but of course, that would invite disaster. Sitting round the dining table, he felt suddenly detached from them all. None of them would understand. He went to bed as early as he could, leaving them all wondering why he was being so moody.

He bottled up his anger until the next day. When he told Segur what had happened, he couldn't believe Peter had been so stupid. 'I saw a woman arrested in the street for giving Poles scraps of food,' he said. 'Leave them alone.'

Peter wondered why they didn't run away. It would be quite easy to escape from a bomb site. Segur said they probably killed them all if one escaped. His father worked with the *Ostarbeiters* at his factory and had a very low opinion of them. 'Vater says they're lazy and stupid, and only do half the work of Germans.'

Peter shook his head in exasperation but he thought he'd be wasting his time pointing out that they had been brought to Germany against their will. They had no reason to work hard. Besides, by the look of them, they were fed barely enough to keep them alive.

'Vater says they work them till they're *verbraucht* – used up – then they pack them off to a concentration camp "for a rest". None of them ever come back.'

Peter thought it best not to return to Wladek and the bomb site, but decided he would carry on helping the *Ostarbeiters* when he could, even if it was just to slip them a couple of boiled sweets when no one was looking.

CHAPTER 14

December 1941

The Kaltenbachs woke on the morning of 8th December to astonishing news. Germany's ally Japan had destroyed half the American fleet at Pearl Harbor the day before, and the two countries were at war. 'The Führer has chosen our allies well,' said the Professor. 'The Americans have been dealt a mortal blow. This will make them think twice if they are considering siding with the British against us . . .'

Later that day Peter and his HJ squad went to watch an athletics display at a sports hall in Charlottenburg. Everybody Peter spoke to seemed quite elated by the news, but they were quickly distracted when a troop of local *Bund Deutsche Mädel* girls came out to perform.

The boys in his squad loved the skimpy outfits the girls wore as they went through their routines, tumbling inside steel wheels or gyrating with wooden hoops, all in perfect formation. A few of the grown-ups in the crowd tutted, especially the grandparents. Such outfits were immodest, Peter heard one of them say. This made some of the boys in Peter's squad nudge each other and whisper lewd remarks.

One tall, dark-haired girl particularly caught their eye. Peter noticed her too. 'Who is she?' he said to Segur.

'Anna Reiter,' he replied. 'Squad leader in the BDM. They live quite close to you. Father is a Colonel in the Home Army. Mother's a journalist on that women's magazine *Frauenwarte*.'

Peter was about to tell Segur that Frau Kaltenbach was an avid reader when Lothar Fleischer poked him hard in the back. 'You can stop ogling, Bruck. Anna Reiter is too good for the likes of you.'

Peter wasn't going to be goaded. 'She's a bit tall for you, isn't she, Fleischer?' he sniggered.

Although Fleischer flushed red with anger, he moved away. They both knew that a fight in a public place like this sports hall would get them into serious trouble. But Peter's jibe had hit a raw nerve. Fleischer had spent many nights thinking about Anna Reiter. That funny little smile she had. The curve of her back down to her waist . . . Anna was his idea of a perfect German female. When he'd asked her out, she'd haughtily told him she only went on dates with Nordic boys. She probably wouldn't even remember his name.

Peter saw Anna again outside the hall when the display was over. Some of the HJ boys made leering remarks. Peter liked the way she seemed utterly above them – as if they were a bunch of crows whose cawing meant nothing to her.

Three days later, Germany declared war on the United States. Professor Kaltenbach heard the news with a satisfied grin. 'That mongrel nation,' he scoffed as the family sat around the dining table. 'Any culture that gives the world *jazz*,' he spat out the word, 'will be no match for the Third Reich.

'I make a prediction. When we're done with the Russians, the Yankees and the Tommies will come begging for peace.'

Herr Kaltenbach's good mood continued for the rest of the month. His confidence was infectious. The German army were the greatest fighting force in history – that was plain to see. Peter and his schoolmates remained convinced that the war would soon be over. Some of them boasted of their disappointment in not being able to prove their fighting skills. Peter smiled to himself and said nothing. Playing at war was great fun – all the HJ boys enjoyed their war games – but the real thing . . . you only had to see the soldiers with missing limbs on the streets of Berlin, or read the long columns of death notices in the newspapers, to know the real thing was quite different.

The third week of December brought heavy snow. In Wyszkow Peter had always dreaded getting out of his bed when the weather was like this. Feeding the animals at that time of year was always an ordeal and shovelling snow from the path from the farm to the road was a never-ending job. Here, in the warmth of the Kaltenbachs' apartment, he could just enjoy how beautiful the snow made everything look, without thinking of the consequences.

On Christmas Eve, Traudl and Charlotte insisted Peter go carol singing with them and some of their friends from the BDM. They asked Elsbeth too, but she refused. 'I have duties to attend to,' was all she offered as an excuse.

As they tramped through the crisp snow and the early evening blackout, candles in jars lit their way. It looked magical. Without the city lights, the stars in the cloudless sky shone bright and clear. It was almost like the winter skies Peter had seen at the farm.

Traudl and Charlotte could not miss the chance to shake their Winter Relief boxes like tambourines as the group sang along to the traditional carols. The songs weren't all traditional. One of the older girls had brought a new version of 'Silent Night' and passed along duplicated sheets, the mimeograph fluid still fresh on the paper.

Silent night, holy night
All is calm, all is bright
Adolf Hitler is Germany's star
Showing us greatness and glory afar . . .

Peter was glad Segur was not there. He would have started to laugh. Looking around at the earnest faces of the other singers, as they sang this peculiar version of the traditional carol, he could see they meant it to their very souls. All of a sudden, he felt very alone. The more he thought about it, the more it distressed him. Fleischer was right. He was always going to be an outsider – an *Ausländer* – with these people. But in his heart Peter knew that was right. Something in him could not accept this unquestioning worship, this unsettling blind faith they had in Hitler and the Nazis.

He felt a terrible disloyalty thinking these thoughts among people who had made him feel as though he was home at last – 'reclaimed for the National Community'. They had helped allay the grief he felt for his dead parents. His mother and father had left him feeling that Germany was always the better place. Germans were always the better people. He desperately wanted to believe it, although the fate of the *Ostarbeiters* was never

101

far from his thoughts. And he still wanted to be part of the Kaltenbach family. He had never really considered what would happen if they rejected him. Would he be sent back to Poland, or would they send him to one of those camps he had heard about? He began to sing at the top of his voice – as if to drive these troubling thoughts from his head.

When Peter and the girls returned home from their carol singing, collection boxes full to the top, Frau Kaltenbach greeted them with an unusually playful smile. 'I have a surprise for you children,' she said. They gathered outside the living room and waited by the closed door. 'Are you ready, mein Liebling?' said Frau Kaltenbach. Herr Kaltenbach asked her to wait a second, then called, 'Come!'

The door swung open. The room was dark save for the lights of the Christmas tree, which had been both delivered and decorated while the children were out singing. The girls gasped with glee. Peter was speechless. Alongside the traditional baubles and tinsel, the tree was festooned with illuminated plastic swastikas. 'Aren't they marvellous?' said Kaltenbach. 'The KaDeWe began to sell them last Tuesday. They sold out in a day. I bought the last box in the shop.'

In the dim light Peter could see the presents under the tree, all wrapped beautifully, and wondered what he would be getting.

They all sat down at the grand dining-room table, with its candles, folded napkins, carefully arranged crockery and cutlery. Frau Kaltenbach had decorated it. She never let the maid near any job like that. Two weeks ago they had dispensed with Elsa, the surly German maid from Neuköln. Frau Kaltenbach was convinced she had been stealing spirits from the drinks cupboard. Now they had Yaryna, a surly Ukrainian who spoke only a few words of German. Traudl had wondered why they bothered to change. 'They're both resentful little miseries. But at least you could make yourself understood with Elsa.'

Elsbeth, much to Peter's surprise, had asked what they should give Yaryna for Christmas. Liese Kaltenbach replied, 'We shall give her the afternoon off. That will be quite sufficient. Besides, I don't want that sullen, moon-faced brat moping round here spoiling our family Christmas.'

'Perhaps we could give her a little chocolate?' said Elsbeth.

Liese snapped. 'Kindness is not something we show to *Untermenschen*. You give these Slavs presents and they start thinking they can steal from your cupboard. When you have your own home to look after, you can make your own rules. But take this advice from your mother. Servants should be treated like dogs. You should always make them feel you are the top dog.'

Elsbeth took this advice with a blank face, neither agreeing nor disagreeing with her mother. Peter watched, intrigued. He never quite knew what Elsbeth would do or say next.

Singing carols out in the cold had given Peter and the girls a ravenous appetite. The stuffed goose, roast potatoes, peas and parsnips were delicious. The adults drank the finest French wine. Peter was allowed a little too. The girls both had a sip and Charlotte wrinkled her nose in disgust. 'Why do you drink it? It's horrible!'

Kaltenbach gave a little chuckle. 'The French would be

delighted to have such fine wine for their own table,' he said to her. Then he stood up and raised his glass. 'We are living at a time when Germany's future will be decided for centuries to come. This war must end with victory. So let us drink to that, my dear ones. To victory in the New Year! Victory against the Bolsheviks, and to a Europe safe in the hands of Adolf Hitler.'

Afterwards, as they sat around the light of the coal fire and Christmas tree, Professor Kaltenbach read a passage from Hitler's autobiography, *Mein Kampf* – In the home of my parents, where the Führer wrote of his earliest years.

Then Traudl said, 'Papa. Can we hear the story we used to hear when we were little? The one about the baby Jesus and the stable and the three wise men.'

Kaltenbach had her come over and sit on his knee. 'My darling Traudl,' he said as she perched there awkwardly, ' "*When I was a child, I spake as a child, I understood as a child, I thought as a child: but when I became a man, I put away childish things.*" Who said that?' He turned to Liese. 'Was it Goethe? Kant?'

She shrugged and shook her head.

'Saint Paul. Letter to the Corinthians,' said Elsbeth acidly.

Traudl, who was much too big to be sitting on her father's knee, looked confused and uncomfortable. Liese Kaltenbach clapped her hands together. 'Now we shall open the presents,' she declared.

Traudl was given a lurid book on the perils of relationships with Jews. She sat in the corner, reading it avidly. Peter sneaked a look over her shoulder. A picture showed a leering fat Jew, cigar in his mouth, monocle in his right eye, in a smart business suit. He was leaning over his secretary, a young, beautiful Nordic girl, who appeared distressed by his close attentions. The caption beneath read:

> *Ignorant, lured by gold,*
> *They stand disgraced in Judah's fold.*
> *Souls poisoned, blood infected,*
> *Disaster broods in their wombs.*

Traudl noticed Peter behind her. 'Hey,' she protested. 'Girls only!'

'We have something for you now, Peter,' said Frau Kaltenbach, and handed him over a brown paper parcel. He knew at once they were books. Peter's mother had always encouraged him to read. He liked his books, but he hoped these weren't *all* about the Nazis.

They had given him six books from the same series – *Kriegsbücherei der deutschen Jugend* – War Library for German Youth. They certainly looked exciting enough. There was *Flammenwerfer vor!* – Flamethrowers in Action – and *Schlachtschiffe im Atlantik* – Battleships in the Atlantic. Peter settled on *Vorwärts, immer vorwärts!* – Onwards, ever onwards! – an account of the opening weeks of the invasion of Russia. He opened a page at random and lost himself in the excitement of battle.

At 5.30 the silence ends. The German side comes alive. Along the whole front, the heavy guns open up. As the sound reaches the bank, the explosions are already visible on the far side. Then the thunder is on the far side. The individual shots can no longer be distinguished. There is a single loud crashing, whirring, banging and whistling. Earth and rock fall into the river. Splinters whizz . . .

Elsbeth handed her father a small parcel that was so heavy she had difficulty holding it with one hand. 'What *is* this?' he said curiously.

The wrapping came off. It was a hefty doorknocker of solid black iron. The hinged circular knocker itself was decorated in embossed oak leaves with a swastika at its centre. Beneath the swastika, where the knocker actually knocked, was a grotesque caricature of the head of a Jew – broad Hebrew features, a huge nose, face screwed into a grimace, supposedly at the pain of the knocker knocking on his forehead.

'Delightful,' said Professor Kaltenbach. He was trying to be polite, but the whole family could tell he didn't like it.

Liese Kaltenbach spoke. 'Elsbeth dear, we have a perfectly good doorknocker.' They had a magnificent brass lion on their front door. Elsbeth was looking hurt.

Kaltenbach saved the day. 'My dear,' he said to his eldest daughter, 'your mother is right. This splendid knocker shall go instead to the Kaiser Wilhelm Institute. I will have it placed on the door of my office.'

In early January, when Elsbeth was out at work, Herr Kaltenbach called Peter over. 'This knocker,' he said in a conspiratorial whisper, 'it's not quite the thing for the Institute. How about taking it to your HJ den? They'll be delighted with it.'

Peter agreed at once. He liked to please Herr Kaltenbach. But he didn't like it either. Walking to his HJ meeting, he tipped it in a dustbin.

CHAPTER 15

February 1942

Later that winter, Peter's HJ squad were doing an evening Winter Relief collection in an apartment block in Geisbergstrasse. It was a large nineteenth-century building, with some of the stairwells and corridors partially open to the outside. Peter had begun to resent the amount of time he was expected to perform this kind of 'voluntary' work. He would rather be reading at home, or studying in the library. When no one else was with him, he always asked for money in a manner that made it clear he was not expecting any. Walter Hertz, his squad leader, often chided him for returning with the lowest amount. But Peter didn't care. He was good at everything else they asked him to do.

Most of the other boys had finished their rounds and gone home. Peter had three more floors to do when he heard a commotion below.

Four floors down, in the courtyard, he could see a small group of HJ boys he did not recognise. They had surrounded another boy in shabby clothes and were prodding and kicking him. 'Jew boy! Bloodsucker!' they taunted. 'What have you been out stealing?'

Struck by a mischievous impulse, and without thinking of the consequences, Peter picked up a potato bag full of rubbish that one of the residents had left outside their door, and hurled it down upon the boys. He watched it burst over their heads and ran for his life as their outraged cries rang through the building. The apartment block was a maze of corridors and stairwells and Peter's first instinct was to go up – after all, he supposed, they would expect him to run away from the building.

He reached the sixth floor and banged on the first door he came to. 'Good evening, madame,' he said to the old lady who opened the door. 'I am collecting for the Winter Relief fund. Could I ask you for a donation?'

She asked him in and he seized his opportunity. Some old people, who lived on their own, liked a chat when the boys came calling. She had some gingerbread wafers she thought he might like to eat. Peter stayed for half an hour as she talked about her grandson, who had been posted to Norway with the *Wehrmacht*. 'Nice and out of the way,' she said. 'Nothing going on there!'

She looked disappointed when he said he had to go. The HJ boys were still there, marching indignantly up and down the corridors in their stained uniforms. 'Excuse me, comrade,' said one. 'Have you seen anything suspicious here? Half an hour ago we were assaulted by a cowardly Jew-lover.'

'I have been visiting my grandmother,' said Peter. 'But thank you for your warning. I have a good sharp knife to defend me.'

On the way home Peter kept sniggering to himself. He didn't quite know why he'd thrown the rubbish and he felt strangely proud of himself. But that night he woke before dawn and worried about what they would have done if they had caught him. At breakfast he looked at Traudl and wondered, if she were a boy, would she have been part of that gang of bullies.

Now she was fourteen she had moved up from the *Jungmädel* to the *Bund Deutsche Mädel* and had been selected as the squad flag bearer. She took her duties very seriously. Most nights, when she was not collecting for the Winter Relief fund, she would be knitting socks and gloves for the soldiers out in Ostland. She had won her 'Life Rune' proficiency badge for First Aid remarkably quickly, and would ask Charlotte and Peter if she could practise splints and bandages on them.

Charlotte didn't mind – it was part of her duty to help her big sister – but Peter always felt uncomfortable when Traudl practised on him. He found her undiluted company increasingly boring. As she worked away, she would chat about who she was supposed to 'Heil Hitler' to when she saw them in the street, and which items of BDM clothing you were allowed to wear outside of meetings and parades.

On the way home from school a few days later, Peter stopped off at the library, as he often did. He wanted to find a book that would tell him more about Poland. He kept hoping one or two would have slipped through the net. But nothing seemed to have escaped the beady eye of Frau Knopf, who had never forgiven him for asking for a Polish author.

In one section of the library there was a small alcove with a desk and chair behind one of the bookshelves. Peter often went there when he wanted to cut himself off from the rest of the world. It was a good place for quiet study. Today he could see through a small gap in the books that the desk was occupied. He recognised who it was at once – Anna Reiter, the pretty, dark-haired girl he had first noticed at the athletics display in Charlottenburg. Segur had said her family lived close by, and Peter had seen her once or twice out in the street.

Peering through the books, Peter relished the moment. Picking up a book from the opposite stack, so as not to disturb her, he pretended to read, all the while watching her through the gap.

Anna was holding a book with a picture of Hitler on the back cover. She held it up and looked on it with disapproval. Certain that no one could see her she began to ape the posture and expression of the Führer. Hand on hip, starch upright, straight back, her face mirroring Hitler's – that of an indignant, petulant child.

Peter could not believe his eyes. Anna, the squad leader in the BDM! Not wanting to be discovered he quietly moved away and began to search for some other books to help him with his studies. When he left the library and began to walk home, she was there, not five metres in front of him. He caught up with her.

'You're the Polish boy, aren't you,' she said, neither friendly nor hostile. 'You live at the Kaltenbachs?'

Peter nodded. 'Yes. It's close by you. My name is Peter Bruck. Perhaps I could be allowed to walk you home? It's a dark night, you never know who might be lurking around the corner.'

She laughed. 'The Führer has made our streets safer, that is for sure.'

They fell into stilted conversation. A man with a large Alsatian dog walked past. 'How the Führer loves his dogs,' she remarked casually.

A rebellious thought flashed into Peter's head. 'Of course he loves his dogs,' he said. 'They are obedient, unquestioning.'

She gave him a sharp look. Then she laughed. 'Well, wouldn't we all like our friends to be like that?' she said.

'I don't know,' said Peter. 'It's nice to have friends who have their own opinions, don't you think?'

She stayed silent. Then she said, 'It is a dangerous conversation we are having, Master Bruck. I'm sure Professor Kaltenbach would not approve of such reckless freethinking.'

Peter felt bolder. 'Professor Kaltenbach would be severely disappointed,' he said.

An awkward silence hung in the air. They barely spoke for the rest of the walk home. Peter began to worry that he had said too much. But when they reached Anna's apartment block she said, 'Thank you for walking me home. This was a most interesting conversation. We must talk again some time.'

When Peter reached the door to his own apartment, he felt like he was walking on air.

CHAPTER 16

April 1942

Anna and Peter saw more of each other after that. They were both frequent visitors to the library, and Peter often stayed there to study. He could get a lot of work done in one of the quiet corners. Professor Kaltenbach approved. He was not totally sympathetic to the Nazi view that boys needed more exercise than education. If Peter wanted to be a doctor or a scientist, after he had done his duty as a *Luftwaffe* pilot, he would have to pass some tough exams.

Anna began to join him at his desk, and work alongside him. She was studious – she certainly didn't sit there to chatter. Then, when it had gone dark, they would walk home together. Sometimes they would talk about friends they both knew, sometimes they would whisper about their homework. One week they both had the same essay: 'How did Adolf Hitler save the Fatherland?'

'There's not a great deal of scope for argument in that question, is there?' said Anna. 'I just trotted out the usual stuff about communists and Jews and Versailles. It took me ten minutes. It would be nice to do something a little harder.'

Peter loved it when she talked to him like that. Her and Segur.

One day in early April, when buds were sprouting on the trees and the sunshine started to feel warm on their faces, Anna asked Peter to come for tea the following

Tuesday. His imagination ran riot. He knew, because she had told him, that both her parents would be away. Frau Reiter was off to Falkenburg, reporting on one of the elite Ordensburgen schools where the cream of the Hitler Youth were sent. Colonel Reiter would be flying to the Führer's headquarters in East Prussia to deliver a report.

Peter did not tell the Kaltenbachs that the Reiter parents were away, although he had a feeling they wouldn't mind. They knew about Anna and had been keen to encourage the friendship.

Peter was nervous. Was she expecting him to kiss her? So far their friendship had been just that – a friendship. But maybe it was turning into something else.

Segur would know. He seemed to be more up on that sort of thing. But when Peter talked to him as they walked home from school, he blushed. 'I'll kill you if you tell anyone, but I've only ever kissed a girl once,' he said. 'When we were on a HJ/BDM hike.'

The day came. Peter arrived with a bunch of wild flowers and two cream cakes. Anna hurried him in, anxious that the neighbours should not see him. 'Frau Brenner,' she whispered and tilted her head to the door across the corridor. 'She'll only gossip . . .'

She made him a lemonade and started to peel potatoes while they talked – about the war, her brother Stefan who was serving out in Ostland, about their friends, about school. It was inconsequential chatter. Peter began to daydream as she cooked. There she was, standing by the window, with her white apron over her blue dress, spatula in hand, turning schnitzels. The smell of hot pork filled the kitchen. He felt very grown up all of a sudden, having someone his own age preparing his supper.

After they had eaten they sat in the living-room armchairs, facing each other and drinking coffee. Peter wondered if she was waiting for him to kiss her. But he didn't feel bold enough.

'Let's listen to the radio,' said Anna. 'See if we can find some good music?'

The radio was on a coffee table by the window. Anna turned the dial and stations flitted by. The news reported U-boat triumphs in the Atlantic, another programme announced increases in tank production, then there was a play . . . Anna left it on and for a brief moment they listened to the tale of a Hamburg girl whose father would not let her go out with an SS man.

Then she came and sat on the arm of his chair and said in a low voice: 'Do you ever listen to the BBC?' Peter was shocked by her boldness, but he was thrilled that she was confiding in him.

'Kaltenbach would have me down at Prinz-Albrecht-Strasse before I knew what had hit me,' said Peter. 'Besides, there's almost always someone in at our apartment. Frau Kaltenbach or Elsbeth. Even the girls would report me at once. Why, do you?'

'Shall we?' said Anna.

Peter was anxious now. 'But what if the neighbours hear through the walls? I'm sure one of them would report you.'

'We'll turn the volume right down and listen with a blanket thrown over us. That should do the trick!' said Anna. 'Mutti and Vati do it too. They don't like me to know, but I caught them once when I got up in the night.'

Anna fetched a blanket from her bed. They huddled together beneath it and she turned the dial. She knew exactly which spot to find.

She'd obviously done this before, thought Peter. Finding the station was easy enough but getting the volume was difficult. It was either too quiet to hear properly, or would leap out loud enough for the neighbours to hear.

The signal was being blocked too, with a piercing whistling noise that rose and fell to make it difficult to hear what was being said. 'They always do that – Vati says it's called jamming,' said Anna. 'To put people off listening.'

'Why would the BBC want to do that?' said Peter.

She batted him round the head, and grabbed his shoulder and shook him.

'Not them, dummkopf!' she laughed. 'It's our lot that does the jamming.'

Peter felt a bit foolish but he liked the way her hand lingered on his shoulder.

'Vati would know how to fix the radio,' said Anna. 'Not that I'd tell him about this. He'd be furious if he knew.'

Eventually, with much crackling and trial and error they settled down to listen. The radio was loud enough to hear the programme beneath the whistle, but probably not loud enough to be heard in the next apartment. They caught the end of a music programme, *Aus der Freien Welt* – From the Free World, playing swing and 'hot jazz' – music that was banned in Germany because most of the people who played it were black or Jewish. The music sounded exciting, but it was difficult to really enjoy it with that undulating whistle. Then it was time for the news.

The newsreader was a British man who introduced himself as Lindley Fraser. He spoke German very well and with only a slight accent, and announced that American troops were arriving in great numbers in Britain.

This surprised Peter. Professor Kaltenbach had told him the Americans wouldn't be interested in fighting the Nazis – just the Japanese. He wanted to say something but Anna was concentrating so hard he did not want to interrupt. They both listened in silence. It seemed extraordinary, to be hearing someone else's idea of what was happening in the world.

When the news finished there was more dance music and they listened with great sloppy grins on their faces, shoulders twitching to the rhythms. Peter was enjoying being this close to Anna. Their heads pressed together against the radio speaker, he could feel the warmth of her body and the moistness of her breath. She shifted her legs a little, then slipped her hand over his. Peter's heart lurched in his chest.

Anna introduced him to her parents a couple of days later, when she invited him round for dinner. Peter found them rather intimidating. Colonel Otto Reiter was a large, imposing man with a steely gaze and brusque manner. Ula Reiter was chic and beautiful, and bristled with a formidable 'can do' confidence.

But they did their best to make him feel at ease. As they sat round the dining table, he noticed how both of them spoke plainly about the war. It was not that they said anything 'treasonable', but it was obvious they spoke their own mind rather than the official Party line.

When Peter asked them how their son Stefan was getting on in Ostland, the Colonel replied, 'I worry about Stefan every day of my life.' There was a long pause, then he said, 'Napoleon invaded Russia a hundred and twenty-three years ago, almost on the exact day we did. He even managed to capture Moscow. Maybe we will too, eventually. But after that, who knows what will happen . . .'

They were fairly frank about the demands of the Nazi Party on their everyday lives. When Hitler's birthday came on 20th April Ula forgot to hang swastika flags from the window. Peter was there when Herr Pfister, the block warden, knocked on the door to demand she put them out. After he'd gone Ula grinned and said, 'We forgot to do that when France fell, too. Pfister was livid. Two hours he gave us, to find a flag to put out, before he reported us to the Gestapo.'

For Frau Kaltenbach this would be a matter of deep shame. For Frau Reiter, it was something to laugh about. Peter got the impression these weren't deliberate acts of defiance. The Reiters just didn't care enough about these Nazi rituals and the obligation to remember them all.

Now, when Peter sat around the dining table with the Kaltenbachs, he wished he could speak more freely with them. These thoughts made him feel guilty and ungrateful and he tried to banish them from his mind.

Listening to the BBC became a shared secret for Anna and Peter. Sometimes they would do it together after school, when they were sure Anna's parents were away or would be back late. 'Best not do it too often,' said Anna. 'If Frau Brenner knew you were here when Mutti and Vati were out, she'd tell them for sure.'

'Why don't you admit to listening? You know they do too,' said Peter.

'I know,' said Anna. 'It's silly. I just think it would be something else for them to worry about.'

Although the news was the important thing, they both enjoyed listening to comedies the BBC put out on their German radio programmes. There was the Berlin char-woman Frau Wernicke, and her grumbling about life under the Nazis. And there was *Gefreiter Hirnschall* – Corporal Numbskull – the reluctant soldier and the letters he wrote home to his wife. 'They're clever, the British,' said Anna. 'These characters, they're not stupid. They're quite sympathetic. It's like the British are saying "We know what it's like for you." '

She had a good point. Peter liked the way the announcers always spoke in calm, matter-of-fact voices. Not like the hectoring tone of the German announcers. It made what they said seem more believable. It was clever, too, he realised, for them to use a British man who spoke German well, rather than a German exile. People didn't warm to traitors.

That spring, the news was good and it was bad. Japan was still on the march in the Pacific, winning a stunning victory in Singapore. The German army were still making deep inroads into Soviet Russia. General Erwin Rommel – the 'Desert Fox' – and his Afrika-Korps were fighting with great success against the British in North Africa. All these things they had heard on their own radio news, and Peter and Anna were both surprised to hear the British announcer reporting them too. It made the rest of what they said more believable. But there was a quiet confidence in the BBC broadcasts. They seem to be saying, 'We know you're doing all right at the moment, but one day the tide will turn.'

Peter had powerfully mixed feelings listening to the BBC. He liked the way the German radio made him feel the war was nearly over and a great victory was almost at hand. That way he could imagine it was unlikely he and Segur and the other boys would ever be called up to fight. But the BBC made him feel it was inevitable. Especially with all those Americans flooding into Britain. The Nazis had stirred up a hornet's nest, and one day he might be one of the boys who would have to take the consequences.

CHAPTER 17

September 1942

When spring turned to summer in 1942, the war was still going Germany's way. Sirens occasionally sounded in Berlin, but no aircraft came to bomb the city. Peter and Anna continued to see each other whenever they could, and Peter always enjoyed his visits for tea with the Reiters.

Although he still liked his Onkel Franz, Peter was beginning to find some of Professor Kaltenbach's opinions preposterous – particularly compared to the measured outlook of Colonel Reiter. He seemed to notice this especially when Anna made one of her infrequent visits. She always felt uncomfortable at the Kaltenbachs' and Peter would be on tenterhooks wondering what she might say. Although conversation never rose above polite formality, she would occasionally make a withering remark which the Kaltenbachs seemed oblivious to. 'What an inspirational painting,' she said as she looked at the print of Hermann Otto Hoyer's *In the beginning was the word*, which hung in the hall. It showed Hitler preaching to early Nazi converts. 'How well the artist has captured the adoration of the people. It reminds me almost of a Holbein or a Cranach.'

Peter would notice at once, and be torn between shrinking in horror and laughing up his sleeve. Sometimes Elsbeth would give her a sharp look but she never said anything.

Franz and Liese Kaltenbach hinted that they would like to meet Anna's parents. Liese had read Ula's articles in *Frauenwarte* and both of them thought the Colonel a very glamorous figure. Peter and Anna knew such a meeting would be excruciating and although Anna always promised she would ask her parents she always came back with an excuse – usually to do with their work commitments.

Anna had joined them for dinner one early autumn evening when Kaltenbach began to splutter about a news report he had just read concerning a group of youths who had been arrested in a Berlin Dance Hall. 'Swing Youth, they call them. They wear their hair long, the boys – what soft eggs – and loud suits and scarves . . . and the girls, they wear their hair down and paint their faces. The Jezebels.

'The music – that awful jazz or "Swing", whatever it's called – what an unholy culture the Yankees have cooked up in that cesspit nation of theirs. This is what happens when you mix the races with such carelessness. And worst of all is the dancing. It's just degenerate. The boys and girls cavort together, shaking their bodies in a frenzy. Sometimes the girls whirl around in their skirts so everyone can see their underclothes. It's sheer pornography.'

The Kaltenbach girls, all three of them, looked suitably shocked.

Peter couldn't believe it. 'WHERE is it happening?' he was bursting to say. 'It sounds marvellous.' He didn't dare look at Anna in case he gave away his thoughts.

Anna spoke up. 'They must be French or Russian workers,' she said with a straight face. 'Surely German

121

boys and girls would not behave like that?'

Kaltenbach ploughed on, venting his disgust. 'Some of them are only fourteen or fifteen.' Bits of food were flying everywhere.

Anna said, 'It is almost unbelievable that some of our young people, all of them brought up in the spirit of National Socialism, have been drawn to behaviour that is so un-Germanic. I cannot imagine anyone I know behaving like that.'

Everyone agreed that this was deeply shocking, but they were lost for an explanation. Peter, in turn, was lost in admiration at Anna's performance.

As he walked her home, she said, 'Mutti told me about the Swing Youth last week. I told her it sounded fantastic. All those people rejecting their Nazi teaching. But Mutti wasn't so impressed. She said, from what she'd heard, they weren't rejecting anything. They just liked a good time. They're all kids like us. Well-to-do parents. They just want to forget about the war.' Then she said, 'Don't you go getting mixed up with them though.' The Gestapo and the *Hitler-Jugend* security squads, they all go out looking for them.'

They walked along in silence, arms entwined. It was one of those lovely crisp autumn evenings when the stars sparkled cold white in the velvet sky. Then Anna giggled and drew Peter's arm tighter to her side. 'Wouldn't it be good to be free to go to a dance like that?' she said wistfully.

Peter saw Segur the next day at school and told him about it. 'It sounds thoroughly disgusting,' he said. 'Especially the dancing. All those flashing legs and knickers and all that shaking it all about. Imagine. People enjoying themselves, while our brave troops make so many sacrifices at the front. It's not very patriotic, is it.'

A few days later Segur said he knew someone, a boy in his block called Dieter, who hung around at a café on Bülowstrasse. There were boys and girls there who looked like the ones the newspaper had described. 'Long hair. Flashy clothes. Girls who look like tarts. Only you know they're not. Too well-dressed. Too rich-looking. They're swing kids, aren't they! Dieter says they greet each other with "Swing Heil!"'

'Let's go,' said Peter. 'I'll ask Anna.'

She reluctantly agreed. 'It sounds good, but let's not get ourselves arrested.'

'It's not a dance,' said Peter. 'Just a café. We can hang around with other people who aren't all hundred-percenters. And if it starts getting too raucous we can make our excuses and leave.'

The three of them went the next week. They all told their parents they were going to a Winter Relief collection meeting.

The place was called Café Lebensart and it did a fine line in cakes and coffee. No beer or wine. At least that was what the menu on the door said. The sign above it read '*The German greeting is Heil Hitler!*'

Although the place was crowded and buzzing with conversation, the door was locked. Peter knocked, not expecting to be heard. An elderly man, short and stubby, made his way to let them in. He greeted them with a smile and a twinkle in his eye, and showed them to a table.

A gramophone behind the counter began to play the most exciting music. Peter had heard something similar on the BBC but now he could hear it properly without the whistling. The music was a little like the sort of upbeat dance-band songs you heard on the request programmes for soldiers at the front. Only it was twice as fast and played with twice the passion. Saxophones or clarinets would take wild excursions over the melody and it was impossible to hear without grinning and tapping your feet.

The owner, who had let them in, was an Italian called Bernardo. He kept a close eye on who came and went, turning the music down to nothing whenever anyone new came to the door.

'So what is this we're listening to?' said Peter, when Bernardo came to take their order.

'It's the trumpet and drum brigade of the Munich *Hitler-Jugend*,' he said with a wink. Some boy behind them, who had overheard, turned and said, 'Benny Goodman. He's just the coolest!'

Coolest? That was a new one to Peter. He supposed it meant good. It was certainly said with enthusiasm.

They ordered their coffee and cakes and sat there enjoying the feeling that they were doing something forbidden. From then on, the three of them managed to visit the café at least once a week. They became familiar faces and one day one of the girls took Anna aside and told her they were organising a dance in the basement of Café Berta, over by Hackescher Markt.

Anna returned to tell the boys. 'We've got to go,' said Segur. He turned to Anna. 'Maybe you can bring a girl for me?'

Anna looked doubtful. 'Is it worth it? This seems harmless enough,' she gestured around her, 'but a swing dance . . . we could end up in prison. Let's think about it.'

Peter grabbed her arm. 'No. Let's go! We've been coming here for a while now, and there's never been any trouble. Come on. Let's have a bit of fun.'

Anna still wasn't convinced.

The next time he saw her, Anna told Peter she had a present for him. 'Unwrap it in secret when you get home. I found it in an old junk shop.'

It was a tie – with a red, yellow and white palm leaf motif on it. The pattern was stupendously vulgar and guaranteed to give Professor Kaltenbach apoplexy if he ever saw it. There was only one place in Berlin Peter could imagine wearing it.

Sneaking out with overcoats over the brightest clothes they could find, Peter, Anna and Segur made their way to the seedy backstreet café where the party was to take place. Segur pretended to be disappointed with Anna. 'I thought you'd find a friend for me!' he chided.

Anna brushed him off with a laugh. 'I don't know any girls disreputable enough to come to such a gathering, or to go out with an oaf like you!'

They started to punch each other on the arm. Segur said, 'Hey, Bruck, you're going out with a hussy. And a violent one at that.'

Anna said, 'Don't worry. We'll find you a girl at the dance.'

She was in high spirits. The train was crowded and they all stood close to the carriage door. When they stopped at Tiergarten Station, she noticed an HJ group leader with a small squad of younger boys standing on the platform. 'He looks very pleased with himself,' she whispered to Peter. Just as the train began to move off she looked him straight in the eye and tapped the side of her head. The boys in his squad noticed and some started to giggle. Enraged, he walked down the platform with the train, shouting and banging on the window.

Everyone in the carriage was looking at them. 'Just an old boyfriend,' announced Anna casually. 'He never forgave me for dumping him.'

They walked into a narrow courtyard off Oranienburger Strasse. Café Berta needed a lick of paint and the tables were sticky. A few others had already gathered there, drinking coffee, eating cakes. They fell into conversation with one lad who wore his hair long at the front, so it flapped over his eye.

'How did you manage to grow your hair so long?' said Peter in admiration.

The boy grinned. 'I wear a hat.'

After a while, when he was sure they were safe, and not *Hitler-Jugend* spies, the lad said, 'I'm Karl. The party will be in the basement. It'll get going when a few more of us arrive.'

Peter had expected to see one or two familiar faces from Café Lebensart. But there was no one here he knew. Anna and Segur said the same thing. 'We're a rare breed,' said Segur. 'The rest of them are all polishing their jackboots or sewing combat proficiency badges on to their HJ jackets.'

It was then that Peter realised how right Anna had been not to bring anyone else. There was no one, apart from Segur, that they could be sure to trust.

Eventually, they were called downstairs, where there

was a basement bar. They piled chairs and tables in one corner to make space in the middle of the room for dancing. Cobwebs and dust covered the place. 'Good thing the light is so low,' said Segur. 'I'd prefer not to see what I'm sitting on!'

Someone had pinned up a big American movie poster – *The Jazz Age* – showing a bright young couple kissing in front of a montage of frantic dancing and a huge bottle of gin. Anna translated the movie slogan for Peter. There were lots of words she could guess but only half understand. An older girl helped her with some of the words. 'A scathing indictment of the bewildered children of pleasure . . . Riding the gilded Juggernaut of Jazz and Gin!!!'

'That certainly sounds very silly,' said Anna. 'I wonder what it means.'

'It means have a shot of this,' said their new friend Karl, who had smuggled in a bottle of gin. They all had a nip and gradually began to feel less nervous.

A record player in the corner blared out jazz 78s. 'Isn't it too loud?' said Anna.

'They'll never hear it down here,' said Karl.

They listened to Duke Ellington, Benny Goodman, Louis Armstrong . . . these were the exotic names the boys and girls in the Café Lebensart had bandied about. It was so exciting to hear the music this loud. Couples started to do extraordinary dances. 'Is that the jitterbug or the boogie-woogie?' said Anna to Peter, as couples threw themselves around the dance floor. They had heard about these American dances, which the Nazis had dismissed as displays of wanton abandon. He could certainly see why they thought that!

127

Anna tugged at his sleeve. 'Would you like to ride the gilded juggernaut?' she asked with mock formality and dragged him into the middle of the room. They couldn't do what some of the dancers were doing – leaping over each other's shoulders – in fact they were lucky not to be hit by flying feet, but they could do the dance where you leaned back on each other's shoulders and waved your hands.

In the corner, a couple were kissing passionately. Peter didn't know where to look. Then Anna grabbed him by the back of the neck and they were kissing too, right there in the middle of the dance floor. Peter blushed, but no one seemed to notice or care.

Segur had found a girl to talk to. She was with a friend who seemed quite odd. They couldn't put their finger on it, until they saw her arm. It was hairy and quite muscular. She was heavily made-up but Peter was sure he could see a hint of stubble. 'She's a he,' said Peter to Anna. He was shocked, but then he began to think it was funny. So, here they were. With all the rebels in Berlin.

They sat down next to Segur and the girl, who he introduced as Lotte. They were swiftly joined by another lad. 'Swing Heil!' he said to them all, with a throwaway Nazi salute.

Lotte said, 'This here's Ralfie. He's been in quite a few scrapes, haven't you!'

Ralfie needed no further excuse to tell them what he'd been up to. 'Me and my pals here, we like to cause a bit of trouble with the HJ. Let the tyres down on their bikes! Smash up their clubhouses! Paint a few words on the walls! Me and Johann are going out afterwards to see what mischief we can get up to. You coming?'

Anna nodded her head. Peter wasn't so sure. He hadn't drunk as much gin as she had.

They kissed again. 'Come on, Peter,' she said breathlessly. 'Let's go mad. It's time we had a bit of fun!'

'Let's see,' he said cautiously. Then someone filled up his glass.

'Down the hatch,' said Anna, and Peter began to enjoy feeling this reckless.

The music stopped. The dancers turned to look towards the record player. 'HJ Patrol,' whispered the boy who had turned it off. He glanced towards the door, white with fear.

CHAPTER 18

The door to the cellar had been locked, and someone was shouting and banging on it angrily.

One of the party organisers stepped forward and spoke quietly and urgently to them. 'There's an exit here out the back that takes us into Gross Hamburger Strasse. This way. Hurry!'

Everyone followed, squeezing through a heavy wooden door and heading up a cluttered passageway behind kitchens and storerooms that stank of stale frying oil and boiled cabbage. *This is what it must be like to be trapped in a fire*, thought Peter. His heart was pumping in his chest but he felt strangely calm. Anna was right behind him, holding his hand. If anyone fell, they would be trampled by the people behind them.

A narrow staircase led up to street level but it was dark now, the only light the open door to the room they had hurriedly left.

Behind them, they heard a splintering of wood as the door to the cellar was broken open. The passageway was packed with bodies – all of them frantic to get away. Some of the party-goers were still there in the room. The crowd behind Peter pressed harder. It was almost impossible to move.

'Give me some space,' said the boy who had led them up the stairs. They pushed back. Peter felt like he was having the life squeezed out of him.

The boy brought out a packet of matches and struck one. In the light of the flickering flame he located a nail at the side of the door with a key hanging from a loop of red ribbon.

A quick fumble and the door sprang open. Cold autumn air flooded in.

The crowd burst out to find themselves in a seedy backyard, lit by bright moonlight. Weeds grew in the broken paving and out of cracks in the mortar of the brick wall. There was an outside lavatory, several wooden boxes, three overfilled dustbins and a narrow wooden door. Someone rattled frantically on the handle. It was locked. Behind them they could hear the sound of splintering wood – tables and chairs – and shouting. Those that had been caught at the tail end of the dash out were putting up a fight. Some of the girls were screaming.

'It's the wall or nothing,' said Peter.

But the top of the wall was covered by barbed wire. It was too high to climb unaided. Peter leaped on to one of the bins, squashing down the lid as he reached up to the wire. 'We can't climb over this. Our hands will be ripped to shreds.'

He put a hand on the wire and tugged. It was so old and rusty it broke. Behind them, the fighting was getting closer. In the distance a police siren began to wail.

Peter frantically pulled at the wire until there was space to climb over. He jumped down to help Anna on to the dustbin but several other boys and girls pushed him out of the way, frantic to escape. After the first two or three had gone over, Peter began to fear for them both. He pushed a boy back so Anna could get up and once she was on the wall he clambered up himself. The boy he had pushed dragged at his trousers and pulled him away. Peter fell hard to the ground as the dustbin toppled over, spilling its contents on the yard. The boy was incensed and began to hit Peter. 'Stop it, you idiot,' yelled Peter. 'Fight them, not us.'

He tried to drag another dustbin over to the wall. The other boy, in a blind panic, was trying to grab it off him. By now the HJ patrol had pushed their way out there and the whole yard was full of flailing fists and boots. Someone in a black uniform dragged away the boy who was attacking Peter, leaving him a moment to vault on to the bin. Peter swung his left foot on to the top of the wall just as a hand grabbed his right foot. He brought his left foot down to kick at the hand and then the head of the HJ who had grabbed him. The boy fell back, clutching the side of his head. That was all Peter needed. He was over in an instant and landed hard on the cobbled street. Ahead was a narrow alley and then the wider Gross Hamburger Strasse. Dancing shadows and a commotion in the street told him the HJ were already out there. The siren they had heard earlier was screaming in his ears.

A figure loomed from a recess in the alley. Peter tensed himself for another fight. 'It's me,' hissed Anna. She grabbed his hand. 'This way!'

She led him away from Gross Hamburger Strasse, through a series of smaller alleys until they emerged into the square by Hackescher Markt. They stayed in the shadows until they were breathing normally. 'You waited for me!' said Peter, and kissed her on the forehead.

'I thought you'd never come over that wall,' she said, stifling something between a sob and a giggle. 'What kept you?'

She was distracted by the sight of blood on her sleeve. 'You've hurt yourself,' said Peter. Then he began to feel a sharp pain in the palm of his hand. It was him that was bleeding. He must have caught himself on the barbed wire. He took a handkerchief from his pocket and wrapped it tightly around the ugly gash. Anna tied it in place.

'I have a special First Aid merit badge from the BDM, don't you know,' she pretended to swank, 'like a good German girl. Nursing our brave soldiers.'

'I'm sorry about your coat,' muttered Peter. That would take some explaining.

There were plenty of people here, milling about or sitting outside the bars and cafés. Anna quickly whipped off Peter's flamboyant tie. They hooked arms and walked to the S-Bahn station as nonchalantly as they could.

'What happened to Segur?' said Peter, suddenly alarmed. Anna stopped in her tracks.

'I didn't see him run away. Do you think he'd tell them we were there?'

Peter said he was sure Segur would not betray them.

'But you can never tell,' said Anna. 'I know how they work. Vati has talked about it. They promise you all the tortures of hell, then tell you they'll let you off lightly if you give them names.'

Peter envied Anna her relationship with her parents. She always called them Mutti and Vati. The Kaltenbachs frowned on such informality. It was Mutter and Vater for Elsbeth and Traudl, except for little Charlotte who still called them Mama and Papa.

It was eight o'clock. The curfew for young people

began at nine, but they were both too excited to go home.

'Let's walk back,' said Peter. 'I'll never sleep after this.'

'We should make it within the hour,' said Anna.

They crossed the Spree by Museum Island and continued down the wide avenue of Unter den Linden. It was a beautiful night. But as they walked the excitement and glee they felt at their escape began to fade.

'I wonder what will happen to the ones who got caught?' said Anna.

Peter shook his head. 'They might get away with a few bruises, I suppose. But I expect they'll be taken off to Prinz-Albrecht-Strasse. The Gestapo will be keen to find out more about them and their friends.'

Anna shuddered at the mention of the Gestapo headquarters. She had been there once with her father, who dropped in to deliver a file from the Home Army office. 'It's so strange,' she told Peter. 'Used to be an art school. It's very grand inside. All marble staircases and pillars. Once upon a time, you went there to attend life classes and learn how to use oils or charcoals. Now you go to be tortured. That's what passes for progress these days.'

Peter jabbed her in the ribs with his elbow. There were two policemen coming towards them. The men walked past with a simple 'Heil Hitler', almost without giving them a second glance.

As they crossed the huge square by the Opera House in front of Friedrich Wilhelms University, Anna said, 'This is where they did the book burning. Just after Hitler came to power. The students, they ransacked the University Library. Anything they could find by Jews, Russians, Poles, out it went on to the bonfire.

Dostoyevsky, Marie Curie, Freud . . . science, literature, the lot.

'Still, as the Führer says, "If science cannot do without Jews then we will have to do without science for a few years." It all makes perfect sense to me.'

Peter didn't know who Dostoyevsky and Freud were and he didn't like to ask.

'Students!' she went on. 'Not thugs like the Nazi storm troopers . . . Educated people did that! I was only five at the time, but my father mentioned it several times when we drove past. What got into them?'

The question hung in the air. Anna said, 'Hitler. He's cast a spell on us all. It's like an awful fairy tale. But some of us are waking up. Even if it's just to dance to swing music.'

As they reached the Brandenburg Gate and began to turn south towards Wittenbergplatz, Anna grew wistful. 'This is such a beautiful city,' she said to Peter, holding him tight with her arm. 'What a shame for all of us that we have to share it with these lunatics.

'If we lived somewhere else, another time, another place, we could just enjoy ourselves without having to worry about it. Go dancing, sneak into bars for a drink, and who would care? The Nazis have taken all the fun out of life. What have we got to look forward to? I don't know how the war will end, but it may not be easy for Germany.'

Peter worried that Anna was upsetting herself. But when he looked at her she seemed quite composed. There were no tears in her eyes. She was just being matter of fact.

'Who knows. Perhaps you will be wrong?' said Peter, and kissed her tenderly on the side of her head.

'But that's the awful thing,' said Anna. 'If I'm wrong and the Nazis *win*, then what hope is there for the world?'

It was a chilling thought. For the first time, and with absolute clarity, Peter could see they were on the wrong side in the war. For him, in a year or two, there was the dark cloud of the call-up. He had still not decided which service to enter. The *Luftwaffe* was still his fantasy but so few who tried were accepted.

So it would almost certainly be the Army or the Navy. Fighting the Ivans in Ostland or firing torpedoes at the Tommies or the Yanks in a submarine somewhere out in the Atlantic Ocean. Somewhere cold and dingy. For Anna, the choices were less stark but no more comforting. Those that stayed on the home front, they would have to wait for death to come to them, rather than go out and seek it.

As they wandered along Tiergartenstrasse they saw a couple of HJ ride past them on bicycles. The boys propped their bikes up against the wall of the Japanese Embassy and went into the large grounds. Peter and Anna peered through the railings and saw them ushered in through the front door.

'Probably despatches of some sort,' said Peter.

Anna looked up and down the street. The moon had gone behind the clouds. It was a dark night and no one else was around. Before he could stop her, she knelt down and began to loosen the valves on one of the bicycles. Peter suppressed a snigger and started to work on the other. With air gently hissing in their ears they hurried, hand in hand, into the bushes of the Tiergarten.

In the distance they could hear angry voices. They carried on walking, half hopping along. Then close to Hofjägerallee they stopped and laughed themselves breathless.

It was getting late. They quickened their pace and parted at Anna's doorstep. Just as they were kissing, the door burst open. 'And where have you been?' said Colonel Reiter in his sternest voice. Peter was tall, but Anna's father still towered over him.

'The Winter Relief Meeting, Vati,' said Anna, trying too hard to sound innocent.

'Not in that outfit, you weren't,' said her father. 'And young Bruck was there too, was he? Short of members are they, the BDM? Open to the Hitler Youth, is it?' His voice was calm but there was no mistaking the sarcasm.

Peter had never seen Colonel Reiter angry before. 'Come in the pair of you,' he said. It was an order rather than a request.

They were ushered into the dining room. Frau Reiter sat there too. She looked like thunder.

'So what's happened?' she said to them both. 'Anna, why is Peter's hand in a bandage?'

Anna looked confused. They had not expected this.

'I fell and caught my hand on a stone on the pavement,' said Peter feebly. He did not like lying to the Reiters. They were good people. People he admired.

The parents nodded without smiling.

'We've been to a dance at the Café Berta by Oranienburger Strasse,' said Anna. 'Perfectly respectable. Nice people.'

'Come, come, Anna,' said Colonel Reiter. He was trying to sound reasonable. 'You would have told us you were going if that was the case. Peter, where have you been?'

Peter wanted to say 'What is this, the Gestapo?' but he thought better of it. He liked the Reiters too much to be rude to them. Besides, Colonel Reiter looked as though he was about to punch him.

'We went to a swing dance. It was broken up by HJ. We managed to get away,' said Anna.

'You silly, silly girl,' gasped Frau Reiter.

Anna, who earlier had been so composed when she talked about the future, was now looking like a tearful schoolgirl. She stared red-faced at the floor.

Frau Reiter turned to Peter. 'You must promise *never* to do this again.'

'Did anyone you know see you?' said the Colonel.

'We went with Segur,' said Peter. 'We don't know whether or not he got away.'

'That's bloody marvellous,' said the Colonel. 'How long d'you think it'll be before he sings to the Gestapo?

'Peter, we trusted you because we thought you were a decent and honourable boy. But you are also foolish,' he said. 'I'll tell you what will happen if Segur gives you away. The Gestapo will be round here. I expect a knock on the door anytime now. I hope you have a good story for Professor Kaltenbach when they come calling for you. I imagine he's going to feel very disappointed.'

Peter was dismissed. He wandered home in deep misery. The evening had been such a roller coaster. It had ended on a wretched low. He came back to the apartment and called in goodnight to the living room. Herr and Frau Kaltenbach called back but had no more to say.

Peter lay awake for a long time, unable to sleep. And

when he nodded off he was woken by the sound of sharp rapping at the door. He sat up in a cold sweat. It was a dream; one he had several times that night. The knock at the door did not come. But by daybreak Peter was still convinced they had got Segur. And what about the poor man who owned the café? Would he tell the HJ he knew nothing about a 'swing dance'? What about the youth dressed as a girl? He was destined for Sachsenhausen for sure, if he survived the kicking the HJ patrol would have given him.

At school the next day Segur was nowhere to be seen. Peter's fear intensified. He waited all day, sure the Gestapo would arrive to haul him out of his classroom. Maybe they had got Anna already? Maybe she would squeal on him? No. That would never happen. Just as he would never betray her – even if they threatened to pull out all his fingernails.

School came to a dreary end. All day he had been caught between livid fear and exhaustion. Twice he had fallen asleep in class to have the teacher's ruler rapped across his head to wake him.

He could stand the suspense no longer. As soon as he was out of the school gates he rode his bike over to Segur's. The boy's mother answered the door. She looked shocked and timid. 'You've come to see my poor Gerhart,' she said. 'See what they have done to him.'

Frau Segur was a ninety-percenter, at least. She was proud of her bronze Mother's Cross, awarded after the arrival of her fourth child. She always wore it on her coat and was most indignant if Hitler Youth boys did not salute her in the street, as they were obliged to do. Peter knew he had to play this one carefully.

Segur was lying in his bed, black and blue with bruises. 'What on earth happened to you?' said Peter.

'A gang of Polack street cleaners,' he said. 'Or maybe they were Ukrainians. They just turned on me for no reason.'

'Gerhart, you must report this,' said his mother.

'I will. I will,' he said. 'Just as soon as I can stand up without wincing.'

She left to prepare them coffee and cakes. Segur beckoned Peter to lean closer. 'They beat me, God in heaven they beat me,' he whispered. 'They got me in a shop doorway and kicked the shit out of me. I couldn't move. But the stupid bastards left me there. Rounded up the rest. Left me. I saw them bundle about fifteen of them into a lorry. Who knows what will happen to them. When I saw what they were doing, I just curled up into the shadows and hoped they'd forget me.'

'Did any of them know you?' said Peter.

'Only by my first name. It's better that way, isn't it.'

'And what's this about "Polacks" and Ukrainians?' said Peter. 'If the police follow that up, there'll be random punishments. Even executions.'

'I didn't think of that,' said Segur. 'I'll say you're going to report the crime. I don't want her to.'

Peter went along with this. He assured Frau Segur that he would go at once to the police station with a report of exactly what had happened. Gerhart had given him a good description, he said. The police would find the culprits.

'Slav scum,' said Frau Segur. 'We give them work and food and spare their miserable lives and what do they do

140

to thank us?'

Peter felt indignant but he had learned to hold his tongue. There were too many people like Frau Segur in the world. He cycled home feeling elated. They were safe. They would not be getting an early morning knock at the door. He went at once to the Reiters' and banged impatiently on the door. Frau Reiter answered.

'Oh, it's you,' she said coldly.

'Can I see Anna, please?'

'Anna is not at home.'

'Can you tell her Segur is all right. I'll tell her more when I see her.'

'You won't,' said Frau Reiter. 'We have decided you and Anna will not be seeing each other any more. But thank you for your message. Goodbye, Peter.'

The door closed with a firm and decisive click.

CHAPTER 19

November 1942

Peter saw Anna in the library two days later. She sat the other side of the reading room and pretended not to see him. He felt hurt, angry even, and buried himself in his studies. After ten minutes or so, he was vaguely aware of someone passing close by his desk. By the time he looked up she was walking back to the far side of the room but a little folded piece of paper lay tucked under one of his books.

Meet me outside. Five minutes.
Ax

It was one of those rainy, cold autumn evenings, when the threat of winter hung heavy in the air. Anna carried a large umbrella and she beckoned him to stand underneath it with her. They kissed and walked off together arm in arm – the umbrella held low to hide their faces.

'Frau Schrader here, she knows Mutter. I don't want her telling on us.'

Anna never called her mother 'Mutter'. *She's angry with her*, thought Peter. *Good*. He was worried she'd be angry with him.

'Your mother,' said Peter, 'she said I was not to see you.'

Anna blew an exasperated stream of air through her lips. 'Yes, we really messed things up going to that dance.

But never mind. It will blow over. Let's be careful for the next month or so. Look, I'll talk to them after they've calmed down a bit. But let's not antagonise them by meeting up like this. It'll just make . . .'

Mid-conversation, two policemen grabbed them either side, abruptly flipping the umbrella away from their faces. 'Papers,' demanded one of the men in a voice so menacing neither Peter nor Anna dared protest.

They produced their identity cards and waited, rain falling down their faces. Peter hoped the men had not overheard anything of their conversation.

'Good,' said one of the policemen, as he handed back the cards. The other laughed. 'It's usually the U-boats who are so keen for everyone not to see them. On your way.'

Both of them were shaken by the incident. 'What did he mean?' said Peter. 'U-boats?'

'It's what the Jews in hiding call themselves,' said Anna. 'When they get their summons, for "relocation in the east" – the shrewd ones know what it means, and they go into hiding.'

Peter was all ears. She was being very indiscreet.

'I wouldn't expect a policeman to use the same term.'

Peter wondered how she knew all this. 'And what does "relocation in the east" really mean?' he asked cautiously.

She sighed deeply, shaking her head. 'I don't know,' she said defensively. 'I'm sorry, Peter. We can't go on talking about this. It's too dangerous.'

She kissed him tenderly on the cheek and then ran off down the street. The more the rain soaked into his clothes, the more bewildered he felt.

* * *

Peter had always enjoyed the autumn. The crisp cold, the frost and mist, tattered trees silhouetted against sharp blue skies. Despite the coming winter, October and November always filled him with hope for the future. He supposed it was because the school year started in the autumn. Then there was Christmas to look forward to, and after that, the promise of spring.

But this year was different. Everyone felt it. The Russians had still not given in. The Americans were over in England, building up their forces. The constant parade of victories that Hitler had presented to the German people had come to a halt. Still, at least in the Caucasus – in the deep south of the Soviet Union – the German Sixth Army were making progress. German and Japanese forces would soon meet up in India. Paulus's troops were within a whisker of taking Stalingrad.

That's what the newspapers said. Before they fell out, Ula Reiter had told him her magazine had been sent a press release announcing the fall of the city with the proviso 'Hold until authorisation from Reich Ministry for Popular Enlightenment and Propaganda' at the bottom of the page. That authorisation never came.

There was something titanic going on in Stalingrad. Traudl was one of the many squads of BDM girls sent to greet injured soldiers from the east at the railway stations. She brought bunches of wild flowers to wounded men in the military hospitals and wrote letters for the ones who were too ill or injured to write themselves. When Peter asked her about it, he expected her to trot out a cheerful line about Germany's inevitable victory. But instead she shook her head and looked troubled. 'There are so many of them . . .' She wouldn't tell him any more.

Peter missed Anna keenly, especially as Segur had been keeping his distance too. The beating seemed to have knocked the spirit out of him. He no longer made those wisecrack put-downs that Peter liked so much. Segur and Anna especially were his safety valve. He could talk to them about anything, which made everything seem a little more bearable. Without them, he had these awful dreams, of standing up in class, or at the HJ meetings, and saying all the wrong things.

Frau Kaltenbach noticed the change in him. 'That lovely girl, Anna. Have you fallen out?' she said to him one day in the kitchen, as he peeled potatoes in the sink.

Peter lied badly. 'Yes. A bit. It was getting a bit too serious. I wanted to spend more time with my friends.'

Frau Kaltenbach laughed. 'She dumped you, didn't she? You've been looking really glum.'

It was not a cruel laugh, and Peter was pleased that she was offering him a little sympathy.

'Well, that's her lookout. She'll have to go a long way to find as fine a looking boy as you.'

Peter blushed. He really wanted to talk about something else.

It was only in early December that Anna finally got back in touch. Since the hurried exchange outside the library, they had seen each other in the street only once or twice, and just once more at the library, although he had often gone there hoping to see her. She had always avoided him. Not even a wave or a smile. It had begun to worry him.

But one day, walking home from school, she had come up to him and slipped an arm in his. Bold as anything. 'I was right,' she said with a grin. 'They relented. Mutti said "I can't bear to see you looking so glum. If you want to see Peter, see him. But no more dances. Nothing silly and dangerous."'

'That means no more listening to the radio either. If we get caught doing *anything* by them, then they'll probably send me to a convent to keep me out of mischief!'

Three days later, she turned up on the Kaltenbachs' doorstep. Her eyes were red from crying. 'It's Stefan,' she said. 'He's back in Berlin.'

'Well, that's good, isn't it?' said Peter. Anna had often talked about her brother and how worried she was about him fighting out in Ostland.

She shook her head. 'He's in a military hospital in Charlottenburg. He's been badly wounded in Stalingrad. Vati thinks he might lose a leg. Come with me to see him. I don't want to go on my own.'

They went the next day, taking the U-Bahn from the Zoological Garden. Anna told Peter all she knew on the way, and he strained to hear her over the clatter of the wheels on the track. 'He's been evacuated from within *der Kessel* – that's what they call it – the cauldron.'

Stalingrad had been in the news a lot. The Sixth Army had almost conquered the city, but now they were surrounded by Soviet troops and fighting for their lives.

Even Peter's *Hitler-Jugend* magazines did not attempt to hide the difficulties facing the troops there. In the sketched illustrations that accompanied the articles, soldiers were shown wrapped in scarves and winter clothing, surrounded by snow and often wounded. They projected an air of heroic defiance, but they were also unshaven and looked close to exhaustion. *If that's what they're showing us*, thought Peter, *what must it really be like?* He thought of the HJ boys who longed to join the military, almost desperate to fight. This would not be what they had in mind.

The corridors of the hospital were unsettling. Relatives, grimly silent, sat in chairs beneath frosted windows. Patients without limbs hobbled by on crutches, nurses and doctors hurried anxiously between wards. Although an eerie quiet hung over the building, the place was bursting at the seams.

Stefan was in a ward with about twenty other men. All of them were badly wounded. Peter guessed this because, although it was visiting time and almost every man had a cluster around his bed, they were all talking in whispers.

The smell of the place, sharp antiseptic and bleach that caught in his throat and nostrils, almost masked another sweetly putrid stench. But not quite. Peter's first reaction was to flee. He thought he was going to be sick.

When Stefan smiled, which he did with some difficulty, Peter could see what a handsome fellow he was. You could tell they were related, he and Anna.

'So you are Peter!' said Stefan, and slowly moved a hand out to shake his. There was no 'Heiling' with him.

'I can barely move, mein Liebling,' Stefan said weakly, when Anna tried to kiss him. 'My leg's got a piece of shrapnel in it and it's badly infected.'

She leaned forward, placing her hand on the bed to

steady herself. Stefan stifled a scream, as the bedding pressed against his injury. Anna jumped back at once, embarrassed by her clumsiness.

They sat down and leaned as close as they could, listening hard to hear his story.

'I was lucky to get out,' Stefan said in a low voice. 'The airfields round Stalingrad are a disaster. Planes crash every day trying to fly in and out in the snow. And they're under constant bombardment from the Ivans. The walking wounded at the field hospitals around the airbases, they're so desperate to get out they'll cling to the wing of a taxiing Ju 52 until they're swept away by the slipstream . . .'

He winced at the memory.

'Don't trouble yourself, Stefan. Just rest,' said Anna. 'We'll stay here and keep you company.'

'No. Hear me out. I have to tell you,' he said.

'So, what happened?' said Peter.

Stefan leaned forward and told them in a low whisper. 'We had our headquarters close to the riverbank. A bombardment came out of the blue, prolonged and intense. We were amazed the Ivans still had that much strength in them. Eventually it stopped. That was the most frightening silence I ever heard in my life . . . then we heard the sound of tanks firing up their engines. Tanks – almost on top of us. They must have come up during the bombardment when we couldn't hear them. It was terrifying. We were trapped in this factory. I can still see it all. The broken bricks and twisted steel rods, and stairs covered in blood and dust and God knows what kind of human remains . . .'

He stopped while one of the nurses walked past. 'They

told us not to tell people what it was like. But I spent my military career gathering intelligence. Now I'm passing it on to you, so you can know the truth. Because I don't think they're going to be telling the German people what's really happening . . .

'I still see it in my nightmares. That stairwell, leading to the floor above. They were there, right above our heads, the Ivans. In my dreams I have to climb that staircase to find out what lies behind the turn on the landing. Or sometimes I'm there, trapped in the workshop while the Ivans tumble down, throwing grenades before them, and it's me lying there on the filthy floor with my guts hanging out.

'We all thought we'd won. General Paulus. He'd even done rough sketches of the campaign victory medal . . . We'd taken almost all of the city. But they held on by their fingernails . . . they're going to hold on until they've driven us out of their land.'

He slumped back. Unburdening himself had wearied him.

He didn't speak for a while, then he tried to sit up. He beckoned them closer and spoke again.

'Now we're like a man who has grabbed a wolf by the ears and daren't let go. This whole campaign, it's been a magnificent disaster. How extraordinary. To take an army from the Reich to the very gates of Asia. It was an incredible achievement . . . But you know, in the early days, when we first arrived, many of the peasants welcomed us as liberators. They came out, the girls in their national dress, all smiles, throwing flowers, offering us bread, holding up their crosses and icons. We were liberating them from Stalin and the Godless Bolsheviks.

But they soon found out we were much worse. All this *Untermensch* nonsense. It was madness treating people so badly – so of course they just turned against us. It's like a fairy tale . . . it's so obvious.

'I was glad to be posted to the front. At the rear, you never know when you're going to be killed. The partisans attack out of nowhere. And whenever they do, we round up and kill entire villages in retaliation. Hundreds . . . thousands, slaughtered like insects. That just drives even more of them into the forests to fight against us. At the front, at least you know who and where the enemy is. And you don't have to concern yourself with the slaughter of innocent civilians.'

He reached out a hand to Anna. 'You carry on doing what you're doing,' he whispered, just loud enough for Peter to hear him. She looked startled, panic in her eyes.

'Hush now, Stefan, you'll wear yourself to a frazzle.'

He turned to Peter. 'She's a good girl. You look after her.'

'We must go,' said Anna. She seemed anxious to get away.

On the U-bahn home the carriage was half empty. Peter could not wait any longer. 'Anna, what is it you do?'

'Nothing,' she said quickly. 'Stefan was delirious, Peter.' She held on to his arm.

Anna didn't take Peter to see Stefan again, which disappointed him as he wanted to go. Whenever he brought it up, she just brushed it aside. 'Stefan needs peace and quiet.'

Peter still asked about Stefan, of course, and in the

150

week before Christmas Anna had some very good news. 'He's doing a lot better now. His leg is healing, so he's not going to lose it. I thought he'd spend the rest of his life hobbling around on crutches. We're all so grateful to the hospital staff. He says they've told him he'll always have a limp though, and will have to walk with a stick. But that's better than we expected. I had hoped he would be invalided out, but he thinks they'll send him back to his unit.'

'Surely they don't expect him to fight?' said Peter.

'No. He'll be working at headquarters. So that's good. He won't be on the front line. Maybe he'll survive the war after all.'

CHAPTER 20

January 16, 1943

When Peter first arrived in Berlin, the Kaltenbach girls had told him excitedly of the air raids they had witnessed. 'Feeble little bombers. Mainly the RAF,' said Traudl. 'The Ivans sent some bombers over too, just before you arrived, but we shot them all down. I saw one of them crash! I don't think they'll be back.'

Professor Kaltenbach had always reassured his family that they were safe in their city. The Soviet front line stretched from Leningrad and Moscow down to the Caucasus, he reminded them. No Soviet bombers could fly that distance. The British were nearer, he conceded. But they seemed reluctant to venture as far as Berlin. The towns and cities to the west had seen some raids but, so far, the *Luftwaffe* and anti-aircraft defences around the capital were formidable enough to keep them away.

But that did not stop the authorities preparing for the worst. In the last year the air-raid sirens had gone off nine times, but nothing had happened. 'Just testing them out, I imagine,' the Professor said.

But soon after New Year, the British took the city completely by surprise.

The Kaltenbachs were all in bed and the sirens only sounded when the bombers were over the city. Peter was deep in sleep and at first the rising and falling wailing seemed part of a strange dream. Then Herr Kaltenbach burst into his bedroom to shake him awake. 'Hurry,

Peter,' he said. 'Get dressed. It's too cold for just a dressing gown. This is a strange time to have a drill, I must say.' But he had barely uttered the words when a distant whistling was followed by explosions loud enough to rattle the windows. Charlotte began to cry and her mother hushed her with a sharp slap on the leg.

'No time,' said Kaltenbach. 'Just grab a blanket.'

The siren wail faded and instead they could all hear the distant drone of aircraft engines – there were scores of them by the sound of it.

The family stumbled down the staircase to the basement, along with other sleepy residents of the block. Peter was surprised, but also a little amused, to see Frau Kaltenbach without her carefully applied make-up. She looked bilious and pasty, like someone who had been constipated for a week.

The basement was locked and the block warden, Herr Schlosser, was nowhere to be seen.

'Obviously, no one was expecting this,' said Herr Kaltenbach. He seemed remarkably calm. Another stick of bombs whistled down, exploding somewhere to the west. Children started to cry, but not Charlotte. She was too frightened of her mother. Her father picked her up and told her what a brave girl she was.

Schlosser came five minutes later. He was dressed and had obviously been somewhere else when the bombs started to fall. He pushed through the anxious residents with a belligerent swagger. Basement door unlocked, they hurried through to sit on the stone floor and wait.

'I shall bring a cushion next time,' said Kaltenbach with a smile. Charlotte and Traudl nestled under his arms, the three of them wrapped in one blanket. He

153

really was brave, thought Peter, and he really loved his daughters. It was quite touching. He felt a twinge of envy for those girls. His own father had never hugged him like that. He was always formal and reserved.

Now there were so many packed into the basement it was impossible to move from where they were sitting. It wasn't as cold as they had feared, though. A lot of people close together generated heat.

Two bare light bulbs lit the room and in the harsh glare Peter glanced at Elsbeth. She was looking sour – irritated at the disturbance rather than frightened. Frau Kaltenbach's face was like a mask. He wondered what was going on inside her head. It was impossible to tell.

Some of the other children started to play a game of 'I see something that you don't see'. They thought this was a great adventure. Their attitude was infectious. People began to chatter and crack jokes in a slightly hysterical way, like students before a big exam. The children got through Cobwebs, Dust and Broom before a huge explosion shook the building and the lights flickered, then failed. There was screaming, and an awful smell – someone somewhere had soiled themselves. It was so dark they could not see their hands in front of their faces.

Schlosser called for silence. He sounded drunk. 'Stay where you are. I shall get some candles.'

As he opened the door another smell wafted in with a blast of cold night air. It was brick dust. In the distance more bombs fell. The aeroplanes could no longer be heard. What they did hear, though, was an ominous rattle that gathered pace and ended with a crash and clatter that went on for ages. That was a building collapsing. Peter wondered where. It was obviously quite near. Then, with terrible alarm, he realised it could be Anna's apartment block.

Schlosser returned with a couple of candles, and closed the door. 'Sounds like they're going,' he announced. 'But we shall stay here until the all clear.'

Peter could see his bloated silhouette in the door frame. He was a great bear of a man with a formidable beer gut. Before Hitler came to power, Peter had heard him boast, he had been a standard bearer at Nazi rallies, marching through the Reds' territory over in Wedding, north of the centre of the capital, spoiling for a fight. *He loves Hitler so much*, thought Peter, *he even has a little Hitler moustache. And how he loves his little bit of power.* Schlosser was not like the other residents. He was as rough as a block of wood.

Anna's parents knew of him too. He often told people he had been a Nazi since 1924. This was his reward, said Otto. A block warden for all these nobs – with his own little apartment and the power to tell these academics, civil servants and haughty hausfraus with their little dogs to put out their swastika flags and 'Sieg Heil' along with the rest of the nation.

They waited another tedious shivering hour before the all-clear siren sounded at 3 a.m. and everyone stumbled back to bed. Peter looked out of his window and could see nothing close to the apartment. He was still desperate to know if Anna was all right, but Kaltenbach had forbidden him to go outside. 'You'll just get in the way of the rescue people,' he said. 'Besides, you'll be fit for nothing in the morning, if you don't get some sleep.'

At first light, the whole family crowded round the

radio to listen to the news. Frau Kaltenbach even allowed them to sit in the living room to eat their breakfast, rather than round the dining table.

The bombing of Berlin was third or fourth down the agenda. The report was entirely positive. The 'terror bombers', the newsreader said, had caused little damage apart from at the Deutschlandhalle, which was a couple of kilometres to the west of Wittenbergplatz. A circus had been performing to ten thousand people. All of them, and the animals, had been successfully evacuated, crowed the announcer, although the building itself had been damaged.

Peter hurriedly finished his bread and coffee and asked Frau Kaltenbach if he could go and see what had happened so close to them. She nodded and he dashed down the stairs. Traudl wanted to go too, but her mother forbade it. 'It might not be pretty,' she said tersely.

Peter ran out into the street to be blinded by the sharp winter sunshine. He just followed his nose, and, as he grew closer, he could see wisps of smoke from the still smouldering ruins. In the street next to theirs the devastation lay spread out before him and small fires still burned, both in the building and among the rubble. Anna's apartment was the other way.

There, on the cobbled street, he watched a burning grand piano with a detached fascination. As the flames ate into its glossy black frame, the tortured strings groaned and then snapped, the tinkly top notes first, then the fatter, lower ones. There was other debris too from last night's air raid, spilled out from the ruined apartments on to the cobblestones: smouldering armchairs, shattered glass cabinets, books splayed open with their pages fluttering in the fierce winter wind . . .

One whole building had collapsed. Next door to it, three of the top floors had tumbled to the street. The smell of ruptured gas pipes and drains mingled with charcoal and burned flesh. Charred bodies lay on the street awaiting identification, not yet covered. Some of the dead were barely marked. They, especially, had a terrible stillness about them. Only the hair on their heads moved in the wind.

Others gathered in clusters, to stare in anxious silence. Herr Schlosser came to take a look too, his boots crunching on the frost and broken glass. He began to rant about the 'terror bombers' and how the British would soon be getting a dose of their own medicine. No one replied. Peter wondered if they were thinking as he was. This was just the beginning . . .

CHAPTER 21

January 18, 1943

The bombers returned surprisingly quickly. Not the next night, although they tried. The radio reported thirty Lancasters and five Halifaxes shot down over Germany with the rest 'scuttling back to England'. But they came back to Berlin the night after that. This time the air defences were waiting for them. Searchlights surrounded the city, their luminous beams criss-crossing the sky. This time the thunder of the anti-aircraft guns matched the roar of the bombers.

Photographs of the British bombers appeared in the newspapers. The boys at Peter's HJ den studied them with great interest. 'Look at these Lancasters and Halifaxes,' said Segur. 'Four engines. Eight machine guns. Seven crew. 10,000 kilograms of bombs. They are quite a piece of work.'

'Yes,' said Peter, 'but you wonder why they haven't put a gun on the belly of the bomber. If we were up there in our night fighters, all we'd have to do is nip underneath and blow them to pieces.'

Lothar Fleischer was eavesdropping. 'You boys haven't a chance in hell of getting into the *Luftwaffe* – they only take the best. And those Tommy bombers aren't a patch on our Condors. And just look at their Stirlings . . .' He jabbed a finger at a photograph of another British bomber there in the paper. It sat on the airfield tarmac, looming over the ground crew like a prehistoric bird of prey. The boys all snorted in derision.

Segur spoke up. 'It's true. The Tommies have ugly aeroplanes and not a patch on our elegant machines, but they carry far more bombs than the *Luftwaffe* ones.'

Fleischer punched him in the shoulder. 'That's defeatist talk, Segur.' Other boys began to jeer. Segur looked wounded. Peter came to his defence.

'It's a plain fact. It's here in the newspaper.'

It was too. The specifications for the planes were there for all to see.

Fleischer sneered. 'If you like them so much, you should join the RAF!' he said and clipped Peter around the back of the head.

Peter saw red. He stood up and floored Fleischer with a swift punch to the side of his face.

The other boys pulled them apart to prevent either of them landing further blows. Walter Hertz, the squad leader, spoke up. 'Save your quarrels for the Yids and Ivans, boys.'

Fleischer, nursing a bloody nose, gave Peter a look that said 'This is not the end of it. Not by a long way.' As Fleischer walked home with his friend Mehler, he said, 'I have a trick up my sleeve. Dig a little into the ancestry of these Polacks and there's usually a Jew in the woodpile. That's what Vater says, and he's been out there long enough to know. When he comes home on leave, I shall have a word with him about Peter Bruck.'

Mehler cackled. 'How does your father stand it – out there among the scum of the General Government? But you are right about Bruck. He lacks the correct National Socialist attitude. He's always reluctant to use the "Heil Hitler" when we meet. It's sloppy, but it also gives away his inner thoughts. I'm sure there's a little Jewboy lurking inside.'

It was not a good start to the year. A few days after the bombing raids, there came more bad news from the Eastern Front. General Paulus's Sixth Army in Stalingrad were facing disaster. Segur had whispered to Peter, 'What they're telling us is bad enough, so heaven knows what it's really like out there.'

At the end of January a message from General Paulus to Hitler was broadcast to the German people. The Kaltenbachs listened in respectful silence.

'On the anniversary of your assumption to power the Sixth Army sends greeting to the Führer. The swastika still flutters over Stalingrad. May our struggle stand as an example to generations yet unborn, never to surrender, however desperate the odds. Germany will be victorious.'

Professor Kaltenbach wiped away a tear and announced, 'With such indomitable will, how can we lose this war?'

Three days later General Paulus surrendered. The German people were introduced to their first major military defeat by hours of solemn classical music, playing across all radio stations.

Peter met up with Anna the next day. 'This bodes ill for the future,' she said. 'A cornered beast is always more dangerous. You'll see. The Nazis will come out of this more fanatical, more irrational, than ever.'

Herr Kaltenbach seemed stunned. In the days after the announcement he wandered around in a daze. One morning he did not even shave. This was unheard of. If any of the girls spoke to him, he would shout at them. Charlotte ran to her mother in tears. Not that she got any sympathy. Frau Kaltenbach seemed even more pinched and closed up than ever. Peter almost felt sorry for them.

A few days later, Peter heard them arguing after the children had all gone to bed. Listening through the wall of his bedroom he heard Frau Kaltenbach say, 'Don't ever say that again, Franz. I cannot believe you, of all people, would betray your Führer and the German people with such defeatist talk.'

Peter was astonished. He pressed his ear tight against the wall. Frau Kaltenbach had calmed down a little now and was talking quietly. But Peter was sure he heard one of them say 'Switzerland' somewhere in the conversation. Perhaps they were planning their escape?

When Peter told Anna about it, she sneered. 'Some of these Nazis, the worst of them, they'll carry on fighting to the bitter end. Let's hope there's more Professor Kaltenbachs out there. The ones who've enjoyed the ride and know when it's time to get off.' Then she stopped scoffing and sounded very upset. 'Otherwise there's not going to be much of Germany left when the war is over.'

Peter had never thought about what would happen if Germany lost the war. The Nazis seemed as solid and permanent as their great swastika-covered stone buildings. Hitler often talked about a 'Thousand Year Reich' but now it seemed there was something flawed in this dream of invincibility.

Since he had been forgiven, Peter had become a guest at the Reiters' again. He had missed his visits. Anna's parents fascinated him. Colonel Reiter asked him how he thought the war would end.

'I've never really thought about it,' Peter replied. 'I suppose the Ivans and the Yanks and the Tommies will make peace with us and leave us to rule some of the new territories in the east. At least I hope that will happen. I want to go back to my farm in Wyszkow.'

Anna spoke next. 'That's just not going to happen, Peter. I listened again to the BBC the other day. Churchill and Roosevelt. They've said they'll only accept an unconditional surrender.'

Something inside Peter tightened up. A little ball of fear. Anna had promised not to listen to the enemy radio. But now she was talking about it in front of her father. And he wasn't chastising her for it. Things must be serious.

'If they won't negotiate peace terms with the Nazis, there'll be no compromise. The war will end with the occupation of Germany. They're stupid to announce it. Now the Nazis will fight to the bitter end,' said Colonel Reiter.

The Colonel shook his head. 'The bombers will keep on coming,' he said. 'The Americans and the British. They'll bomb us like we did to Warsaw and London and Rotterdam . . . And then, one day, the Russians will arrive and God knows what they'll do to us after what we've done to them. And people like you and me, we'll be right there in the middle of it all. And if we survive the bombing and the street fighting it will be too late to say to the Soviet soldiers, "We never liked the Nazis. Don't kill us." Everyone will be saying that then, even the wild-eyed fanatics, and the foaming Jew-haters.

I don't think the Soviets will be inclined to make a distinction.'

In early February, the Nazi regime spelled out how they intended to react to the catastrophe of Stalingrad. The propaganda minister Joseph Goebbels made a major speech on the radio. This was trailed all day, in the manner of the 'special bulletins' that had reported army successes in the heady early weeks of the Soviet campaign.

Once again, the Kaltenbachs gathered around their radio and listened in silence.

Peter could see they were spellbound. Goebbels was speaking in the packed Sportpalast in Berlin. Kaltenbach several times voiced his disappointment at not being there in person. The atmosphere in the hall seemed feverish, hysterical even. The crowd cheered Goebbels's every strident utterance. The Jews were to blame for this war, he reminded his listeners, and a wave of hatred swept through the audience – so profound and vicious you could almost feel it through the static of the radio waves. 'Two thousand years of western history are in danger,' he told them. Now the Bolsheviks were coming, Germany was Europe's only hope.

'Do you want Total War?' Goebbels asked the crowd. They cheered wildly. 'Then people rise up,' he barked. 'Let the storm break loose.'

The Sportpalast erupted in a frenzied ovation.

'Now the gloves are off.' said Kaltenbach. 'We've barely been trying. The world will soon find out what a formidable foe Germany really is.'

Frau Kaltenbach seemed as jubilant as her husband,

but the girls were subdued. Peter wished he could ask them what they were thinking.

Hearing Goebbels was exactly the tonic Kaltenbach had needed. 'The lousy Jews who started this war won't know what's hit them. Now we will teach them a lesson they'll never forget.'

CHAPTER 22

February 3, 1943

The air raids grew more frequent. It wasn't just the big bombers now. The British had invented a fast two-engine warplane called the Mosquito. It was aptly named, as it buzzed low over Berlin causing havoc. Peter had first seen these aircraft at the end of January. One had flown over the apartment and he had immediately been struck by its strange shape, with the wings well forward on the fuselage. Now, whenever the air-raid sirens went, nobody knew whether they were getting a single Mosquito or hundreds of heavy bombers.

Everyone's life was affected in some way by Goebbels's 'Total War' speech. The Kaltenbachs lost their maid. Yaryna was conscripted by the armaments ministry and sent to work at a factory in the west of the city. Frau Kaltenbach was unable to find a replacement. Now all the family were expected to help with the chores – especially the younger girls. 'Why shouldn't Peter help with the dishes and dusting?' said Traudl, whose extra household duties were cutting into her swimming routine.

Professor Kaltenbach chuckled benevolently. 'Our Führer has said a good German girl's life should be focused on her home. You should see your chores as part of your National Socialist duties. Besides, Peter is required for more hazardous work.'

Boys in the Hitler Youth had been ordered to join the Berlin *Luftschutz* – the anti-aircraft defences. Some of

Peter's school friends had to man the guns, others made up squads of firefighters. It was potentially dangerous work. Even in training some of the boys on the guns ended up with crushed fingers or mangled arms. The firefighters could find themselves in collapsing buildings. Peter was glad he wasn't doing that. And, it was whispered, they would also have to pull dead bodies from the rubble and stack them out in the street after a raid, so they could be identified. This wasn't a job for boys, surely?

Peter volunteered to be a messenger. If phone lines between gun batteries or fire-observation stations broke down, then it would be his job to get on his bicycle and deliver instructions. This appealed to him. It might be dangerous but he liked the idea of doing something to protect people from the bombers. Anna was impressed.

'They've got jobs for us too, in the BDM,' she told him. 'We're to be employed in the *Katastropheneinsatz* – disaster action. We're supposed to give out food and other assistance to the people who have been bombed out of their homes. They're really expecting the worst, aren't they?'

Then she said, 'I'm glad that they're using us to do something worthwhile. We spend so much time collecting money or materials for the war or listening to nonsense lectures about being better National Socialists. Now we'll be doing something useful.'

Anna said she'd heard that thousands of anti-Nazi leaflets had been handed out in Munich. Peter got very excited about this. 'Wouldn't that be a brilliant thing to do!'

He spent half the night wondering about it. All those

times when he wanted to speak his mind but had had to hold his tongue. He was bursting to do something like that. To tell the world what he was really thinking. His messenger job gave him the perfect opportunity – when he was out on his bike during air raids, he could leave leaflets in apartment hallways. Everyone would be hiding in their shelters and basements. Who would see him? Anna would be impressed.

When he told her the next day, she was wary. 'But what about the paper shortages we're having? Every scrap has to be accounted for. Have you thought of that?'

Peter shook his head. 'But we've got to do something!'

She paused and made a little bridge with her slender hands.

'Those sort of leaflets, they're only telling people what they know already,' she said.

'They're not.' Peter felt exasperated. 'They're telling people that we're not all Sieg-Heiling robots. They're offering them a glimmer of hope. I think we should do it.'

'We can't do it on our own,' said Anna dismissively. 'Who would we ask to help us? Segur? He's not been the same since that beating. Look, we'd need spare paper and a printer.'

'We'll find something. My school has these things. We could break in after dark.'

'Peter, you're being silly.' Now she was cross. 'It's just too dangerous. Don't you remember the posters back in the autumn? That boy, Helmuth Hübener, he was sixteen, and they executed him because he did exactly the thing you are suggesting.'

Anna started to speak in a deliberately calm voice, but there was a hint of scorn in what she was saying. 'If you get caught with a hundred leaflets saying "Down with Hitler. Surrender Now", what are you going to say? You found them in the street and you were just going to put them in the bin? You'd be in Plötzensee Prison before your feet touched the ground and you'd be facing the guillotine within a fortnight.'

She was right. It was a stupid idea, though he was too sheepish to admit it. They parted without their usual kiss.

A few days later they met again at the library. She gave him a big smile – one that said 'all is forgiven'.

'Coffee and cakes on me?' she said, and they walked arm in arm to a local café.

It was a rainy winter afternoon. The café was almost deserted. A radio played dance music loudly, as if to make up for the noise of absent customers. They huddled on a table as far from the counter as possible.

Anna began to speak cautiously. 'If you really want to do something . . . something to get at the Nazis . . .' she was watching his face all the time, searching for reassurance, 'then you can help me.'

Peter leaned closer. For some time now, he had thought Anna was up to something. Was she finally going to tell him?

'I know some people,' she said in a whisper, 'people who help the Jews who are hiding here.'

Peter felt a shiver right down to his soul – the sort of shiver you read about in ghost stories when someone thinks a spirit has passed through them. This was no longer playing at rebelling against the Nazis. This was the real thing.

He wanted to ask if they were people he knew. Then he thought, if she wants to she'll tell me. Besides, he was almost certain she meant her mother and father.

'They're really struggling, especially since the Goebbels proclamation.'

Peter had heard the announcement too. Who hadn't? Goebbels had used the chilling phrase *judenrein* – clean of Jews – as if they were an infestation of lice or a bacterial infection. They would all be gone, he had said, by Hitler's birthday in April. At the time Peter had thought little of it. Surely by now, all the Jews in Berlin had been relocated to the east?

'There are still some left,' said Anna. 'Ones with special skills – like engineers, machine builders. They're helping the Nazis, to save their lives. But it's been a poor bargain and now their luck has run out. And then there are hundreds, maybe thousands, who have just gone underground. You know, the U-boats the policeman mentioned. Well I help them. I bring them food. But there's so many now, it's difficult to keep up. I thought you might be able to help me?'

Peter was stunned. He didn't know what to think. All the bravado he felt evaporated. What was left was fear.

They sat there in silence. After what seemed like an age, Anna said, 'Let me buy you another coffee,' and got up to go to the counter.

'Lovers' tiff?' said the matronly lady behind the counter, and smiled sympathetically.

'We'll get over it,' said Anna in a tone that invited no more conversation. She'd been watching them, she thought. We need to be more careful.

Peter was watching Anna too. He thought of how

much danger she was putting herself in, and felt a powerful urge to protect her. Yes, of course, he would help. The more he did the less she would have to, and the safer she would be. But he was terrified. Swing dancing might result in a beating or temporary imprisonment. The punishment for this was torture and execution.

When she came back with two coffees, he said, 'Anna, how do you find the courage to do this?' He had abandoned his leaflet idea the moment Anna had pointed out the consequences.

She held his hand. Her eyes filled with tears. 'She thinks we're having a lovers' quarrel,' she said. 'But we'd better be careful what we say here. I'll tell you on the way home.'

For now, they could think of nothing further to say. So she sat next to him and nestled her head on his shoulder. Peter loved the smell of her hair and how warm she felt. He wished they could stay there like this for ever.

By the time they left the café, the rain had stopped. They walked home, holding hands.

'Why didn't you tell me before?' said Peter.

She hugged his arm tighter. 'Mutti and Vati made me promise not to. The more people who know, the more dangerous it is. They decided to tell me a few days after we came back from that dance. They said that anything that drew the attention of the Gestapo to our family was putting us all at risk. And the people they were helping.'

'Aren't you frightened?' asked Peter again. He certainly was.

'A few months ago, when I first started doing this,' began Anna, 'I was really frightened. So I thought about

170

a photograph Stefan showed me that he had confiscated from one of the soldiers in his division. It's the most awful thing I've ever seen in my life.

'It was blurred and tattered, but what was going on was clear enough. A group of women were huddled in their underwear with their backs to the edge of a wide trench. I don't know where it was. Somewhere out in Ostland. And in the trench, there was a heap of dead bodies. Can you imagine that? Standing there waiting for a bullet?'

She stopped for a moment, trying to compose herself.

'But what made that picture more terrible was . . . there was a little girl there, among the women. Maybe she was eight or nine. And she was turning to look at the pile of bodies in the pit behind her. I couldn't see exactly, but she looked like she was wringing her hands, clasping them tight to her chest. She must have been utterly terrified. That a child should see something so horrific, should have THAT done to her, it's inconceivable . . .'

Then she said, 'Mutti is sure they were all Jews. She hears terrible rumours of death camps out in the east, where they kill Jews in their thousands behind barbed wire, rather than out in the open. We had to do something to help.'

It was too horrible for words. Peter held her tight and swallowed hard. 'What can I do to help?' he said, sounding far braver than he felt.

CHAPTER 23

February 14, 1943

Ula Reiter played nervously with the telephone cable as she spoke. 'And how is Onkel Klaus?' she asked, trying to keep her voice calm.

Otto Reiter winced as he listened to the agitated response rattle from the earpiece. 'Onkel Klaus' was the code word they used when talking about the Jewish families they were helping. He could not quite work out what was being said, but it did not sound like good news.

'And the rest of the family?' said his wife. 'Very well. We shall see what we can do.'

She placed the receiver on the handset with a heavy sigh and turned to Otto. 'We need to make another collection of food stamps. Frau Niemann is at her wit's end. The Abrahams are all ill and she's convinced it's from lack of food.'

'A couple and five children . . .' said Otto, holding up his arms in exasperation. 'You'll just have to tell them it's not practical. They can stay together, have the people who've been helping them arrested and executed, and then all get packed off to Auschwitz, or they can see some sense and split up.'

He was always matter of fact about these things.

Ula went to the biscuit tin where she kept the spare coupons and made a quick inventory. 'We have enough for a kilogram of meat, five hundred grams of margarine, three kilograms of bread, and two kilograms of canned goods. That'll barely keep them alive for a week.'

Otto nodded. 'We are having the Schafers over tonight. I am sure they will be able to contribute.'

Colonel Ernst Schafer was Otto's friend at the Home Army headquarters. He and his wife, Magda, were always prepared to help.

Most of the Jews the Reiters and Schafers knew before the war had managed to get out. Like them, they were professional people. They had the kind of influence that helped them obtain exit visas. What a lottery that was. Some had gone to England or the United States. They were the lucky ones. Others had gone east to Poland or Czechoslovakia; they would be in worse trouble now, if they were still alive. Awful stories from the east continued to reach the Reiters. Stories, almost too horrible to believe, of mass extermination in special camps. The ones still living in cities were starving in ghettos that they were forbidden to leave.

Some of the Jews who had not managed to get out had gone underground, but people who were prepared to help them, like the Schafers and the Reiters, were few and far between. The ones with big houses hid them in their attics and basements. They moved from house to house, which was always a terrible risk, particularly for the ones who looked especially 'Jewish'.

The Reiters, who lived in an apartment, only rarely had 'guests'. It was too risky. So they helped as much as they could, with food and clothing stamps. A little bit from several people could just about feed a small family without depriving the donors of too much of their allotted rations.

Berlin's remaining Jews were being picked off in small

groups now. They couldn't stay indoors all the time. When they went out, the Gestapo picked them up in the street. Bundled them into a black van. Sometimes there were shots. Cold-blooded murder, right there on the streets of Berlin.

There were raids on safe houses too. 'If you ignore the knock on the door, they go away,' Frau Niemann had said. But that was wishful thinking. The Reiters had heard accounts of these incidents. A car arrives – almost always after dark. Men jump out and run up the stairs. There is a lot of banging and shouting. The doorbell rings constantly. The phone inside rings. If there is no answer, the door is broken down. The poor souls inside are led off in handcuffs. Ula could well imagine those final moments.

Ula had always felt she would not survive the war. God would be her protector, up to a point. But there were too many other terrible things going on in the world, she realised, for Him to concern Himself with saving Ula Reiter. Her own life she was, by now, reconciled to losing. The grief she felt was like a mild toothache or headache. How her death would come she could not imagine.

Otto was different. The first time she met him he had told her he felt as though he was living on borrowed time. As a young officer in the Great War he had served in the trenches on the Western Front. Nothing, he sometimes said, could ever be worse than a week-long artillery bombardment. When the war ended and he found himself still alive he had treated every extra day of his life as a miracle. Ula knew Otto was tough and could look after himself, and although she loved him, she did not worry about him. But when she thought about Anna, and what the Gestapo might do to her, she felt sick with fear.

Recently Ula had heard about a young girl called Maria, not much older than Anna. She had been arrested for hiding army deserters. She wished Otto had not told her about it. Maria was sent to Plötzensee and guillotined within a week. Once the People's Court passed a guilty verdict in cases like that the sentence was swiftly carried out.

Such thoughts often kept Ula awake at night.

Otto kept reminding her they would be all right as long as they were careful. As a senior officer in the Home Army, he reasoned, he was beyond suspicion. She was a trusted journalist. They just had to play the game. Say the right things to the right people.

There was a rattle at the door. It was Anna, home from the library.

'You look troubled, Mutti,' she said. 'What's happened?'

Ula explained about the Abrahams family being ill and needing extra rations. 'It means more deliveries.' She sighed.

'We need some help, Mutti,' said Anna.

Her mother shook her head. 'It's too difficult – you never know who to ask.'

It was a subtle, almost magical art, being able to tell who was safe and who was dangerous. You could never be sure. One slip could mean the whole network of friends and family would come tumbling down.

'We should ask Peter,' said Anna. 'You know he is a safe one. He won't betray us.'

'It's not right, Anna,' she said. 'It's too dangerous. How would you feel if he was arrested and executed?'

'I asked him already,' she said. 'He wants to help.'

Ula was too tired to feel angry. She knew she ought to be livid with Anna. Now there was another person who knew about what they did. Another person who might betray them to the Gestapo under torture. And although she liked Peter, she thought he was a hothead and too young and silly for such dangerous work. But she was so exhausted she almost felt detached from her body. 'Very well,' she said with a sigh.

Anna took her mother's hand. 'He'll be careful. He can go about his deliveries in the air raids, when no one is out on the street.'

'Don't be stupid,' said Ula, venting some of her irritation. 'He can't turn up for duty with a bag of groceries to deliver.' She regretted the words as soon as she said them. She felt dreadfully guilty about her daughter being involved in work like this. But right now, the network was barely coping and they needed all the help they could get.

Anna asked Peter to drop in at the apartment after school the next afternoon. There was food to be delivered to a flat in Salzburger Strasse. The Webers, old friends of Otto and Ula, had another Jewish family to hide. They were all starving on the rations they had to share.

When he got to the Reiters' flat, Anna was out on a delivery herself and Ula sat him down and made him a coffee. 'You don't have to do this, Peter,' she said. 'But there are many drops to be made so it is a great help to us all.'

Before he left she said, 'Has Anna told you about our emergency plan?'

Peter shook his head.

'If the Gestapo latch on to us, we have a safe house. So, if anything happens and we have to go into hiding, I want you to remember this number,' she said. 'Kreuzberg 1791.'

'I'll write it down,' said Peter.

'You'll do no such thing,' she scolded. '1791. That's easy. It's the year Mozart died. You ring that number and ask for Wulfie. Got that too? That's Wulfie as in Wolfgang Amadeus Mozart. Very important to remember that, Peter. In case anyone is listening in.'

As she handed him a small parcel of food, she gave him a kiss on the cheek, 'For good luck', and he set off to the address she had made him memorise. Being stopped was not a great terror. He could always say he was bringing provisions for his grandmother. The real risk was that the safe house would be under observation and the Gestapo would pounce when he arrived.

When he got there and knocked on the front door, his heart was beating so hard he imagined other people would actually hear it. The door was swiftly opened. He went in and handed over the provisions to a middle-aged woman. He was trembling so much he dropped them and broke an egg. After a muddled apology he was gone. Nobody was waiting to arrest him. It had all gone well.

As he walked home, Peter tried to remember the face of the woman who answered the door. She was so ordinary, so nondescript, he did not even think he would recognise her if he saw her again. He did remember the Nazi Party badge she wore on her cardigan and the thought of it made him smile. As he looked around at the other people on the street, he wondered how many were like her. It could only be a handful.

Coming back to the Kaltenbachs' for supper, after that, was almost as unsettling as making the delivery. Sitting round the table he felt entirely disconnected from them. Every one of them, he reflected with mounting anger, if they knew what I'd just been doing, they'd betray me to the Gestapo without a second thought. He felt a deep longing for his parents and the safe life he had known on the farm.

He forced himself to smile and asked Traudl about her hockey match that afternoon. 'We lost four nil,' she said without looking at him. No one else spoke. Peter realised they were all as wrapped up in themselves as he was.

CHAPTER 24

March 2, 1943

The British came back again in force on the night of 2nd March. When Peter heard the wailing rise and fall of the air-raid siren, he was just getting ready for bed. He was already exhausted and desperate to sleep, having made another delivery for the U-boats that evening. The task itself was not hard work. But the worry, the fear of being caught, the excuses he had to make to the Kaltenbachs to cover his tracks, they were more draining than a twenty-kilometre HJ route march.

He threw his clothes back on, hopped on his bicycle and pedalled for his life. The Fire Observation Station was a mere five minutes on his bike. By the time he arrived, there were still people hurrying home from the theatres and the bars to the shelter of their basements.

There was trouble in store. When the siren went during the day, it was almost certain to be a false alarm or one or two Mosquitoes at most. Unlucky for whoever caught the bombs they dropped, but a pinprick on the rest of the city. But night raids promised something more dangerous. 'It's a big one,' said the Fire Observation Officer. 'Should be here in half an hour. Unless they change course and go to Stettin or Rostock.'

They didn't. This was much worse than the raids they had had back in January. Judging by the thunder of engines, there must have been hundreds of heavy bombers up there. The watchers up on the roof could see explosions and fires raging in the south-west of the city. Peter spent the night listening to the distant *crump* of high-explosive bombs and praying they did not come any nearer. At first light he was despatched to Wilmersdorf, the nearest district to have been damaged in the raid. 'Go and see if you can do anything to help,' the officer told Peter. 'I hear there's been a lot of damage.'

As soon as he ventured out into the cold winter dawn, the sulphurous smoke caught in his throat. There seemed to be a strange yellow fog over the city, which the light of the morning did little to dispel. This he had never seen before, even in the raids back in January.

Wilmersdorf was twenty minutes' hard riding away, and when he arrived at Detmolder Strasse, he was faced with a scene of utter devastation. Before, he had seen one or two apartment blocks or town houses destroyed by stray bombs. Here, whole streets close to an electrical machinery factory had been gutted. The fire services were still struggling to put out blazing buildings, and many others were still smouldering. The awful smell of fire and drains and leaking gas mains filled the air.

People walked amid the smoke and debris like zombies, their clothes and faces blackened by soot and smoke. Others screamed hysterically. The whole width of the street was filled with rubble and furniture. Some of it barely recognisable, some of it still intact. A wardrobe here, a metal bed frame there. Peter thought of Charlotte's doll's house. It was as if a giant's hand had swept through the homes, scattering their possessions out on to the street.

There were bodies too, already laid out for identification, including quite a few children. Some were charred and contorted. They looked like grotesque, brittle statues. Others, virtually untouched by death, had that terrible stillness he had seen back in January. Occasionally, the air would be pierced by the cries of a relative or parent, finding a loved one in that grisly parade. It didn't seem right to Peter that children should be killed in these raids. He felt a violent anger towards the British for perpetrating this atrocity.

Although he had long ago lost patience with the endless HJ training and the Winter Relief collection, he felt what he was doing here, assisting these victims of the air raid, was noble work. He helped a local HJ squad fill wheelbarrows with rubble from a collapsed apartment block, until he was faint with hunger and thirst.

'Attention!' called an HJ squad leader, holding up his hand for silence. 'There's someone underneath here.'

He called down into the rubble. 'Can you hear me?' Then he shifted a few more bricks and pulled out a pale hand. 'He's cold,' he announced plainly. 'Let's get him out anyway, stack him over with the others.'

Peter came over to help. As they cleared away the bricks, the dead boy began to look naggingly familiar. His head was shaved and he was terribly thin – gaunt face and a flimsy jacket torn open to show ribs stark against sickly white skin. It was Wladek.

'It's a lousy *Ostarbeiter*,' said the squad leader as soon as he saw the blue triangle on his jacket with a P on it – showing he was a Polish worker. 'Forget him. Carry on looking for our own people. He's probably crawling with lice, anyway.'

Peter tried to keep the anger from his voice. 'I'll dig him out,' he said.

181

'Very well,' said the squad leader. 'We can't leave him there for ever.'

Peter carried on clearing rubble from around the body. How long had it been since he'd last seen him? It was that awful night in Gleisdreieck when the other Polish boy had held a blade to Peter's throat.

Wladek had changed in those eighteen months, but not as growing boys would usually change. He had grown skeletal. There was so little flesh on his bones, Peter wondered how he had managed to walk, let alone work. He wondered what he was doing here, out in Wilmersdorf. Maybe he had been at the electrical factory, or on another building or bombsite. His hands were scarred and rough from hard physical work, and his body was covered in small sores and abrasions. Peter thought about the ancient seafarers he had read about and how their bodies were ravaged by scurvy. Poor Wladek's body had suffered similar torments. Peter remembered the German official in Poland, when they had first selected him, talking about giving food to Germans and not Poles. They'd been true to their word. But Wladek looked peaceful now. Peter hoped he'd just been caught by a bomb blast and died in an instant.

Once he'd cleared away enough to free Wladek from the rubble, he picked him up and carried him to the side of the road where the other bodies were laid out. There was so little of him, Peter thought, he could have carried two of him. He placed him down gently with the other bodies, his head resting on the kerb, and then straightened his legs, closed his eyes and crossed his arms on his chest.

'Stop wasting time with that Polack,' barked one of

the squad leaders and ordered Peter over to a building on the other side of the street. He worked on for another hour, trying not to think about what had just happened.

Too tired to cycle home, Peter caught the U-bahn, which, he was surprised to find, was still running. Although he was exhausted, he could not let himself go to sleep until he had scrubbed the acrid stench of sulphur from his hair and body. Even then, as he lay in clean sheets, he kept thinking of Wladek. The airmen were murderers; it was true what the Nazis said. The British bombers killed indiscriminately. But he detested the Nazis too, for starving that poor boy before a British bomb put him out of his misery.

The next day, the city was full of rumours. Thousands killed, a hundred thousand made homeless. The radio news said there had been some damage but casualties were not as bad as feared. For once, especially having seen some of it, Peter took the official view over the rumours. But it irritated him to hear the announcer declare that the people of Berlin had helped to clear the damage in 'a magnificent expression of National Socialist enthusiasm'.

The air raid in early March shocked a lot of people. Even Peter's HJ squad were muted for days afterwards. Many of them had been dispatched to the nearest bomb-damaged areas, and most had now had their first direct encounter with death.

A week later, when he was invited to tea, the Reiters told Peter there had been rumours of mutinies – soldiers refusing to go to the front – but discreet enquiries at Bendlerstrasse had revealed this story to be pure fiction.

'Still,' said Peter. 'There's grounds for hope. Like those thousands of leaflets they gave out in Munich.'

'That story has a rather unhappy ending,' said the Colonel. He had also heard about this through his colleagues in the Home Army. 'It was a group of students calling themselves "The White Rose". They scattered leaflets calling for the overthrow of the Nazis. One of them – a girl I heard – threw a whole stack of leaflets from the stairs of the university entrance hall,' said the Colonel. 'She must have had a death wish. There have been four executions – I think within a week of the arrests.'

The Reiters took some comfort in the continuing misfortune of the German Afrika-Korps in North Africa. 'Perhaps, if we are lucky, the war will be over in six months,' said Ula. Colonel Otto shook his head. 'No. The Nazis will fight right to the end.'

Despite the bombing, and the imposition of stricter food and clothing rationing, it was still possible to forget there was a war raging around them. In the final week of March, Professor Kaltenbach took the whole family to a concert at the Beethoven Hall. The celebrated Dutch pianist Karlrobert Kreiten was playing. As they sat there in the packed auditorium, Kaltenbach whispered to Peter, 'Kreiten was brought up in Germany, and his mother is German. But his father is Dutch so he's considered a Dutchman. Ridiculous really – he's one of us. You can tell by the way he plays German music. It's just engraved in his heart.'

Kreiten did indeed play beautifully. His programme was exclusively German or Austrian – Beethoven,

Mozart and Bruckner. The Bruckner particularly pleased Herr Kaltenbach. 'No one understands the German soul quite like him,' he said.

Peter sat next to Elsbeth and was surprised to see her wiping away a tear during a Mozart piano concerto.

CHAPTER 25

April 1943

Whenever the air-raid siren sounded, Peter and all his schoolfriends were expected to hare off to their stations. It played havoc with their school work, but nobody seemed to care. 'The defence of the Fatherland is our primary concern,' said the Headmaster to them all in school assembly. 'You will have plenty of time to catch up on your schooling after the war.'

The air raids were happening with increasing frequency, although they were mostly nuisance raids – rather than the heavy bombing the city experienced in January and March. Peter was sometimes on standby all night, snatching a few hours' sleep in a bunk in the Fire Observation Station. So far the phone lines had not been damaged, and he had not had to go out on his bike during a raid. Sometimes he went to school. When he was too tired, he came home. The rest of them would be out, although Elsbeth, who worked shifts at the post office, was sometimes at home.

He came back one mid-morning and caught her wandering naked between her bedroom and the bathroom. She shrieked and ran back to her room. 'Stop staring at me, you horrid little boy,' she shouted. Peter was too flustered to respond. He felt angry at her constant hostility, but he was still mesmerised by the sight of her.

Why did she dislike him so much? He mentioned it to

Anna. 'Elsbeth doesn't like anyone, Peter,' she laughed. 'She's an icy one, isn't she. But she's got something. She looks like a wicked fairy, with that black hair and milky skin. Whooo! She'll put a curse on you if you don't watch out!' She waved a hand around, as if she was holding a magic wand.

It wasn't just Elsbeth that made the apartment an uncomfortable place to be. Charlotte had recently joined the *Jungmädel* and she was often fractious and exhausted after an evening or afternoon of their activities. Liese and Traudl both chided her when she showed little interest in knitting gloves for the troops or making straw slippers for the soldiers in hospital. Peter felt sorry for her. She was only ten and tired enough already from school. But he didn't dare say anything.

Mealtime conversation, when they could not avoid talking to each other, was sparse and sullen. Gone were the days when the Professor would hold forth about the great opportunities available in Ostland, or the best scientific methods for ridding Germany of its social parasites.

Sometimes, though, Kaltenbach still fumed about something he had read in the newspaper. Peter would sit there bursting to disagree with him and wondered how much longer he could hold his tongue.

In early April the papers reported that the concert pianist Karlrobert Kreiten had been arrested. The charge was 'undermining military strength'. Peter was flabbergasted. He remembered Kreiten as a rather effete young man, with a great floppy fringe that fell down over his forehead as he played. How could he have undermined Germany's military strength?

187

Kaltenbach read the piece to the family. Kreiten had been additionally accused of 'paralysing and undermining the will of the German people' and 'making malicious remarks about the Führer'.

'His head will roll for this,' said Kaltenbach.

'You mean they're going to kill him?' said Peter. 'How can a little man like that be so dangerous?'

Kaltenbach looked at Peter with a quizzical frown. 'Don't they teach you anything in school or at those HJ meetings?' he said impatiently. 'In the last war, the German nation was brought to its knees by traitors on the home front. We were undefeated in battle, and no enemy soldiers had set foot in the Fatherland, yet we had to surrender. The Führer is determined not to let that happen in this war. That "little man" should know better – spreading defeatist poison. And him in a privileged position too – playing his music while other young men his age give their lives to defend our country from the Soviets.'

Peter shook his head. 'But it was us who invaded Russia. We attacked them!'

Kaltenbach snapped. 'That is Bolshevik poison, Peter. The Führer ordered our military action in self-defence.'

'Onkel Franz,' said Peter. 'I was there when it happened. My family's home was close to the border. There was no Soviet attack.'

'Go to your room and do not join us at the table again until you have apologised for your traitorous talk,' said Kaltenbach. 'And if I hear another word against the country that has taken you into its arms, then you will be on the first train back to Warsaw.'

Peter fled before he lost his temper. *This is a*

madhouse, he thought. *You are all mad.* And that pianist – that harmless little man who had probably just said some home truths everyone knew but no one wanted to hear – he was going to be killed for it.

Franz and Liese were reluctantly coming to the conclusion that their project was failing. Peter had many qualities they wanted in a son – he was tall and Nordic, brave and bright. But he was never going to be the 'political soldier' and standard-bearer for National Socialism that they had hoped to mould. He was too good-natured. Too much of a 'soft egg'. He had too much sympathy for the underdog.

'It's the Polack in him,' said Liese, just before she and Franz went to sleep. 'He lacks the German ability to apply himself to a task until it is done. And I've seen him staring at the *Ostarbeiters* in the street. He looks sorry for them.'

Kaltenbach nodded in agreement. 'And when I talk to him about our politics, he always trots out the party line – but he's just saying what he thinks we want to hear.'

'Never mind,' she went on. 'Next year he will be going to his army training and that will knock some sense into him. We'll see a change for the better then. Just you see.'

Kaltenbach softened. 'He's not been a total disappointment though. At least he has a decent girlfriend. And from a good family too.'

Liese gave a rare smile. 'The Führer himself would surely approve of the match.'

Peter slept so badly these days, he was usually awake when the birds started to sing. Over long restless nights

189

he would worry about when Frau Reiter would ask him to make another delivery or whether the Kaltenbachs would send him back to Poland. Since the defeat at Stalingrad they had been especially brittle with him. Perhaps it was their pride. They didn't want to admit to friends and neighbours that Peter had failed to flourish under their guidance.

Stalingrad had shaken them all to the core. One evening, Charlotte was looking particularly distracted. Eventually she asked her father, 'Do you think the Ivans will come and kill us?'

Kaltenbach smiled indulgently. He went to fetch an atlas. 'Look, mein Liebling, Stalingrad is there.' He pointed to a spot past the Black Sea and close to the Caspian. 'We are here. Look how far away they are.'

Frau Kaltenbach spoke. 'The Führer will protect you, meine Kleine.'

They all talked about 'finishing the job with typical German thoroughness', a phrase they had borrowed from one of Goebbels's speeches, and told themselves over and over that the German army was the best in the world.

'The Russians will never triumph. They're *Untermenschen*,' said Frau Kaltenbach. 'Eventually we shall grind them down. Our soldiers have been poorly led by commanders who lack the correct National Socialist spirit. I am sure the Führer is doing his utmost to rectify this problem.'

One early spring day Peter returned from an exhausting shift. He had been up all night 'on standby' just hanging around in case he was needed. It was the boredom that wore him out, just as much as the odd hours he was expected to be there. Since the March raids, the Tommies had only been back with their Mosquitoes.

The front door to the apartment was double-locked, a sure indication that no one was home. At first, all he wanted to do was run a bath and then collapse into his bed. But he liked being alone in the place, so he took his time eating his breakfast and sitting in the bright sunshine that poured into the living room.

The sunlight put him in a good mood. He had an HJ athletics match to attend that evening and was even looking forward to it. Lothar Fleischer had recently left Berlin and Peter enjoyed the HJ meetings much more without him there. All boys Fleischer's age were sent to a military fitness camp for three months, in preparation for the armed forces. Peter wouldn't have to worry about that for another year.

On the way to the bathroom he noticed the door to Professor Kaltenbach's study had been left ajar. This was unheard of. Kaltenbach always locked the door. When Charlotte asked him about it, he said, 'Top secret work, mein Schatz! Top secret for the good of our Fatherland.' He must have left in a terrible hurry that morning. The key was still in the lock. Maybe he had had a row with Liese and felt distracted. They quarrelled frequently these days.

Peter had never been in the room in his life. No one was allowed in there except Frau Kaltenbach. All the children knew never to disturb their father when he was working in his study.

Peter stood outside for a brief moment, straining to hear if anyone was in there. Then he pushed the door with his little finger. It creaked terribly as it swung open just enough for him to peep inside. The noise made him wince and he felt a terrible gnawing in his stomach. 'Stop! Don't do this!' a little voice in his head kept telling him. But he felt drawn inside, as if by a magnetic force. The study was a bright but narrow room, with a large window at one end, in front of which sat a hefty roll-top desk bursting with scattered papers, files and books. Bookshelves lined the walls along with several metal filing cabinets. There was barely room for Kaltenbach's mahogany and leather desk chair. The only space on the walls not crammed with books and files was filled by a framed photograph of the Führer.

Peter moved inside, all the while his ears straining for any sign of the door opening. If anyone came home, he would be caught red-handed. The front door to the apartment looked straight down the corridor into the study.

There was a strange, dream-like quality to all this. The brightness and heat of the sun. The stillness of the room. The awful foreboding. The voice in his head kept saying, 'Go! Get out!'

On one of the letters on the cluttered desk Peter noticed the slogan *'Sterilise the Jew. Then healthy and filthy blood will no longer mix'* stamped on the back of the envelope in dark Gothic letters.

He picked up a journal and flicked through its pages. Wolfgang Abel – he was one of Kaltenbach's colleagues – had written an article. Abel had come to dinner not six weeks ago. He was reporting on an anthropological survey he had conducted on Soviet prisoners of war. His findings, summarised in a neat paragraph at the start of the piece, were alarming. Among the Russians there was a higher component of the Nordic race than had previously been thought. This made them a more formidable opponent than the Slavs of eastern Europe. Peter shook his head and put the journal back in the exact spot he had picked it up.

There was a file on the desk that was half open, with neat typewritten pages spilling out. The top of each page was headlined *TOP SECRET – SACHSENHAUSEN MEDICAL FACILITY*.

Peter looked at the pages, hardly daring to pick them up. He tried to make sense of the information on them. Scanning down the top page he picked out words and phrases: 'In order to enlarge our knowledge . . .', 'Epidemic Jaundice Vaccine . . .', 'casualties should be expected . . .', 'human material . . .' and then reams of figures for Jews, Poles, Russians, Romany, Asiatics, Caucasians, each of them further subdivided into blood groups A, B, AB and O. Peter knew about that, at least. They had been told about blood groups in their HJ First Aid training.

There was a note scribbled at the bottom in black ink.

So far there are no indications that racial origin and/or blood group of those infected offer any suggestion of expected fatalities. Test no more conclusive than human/animal infection. F

Was Kaltenbach involved in this or was he just reading about it? Peter wanted to believe that this man, who had looked after him, who had taken him into his home and rescued him from the orphanage, could not be part of any vile experiments. But he could also imagine it was the sort of thing the Kaiser Wilhelm Institute would take an interest in.

'You sly little busybody.'

Peter jerked bolt upright and the paper dropped from his hand. He felt rigid with fear. The voice was Elsbeth's.

'What are you doing snooping around in Vater's study? You know it's forbidden.'

He turned slowly to look at her. She had a terrible, triumphant look in her eye. 'Now I've got you,' it seemed to say.

Peter tried to say something. 'The door was open. I haven't touched anything . . .' It sounded too ridiculous to continue.

'You snake. You'll not get away with this. As soon as Vater finds out you'll be on the next train back to Polackland – unless they hand you straight over to the Gestapo. You know! You know you should never go in here. This is all top secret. You Polack traitor. You're spying, aren't you?'

She was taunting him now.

Peter was almost too frightened to think. But somewhere in his head he managed to string some words together. 'This . . . just look at it. It's experiments. It looks like experiments on human beings . . .'

She stopped for a second. 'I don't care what it is. You, especially, are not allowed to look at it. You are a spy. You should be shot. And to think, we took you into our home and treated you like a brother.'

But for Peter, anger was taking the place of fear. 'Elsbeth, you trained as a nurse. Look at this. You know it's wrong.'

'It is not my place to look at secret information.'
'Look,' said Peter. 'Tell me what this is about.'
He read out the foreword to the report:

The General Commissioner of the Führer, SS Brigadeführer Professor Dr Brandt, has approached me with the request to help him obtain prisoners to be used in connection with his research on the causes of Epidemic Jaundice which has been furthered to a large degree by his efforts. In order to enlarge our knowledge, so far based only on inoculation of animals with germs taken from human beings, it would not be necessary to reverse the procedure and inoculate human beings with germs cultivated in animals. Casualties must be anticipated . . .

He looked up at her. The malice had gone from her face. For a moment she seemed lost for words. Then they came tumbling out. 'It's none of our business. Whatever it is is for the good of Germany. It will be to keep our soldiers alive. I don't care if they kill *Untermenschen*, they can kill a thousand *Untermenschen* if it saves the life of a single German soldier . . .' but she began to cry when she said it.

Tears flowed down her face and, leaning against the wall, she slid to the floor. Peter was flabbergasted. What was he supposed to do now? He stood there for a minute while she sobbed to herself. Then he said, 'We should go out of here,' and walked towards the door.

She began to compose herself, and wiped the tears away. 'No. Let me see,' she said. She moved over to the desk and swiftly leafed through the report. After a minute she said, 'It's a medical experiment. They're infecting the prisoners at Sachsenhausen with jaundice. Then they're seeing whether their blood group and racial type have any bearing on the progress of the disease. It's the sort of thing pharmaceutical companies do with animals when they test new vaccines, new drugs. Instead they're testing directly on humans. That's why Vater has the report. To see if different races have a greater or lesser resistance to pathogens.'

She had never talked to him like this before. Peter started to wonder if she was still going to betray him.

'My God, look at this,' Elsbeth said, as she carefully picked up papers from another open file. Peter stood next to her, hardly daring to breathe, as she swiftly read the first page. Then she picked up a form with a photograph attached of a dishevelled, dark-haired young man, staring mournfully into the camera.

'This is Doktor Magnussen's project,' said Elsbeth. 'I've met her – she works with Vater at the Institute. She's trying to discover if there's a link between race and the patterns of the iris.'

Peter looked puzzled.

'The iris, dummkopf,' she said, pointing at her eye. 'So they are sending her eyeballs from one of the camps. This young man, he's Sinti – they're one sort of gypsy. This is the form that came with the eyes. They probably killed him just after they took the picture. I dare say they're sending Frau Doktor eyeballs from Jews, Slavs and Russians. And some Germans, too, who have come to the attention of the Gestapo. I cannot bear to look any more,' she said.

She put the papers back on the desk and walked out. Peter rushed over, hurriedly trying to put the desk back exactly as he had found it.

While she fussed in the kitchen, Peter said, 'I thought you were all out. The door was double-locked.'

'I do that sometimes, when I'm here on my own. I don't feel safe unless the door is secure.'

They sat together in the living room, drinking coffee. Peter wondered if she might still tell her father. But she had looked. She had become his accomplice. She was guilty too.

'I wonder how much the Führer knows of these medical experiments,' she said. Then she corrected herself. 'No. I can no longer pretend. I'm sure the Führer knows. What I do not understand is how something so good and right for Germany could turn into something that has become so misguided. I remember, when I was a small child . . . before you were born, how awful it was to be in this country. We were always hungry. My grandparents' life savings couldn't buy a loaf of bread. There was fighting on the streets. And the Führer came and saved us from all that . . .'

All of this trotted out in a flat monotone. Face blank. No eye contact. Peter wondered what had turned her into such an empty shell.

CHAPTER 26

'I did everything right,' said Elsbeth, sitting back in the armchair with her eyes closed. She lit a cigarette and blew plumes of smoke up to the ceiling.

'I was the perfect National Socialist. *Jungmädel* at eight. Group leader in the *Bund Deutscher Mädel* at fourteen. I was chosen from our squad to meet the Führer. He looked right into my eyes and I swore then I would dedicate my life to Germany. I even tried to give the Führer a baby when I met a young SS officer. I knew Mutter would understand and arrange a place for me in one of the *Lebensborn* hostels.

'But the baby didn't happen so I enrolled as a nurse and volunteered for the difficult work – with the incurables, the feeble-minded, the cripples. Someone has to do it and I felt I was serving our country.

'They told us we were to report every child up to the age of three who wasn't right. They got taken away from the hospital to a "specialist centre". They came to collect them in a big old van with all the windows blacked out. We told the parents they would be better looked after there.

'It was whispered among the staff that they were put to sleep, like sick animals. Morphine. Veronal. Luminal. The right amount of one of those would do the job quick enough. "Mercy deaths" they call them. I was shocked when I first heard about it.'

Peter watched as she stubbed her cigarette out in the ashtray, then got up to tip it in the bin. He was astonished that she was talking to him like this.

'But then, after some reflection, I thought it made sense,' she said, returning to her chair. '"For the good of the Fatherland", that was the term we used. These children, they were "life unworthy of life" or "the useless eaters". I trotted out all that when Doktor Knodel asked me about it. He was one of the doctors at the specialist centres we sent them to. He came to the hospital sometimes, to see the patients first-hand. He must have liked my attitude because he asked if I would come to work with him in Brandenburg.

'He said that because of the sensitive nature of their work, they were looking for staff who were capable of great discretion.

'So I said I would go. Vater had told me so much about his work and how Racial Science was at the centre of the Nazi revolution. I remember the little speech he gave me, almost word for word. "Imagine a world without illness, or weakness. A world without misery. That is what we can create now the Nazis are in power." Wouldn't you do it, Peter? If that's what you thought? He said modern humanist values favour the weak, the worthless. We must return to nature's way and weed out the inferior, that nature's tools no longer do this in the modern world. So we must do it with our political will.'

Peter said nothing. He tried to keep his face as neutral as possible. He didn't want her to see him looking disgusted and then clam up. He needn't have worried though. She wasn't looking at him. It was as if she were talking to herself. This speech, this monologue, it poured out with so little hesitation, he wondered if she had sat here alone on many other occasions, just talking out loud to herself, running over the same grisly story.

'So I went over to the other side. Instead of helping select the children who would be sent to the specialist centres, I went to work in the one at Brandenburg. It was an extraordinary place. An old psychiatric hospital surrounded by a high fence and signs saying "Danger of Disease", to warn off the curious.

'I became the nurse in the big van with the blacked-out windows. We visited the hospitals of Berlin, and the towns and villages to the west. They used to collect the post, those vans. Now we collected the "useless eaters". We used to say to ourselves we were turning them into angels. It's amazing, isn't it? How sentimental people can be. Even doing something like that. Not Doktor Knodel, though. He called them "an assemblage of malfunctioning parts", like they were faulty automobiles fit only for the crusher.'

She lit another cigarette.

'I coped for a while. My staff nurse told me "Where there is no suffering there can be no pity." But then I started to doubt that. There's not many who have no sense of where they are. Even the really hopeless ones, the ones who can't talk or feed themselves and wear nappies all the time. Even they like a cuddle. When they're agitated, they'll calm down if you stroke their hair. And the scenes at some of the asylums, when we'd come and take them away . . . Some of them thought they were going on an outing! They were so excited. But others, they had to be prised away from their helpers. There'd be tears, screaming, hysterics. As I had done, some of the nurses knew exactly what was happening and they'd hiss "Murderers" at us. We were supposed to report them, but I didn't see the sense in that. They weren't betraying the Fatherland. I just thought they were too ignorant to appreciate the value of the work we were doing.

'We tried to keep it a secret but then people started to find out. We took so many of them to Brandenburg there were bound to be slip-ups. "Disinfected", that's what we used to call it. They'd been "disinfected".'

She spat out the word, sickened by her own callousness.

'People got careless. Some of the parents were told their children had died of measles, when they'd had that illness years before. Well, no one gets measles twice, so you can imagine the stir that caused. Or we'd say some died of a burst appendix, but they'd already had it taken out. We always cremated them as soon as they'd been "disinfected". That saved a lot of bother. No chance of an autopsy then.'

She gave a mirthless laugh.

Peter, no longer able to conceal his feelings, was shaking his head in utter disbelief. 'So what happened when people complained?' he asked.

'If it was just the parents, we could handle them. We'd say there were many patients under our care, and regrettably, very infrequently, mistakes were made. If they persisted, we'd remind them that the Fatherland was at war and our medical resources were stretched to the limit providing for our wounded soldiers. That worked in most cases. But the more persistent would bring in lawyers or priests or other professional busybodies.'

Peter, who had been listening to every word with an appalled fascination, began to lose concentration. It was just too much to take in. He turned to gaze out of the window.

'I cannot be boring you, surely, with this sorry tale?' she said.

Peter looked back to Elsbeth and shook his head. He was too dumbfounded to actually speak.

She was determined to finish her story. 'The Bishops got involved. Sermons were preached from the pulpits. The programme became common knowledge. Word came down from on high to stop, but we'd done much of our work already . . . the job was almost completed.'

She paused. 'So did you kill them all with the drugs?' Peter blurted out. He was reeling, barely believing what he was hearing.

Again, the mirthless laugh. 'Heavens, no,' said Elsbeth. 'That would have taken for ever. We gassed them. They turned a shower room into a gas chamber. All black and white tiles. Instead of water, gas came out of the shower heads. Much quicker, and you could do a group of them at once.

'They'd come off the bus, and we'd take them one at a time into an examining room. They'd get undressed and the doctor there would make sure we'd got the right ones. Then, if they had any gold teeth or gold bridge-work, he'd mark them with a little cross between the shoulders. Then we'd stamp a number on their hand – with one of those date stampers you see in libraries – and then they'd have their photo taken.

'All this seemed to calm them down. They'd have no idea what was going to happen next. Then we'd tell them they were going for a shower. Ten minutes later they'd be dead. The stokers – that's what they called the staff who dragged them out – they'd go in and take them to the death room. They'd take the teeth and sometimes the brains and other organs. They got put in clear glass jars, to send to Vater's office or another of the Racial Science Institutes. I can never see those glass storage jars in the kitchen without thinking of brains . . .

'Then the bodies went off to the ovens and that was it. Not a trace. They used the ash for fertiliser, although some of it was kept for the urns. Once they'd been informed, most of the relatives wanted an urn full of ashes. Too bad they never got the right ones.'

'Have you told anyone else about this?' said Peter.

She waved a hand dismissively. 'When I came back home, I talked to Mutter and Vater. I tried to explain why I couldn't do it any more. They didn't want to know. "It is not cruel," Mutter said. "Your work has a solid basis in scientific fact. You should develop a detachment from these petty moral judgements."

'Vater had been especially proud to have a daughter in the *T-4 Aktion*. That's what they called the programme. It was an open secret among his colleagues that his daughter was part of it, and it embarrassed him terribly when I stopped.

'Vater and Mutter made me feel like a failure. That's why they wouldn't help me get a decent job here. That's why I work for the post office with all the dunderheads and the drudges.'

'So why did you stop?' said Peter. 'What made you leave?'

'It was the mental patients,' she said and lit another

cigarette. 'The schizophrenics, the shell-shocked soldiers. A lot of them arrived with suitcases, and one of my jobs, it was sorting through their personal possessions. The watches, the brooches and bracelets, the combs and hair-brushes. These were people – ordinary everyday people who cared about their appearance. Some of them had rosary beads. Or a little teddy bear or doll they'd kept since childhood.'

She started to cry silently, tears trickling down her face.

'Then I started to think about the people who might have given them these things as presents. Doktor Knodel, he used to say the schizophrenics were empty shells. That there was nothing there. But I could see that wasn't true from what they'd brought to the hospital. That was it. I had to stop.

'And the funny thing was, they understood. Knodel didn't try to dissuade me. He just thanked me for performing a valuable service for the National Community.'

Peter felt repulsed. She came over and sat down next to him. She put her hand on his arm. 'Thank you, Peter,' she said. 'For listening to me. I had to talk to someone. Someone who wouldn't report me. Wouldn't admonish me for being weak. Sometimes I wish it had been me who died instead of them.'

Peter couldn't help himself. Rage boiled up inside him. He shook her hand away. 'Elsbeth, how can you live with yourself?' He was red-faced with anger. 'You trained as a nurse. You're supposed to look after people. What sort of world is it where the nurses go around killing the patients?'

She was angry now. 'At least we killed them quickly

and quietly. In Poland I heard they just got the SS in to shoot them. At least we didn't do *that*.'

Her icy calm returned. The tears from earlier were not coming back. The scorn returned to her voice. 'You are right, Peter. I am a monster. And I do find it difficult to live with myself. Now this shall remain between you and me, or Vater shall hear about your trespassing.'

She left the room. Peter sat in stunned silence. He regretted getting angry with her, but he couldn't help it. Her story was vile beyond words. For now, though, they were co-conspirators. He had done something unforgivable in the Kaltenbach household and she was going to keep it secret. He wondered for how long.

A few minutes later he heard footsteps in the hall and then the front door slam. She had gone out. When she came back later that day, it was as if nothing had been said between them.

CHAPTER 27

May 1943

Now whenever Peter approached the great wooden doors to the Kaltenbachs' apartment block his heart sank. How he wished they were more like the Reiters. They had all been in enormously good spirits recently. 'Stefan's been sent to Italy,' Ula had told him. 'Right down in Sicily. The sunshine will do him good. He's going to be doing liaison work with the Italian divisions there.'

But Kaltenbach had become more like his wife. That awful, impenetrable carapace she had. That coldness. Recently Peter had noticed how his hands shook. And his temper was just awful.

The girls were distracted. They no longer carped about the poor payers to the Winter Relief fund. It was as if they could sense the tide turning. Elsbeth had been utterly aloof since that odd morning. But she no longer sniped at him as she had done. Traudl, who had been so friendly when he had first arrived, no longer asked him to come along to anything.

Charlotte had begun to have nightmares. She woke them all with her wailing. When Frau Kaltenbach chastised her over breakfast she broke down in tears. 'Mutti, I don't want to be killed when the Tommies come to bomb us.'

Some of Professor Kaltenbach's old kindness returned. 'Charlotte, mein Liebling. Our aircraft defences are getting better by the day. Besides. We have Peter here to protect us!'

Peter was surprised to hear his guardian talk about him so generously. He had been distant with him recently. Charlotte was not convinced. 'He won't protect us. He's a traitor. He listens to that dirty jazz music when you're not around!'

Despite himself, Peter blushed. It was true. When the other Kaltenbachs were out and he was left to look after Charlotte he would put on a jazz 78 he had bought from Segur.

Kaltenbach looked at him coldly. There had already been a row about music earlier in the week, when Peter had played one of Mendelssohn's 'Songs without Words' on the apartment piano. Traudl and Charlotte had come in to listen and had both curled up on the sofa, beguiled by the wistful melody. When he was younger, Peter had learned the piece by heart and had played it so often his parents groaned aloud when they heard it. He had not touched the Kaltenbachs' piano since he arrived in Berlin – he thought it would stir up too many painful memories.

The girls urged him to carry on, but as he began another piece, Herr Kaltenbach had stomped into the room and all but slammed the piano lid down on his fingers. Peter looked so astonished the Professor realised he did not know what he had done wrong. 'Mendelssohn is a Jew,' he snapped. 'Do you not listen to your school-teachers? They must have told you?'

Peter had lost his temper. He stood up and shouted, 'Well I did *not* know that. And if I had any time at school these days, instead of hanging around doing nothing at the *Luftschutz* station, I'm sure I would have found out.'

Charlotte began wailing. 'But it's such a pretty tune, Vati.'

For one moment, Peter had thought the Professor was about to hit him. He had never been so openly defiant. But Kaltenbach seemed embarrassed at his own behaviour.

'We do not soil the air of our household with the polluted outpourings of a Jewish composer,' he said, straining to be calm as he walked out of the room.

But listening to swing was different. This was blatant rebellion.

'Is this true, what Charlotte says about you listening to jazz?' said Kaltenbach. The whole family were all staring at Peter.

'I would never do anything like that,' said Peter.

Charlotte began to sing. 'Izz yoo izz or izz you aynt mah baybe . . . That's the one. He puts that on and dances around the living room like a Hottentot.'

Peter back-pedalled desperately. 'Well, I found it in the market, on a second-hand stall. I didn't know it was "forbidden".'

It was a feeble excuse. 'I will not have degenerate music in my house,' hissed Kaltenbach. 'You, my friend, are sailing very close to the wind. If this happens again, I will take you to Prinz-Albrecht-Strasse and hand you over to the Gestapo. Now give me that record.'

Peter found it in his room and meekly handed it over. There, in front of them all, Herr Kaltenbach wrapped it in the morning paper and smashed it to slivers with a hammer.

CHAPTER 28

June 1943

Peter visited the Reiters' at least a couple of times a week now. He needed more than ever to escape from the Kaltenbachs, who just assumed he was seeing Anna, and thought no more about it. Most of the time he was, but perhaps once every two weeks he would visit families who were hiding U-boats.

Today he knew Anna would not be home and he was expecting to visit the Webers again, in Salzberger Strasse. When he arrived, Ula came to the door looking distracted.

'We've had a telegram,' she said. 'Stefan is missing in action. I don't know any more about it.'

Peter was lost for words. Everything he could think to say just sounded too trite. He stood there feeling useless and embarrassed. Fortunately, Ula was in a hurry. She had to report on a Nazi Party rally for *Frauenwarte* and was worried about being late. Peter picked up his parcel and they both left the house together.

Peter had been back to the Webers' several times since his first visit in February. Every time it was the same. He handed the food or the coupons over in the hall and went at once. Barely a word was spoken. But on this occasion, rather than have him stand in the hall, Frau Weber asked him to come into the dining room and sit down. She was wearing her Party badge again – and looked no different from the many women Peter had seen proudly wearing their mother's medals on their winter coats.

'Can you tell Frau Reiter we have a problem,' she said in a matter of fact way. 'One of our lodgers has had an accident. He was cycling to work and fell off his bike. Now he has a great gash on his forearm and its turning a horrible colour. I'm hoping Otto or Ula will know a doctor who we can rely on.'

Peter nodded. He could not contain his curiosity. 'How many lodgers do you have?' he asked.

'There's five of them at the moment. We have a big attic.'

'If I may say so, Frau Weber, you are very generous,' said Peter.

She shrugged. 'The Gestapo will arrest you for helping one or a hundred – so what difference does it make? They can only kill me once.' She gave him a humourless smile.

'Why was he out on his bike?' asked Peter.

'They have to work. If they don't work, they don't get paid and if they don't get paid it's difficult to find enough to feed them. It's a horrible risk going out everyday, but what else can they do? Starve to death? There are people out there, good people, who will give a Jew a job and keep quiet about it.'

She patted his arm. 'You're a good boy, Peter. And a very brave one too. Now off you go.'

Otto Reiter went to the Webers' house early next morning. He had a good knowledge of basic first aid from his time in the trenches. He knew the family – they were old friends. He and Herr Weber had known each other since the early 1920s. That was how these

210

networks operated. You had to trust someone very deeply to ask them to hide Jews.

He did not burden Frau Weber with the ominous news about his son. 'Peter told me about your casualty,' he said, and Frau Weber took him to an upstairs bedroom. 'This is Herr Lichtman,' she said.

'Guten Tag,' said a middle-aged man as he stood to greet him. 'You'll forgive me if I don't shake your hand.'

There was something in his bearing that Otto instinctively recognised. 'I would guess you are a military man, Herr Lichtman,' he said. They were a similar age and Otto discovered he had been a Major in the army and had fought from the Marne to Passchendaele during the Great War.

'111th Division,' said Lichtman proudly.

'I was only a few kilometres down the line from you,' said Otto. 'And now this is your reward.'

'I thought my Iron Cross would save me, and my family too,' said Herr Lichtman. 'But they came for us in the end.'

Otto carefully unwound the bandage and was immediately struck by the pungent smell of the wound, which had turned a livid green around the edges. 'It's ulcerated. How long ago did this happen?'

Lichtman winced as Otto took the final strips of bandage from his arm. 'Two weeks ago now. I fell off my bike on to a gravelly road and didn't bother to clean it until I got home.'

One look was enough. 'You need a doctor, or at least some sort of anti-bacterial medicine like Prontosil. I shall ask around.'

* * *

His visit completed, Otto hurried to work. It was an eventful day. Just after noon the air-raid sirens went. As Otto and his comrades at the Home Army in Bendlerstrasse hurried across the inner courtyard to their underground shelter the unmistakable shape of a Mosquito flew low over the building. 'He's got it in for us,' shouted Otto as they threw themselves to the ground. A huge explosion followed, showering the soldiers in the courtyard with debris. After the fragments had settled they picked themselves up and beat the dust from their hair and uniform. A lot of men were coughing but no one was crying in pain or asking for help. Otto looked up. Windows had been broken, but the damage was not too bad. The bomb had exploded on impact, right on the roof. If it had penetrated and done its work from within the building, they might all have been killed.

Then he noticed the soldier at his feet. It was one of the telex operators. He crouched down and shook the man gently but he did not move. He had a stillness about him Otto had often seen on the Western Front. 'This man is dead,' he called out. What terrible luck, and none of the rest of them even injured. Otto turned him round. There was a bright red wound on the back of his head. A brick or metal fragment from the roof must have struck him with some force in just the exact spot to kill him.

And Otto was right beside him. This sort of thing happened often in combat. Almost everyone who fought had stories to tell of comrades right next to them, shot by a sniper or caught by shrapnel. They always shrugged it off when they related these tales. Fate could be cruel or

212

kind, they would say, or these were the fortunes of war. But Otto knew from personal experience that such incidents were the stuff of nightmares for years to come.

He told Ula about the incident with the Mosquito that evening, missing out the part where the man next to him was killed. She had enough to worry about with Stefan. Then he mentioned Herr Lichtman. 'Who can we ask?' he said. They both agreed their own family doctor, Fruehauf, was a hundred-percenter, and not a safe man to ask. 'I know there's a Doktor Glöckner who lives downstairs,' said Otto. 'I've seen his name on his doorbell. I've nodded at him on the stairs when I've passed him, but otherwise I don't know a thing about him.'

Ula said, 'Can you ask him for the medicine yourself? Pretend it's for you?'

'He'll want to have a look. What shall I do then?'

'Tell him it's for a friend in the Army, who's afraid his old war wound will lead him to be taken off active service. He wants to treat it himself.'

'It's worth a try,' said Otto. He felt the gods were with him today. This might be simpler than they expected.

He went immediately and knocked on the door. Glöckner's wife answered and Otto noticed at once she wore an enamel Swastika badge on her blouse. She showed him into Doktor Glökner's study.

'Heil Hitler,' barked Glökner.

'I am sorry to bother you, Herr Doktor, at this late hour, but I am your neighbour from upstairs.'

Glökner nodded. 'We've met on the stairs, yes, yes.' He seemed impatient.

Otto told his story. Glökner looked on, stony-faced.

'And you, an officer of the Weremacht,' he said when Otto had finished. 'I had always taken you as a man of honour. I will not be party to this deception. Now leave at once.'

Otto returned to the apartment feeling shaken. 'I don't think he believed me,' he said to Ula.

'You'll just have to deny you ever talked to him,' she said.

'Frau Glökner saw me in,' said Otto.

'Then we'll just have to tell the Gestapo, or whoever else might want to know,' said Ula, 'that the Glökners are a cranky old couple who have a grudge against us. It's your word against theirs. I don't think we need to worry.'

'And what of Herr Lichtman?' said Otto.

'I shall ask around at work,' said Ula. She knew a lot of people at the magazine, and a lot of them were not hundred-percenters. This always surprised Otto, considering the relentless Nazi propaganda the magazine produced. But then every magazine and newspaper produced the same kind of thing. There was no telling what the writers really thought.

Ula asked around at work – there were several people there who 'thought their own thoughts' and would ask no questions. A day later, word came back that a doctor in Pankow would provide the medicine for a greatly inflated price.

'Crooks or fanatics,' said Otto. 'I'm sick to death of having to deal with twisted people.'

'We need to get hold of 400 Reichmarks,' said Ula.

The Reiters had the money to hand but Otto was reluctant to spend it on his 'Onkel Klauses'. Ever practical, he said, 'If we start spending that sort of money on these people, where will it end? Besides, I want to keep as much as I can for when we might need it. If you or I are arrested, we might want every pfennig we can scrape together to bribe our way out of trouble.'

Ula had seen Frau Weber that morning. 'Herr Lichtman is now really poorly – his wound is making him delirious. He needs the medicine as soon as possible.'

Otto made a quick decision. 'We'll pay for it, but I'm going to ask Herr Lichtman to pay me back.'

Ula and Otto both knew that many of the Jews they helped had things of value with them when they went into hiding. It might be jewellery, high-denomination bills, even an ornament that a collector might want. Lichtman would probably have something like that.

The medicine came the next day. Ula and Otto were both very busy with their work so Ula asked Peter if he would make the delivery. She made it plain it was a more dangerous job than taking food. 'The doctor will swing if they ever catch up with him. These pills are army issue, they've got army insignia stamped all over them – on the box, even on the pills themselves. If you're searched and they find them, you'll be in deep trouble.'

Peter felt uneasy, but he had made several visits to the Webers' now and had convinced himself that if he 'acted normal' then there was no reason for him to be stopped in the street.

'One more thing,' said Ula. 'Can you mention to Frau Weber that the medicine was 400 Reichmarks. She'll talk to Herr Lichtman about it. They'll understand they'll need to pay us back.'

Peter whistled aloud at the cost. That was a month's wages for a factory worker.

Peter visited the Webers' again a week later, with some milk coupons and a bread voucher. 'Herr Lichtman wishes to talk to you,' said Frau Weber, and Peter was shown upstairs.

Lichtman looked much better. The medicine was working. His arm was still bandaged but he said the wound had lost its livid colour.

'Thank you very much, to you all, especially Colonel Reiter,' said Lichtman. 'I am very grateful and would like to pay him back for the cost of the medicine as soon as possible.'

He looked at Peter, sizing him up. 'Can I trust you to help me here?'

Peter felt uneasy. Taking food and medicine to a house was one thing. What was he getting into now?

Lichtman took out a small envelope.

'Have a look at that,' he said with a smile.

Peter tipped out the contents – a single red stamp from Cameroon with a value of 40 pfennig and a picture of an ironclad battleship on it.

'1900,' said Lichtman. 'If it had been franked it would be worth maybe 50 Reichmarks. But unfranked, it's worth four or five hundred. Can you ask around, see if anyone wants it?'

'I know nothing about the world of stamp collecting,' said Peter. He was wishing he had never volunteered to come.

'I can see you're a resourceful boy,' said Lichtman. 'And I do trust you. Get the best price you can.'

*　*　*

Peter talked to Anna about it the next time he saw her. She shook her head. 'I haven't a clue where to start, but I bet Segur will know.'

Segur was as good as any other person to ask, although Peter and Anna had seen a lot less of him since his beating.

They arranged to meet for a coffee after school. Peter asked Segur if he knew anyone who was interested in stamps. 'I might do,' he said. 'Who wants to know?'

'I have a rare Cameroon 40 pfennig to sell,' said Peter.

'You've never been interested in stamps before,' said Segur. 'Why start now?'

Peter was affronted. He wasn't expecting to be quizzed about it. He hadn't thought of a cover story.

'Just curious,' said Segur. 'Can you show me?'

Peter took the stamp from his pocket.

Segur said, 'I'll take it to show my uncle. He knows a thing or two about stamps.'

'You'll be careful with it?' said Peter. 'It's worth a lot of money.'

'How do you know?' said Segur.

'Just what I've been told.'

'So where did you get it?'

'Oh, let's just say a friend and leave it at that,' said Peter. He didn't like the way the conversation was going.

'What are you expecting for it?'

'He said about 400 Reichmarks,' said Peter. 'Anna's father reckons it's worth 600, though.'

He stopped himself suddenly and began to worry that he had said too much.

After that, Peter ran out of things to say. In the past he

had been able to talk to Segur about anything that came into his head. Today, they seemed like strangers who had started to talk at a bus stop, then suddenly became conscious that they had no common ground.

Segur was in a hurry. He swigged down his coffee and slapped Peter on the back.

'I'll see what I can do,' he said.

CHAPTER 29

July 1943

Gerhart Segur did have an uncle who knew about stamps, but not in the way Peter imagined. Onkel Gustav had introduced himself to Segur the day after the HJ raid at Café Berta. Segur had been too frightened to tell his friends what had really happened on that night. He wished he really had been left in a shop doorway, but the HJ patrol had not actually been so careless. Instead, Segur had been taken to Gestapo headquarters at Prinz-Albrecht-Strasse with the rest of those who had been caught, and was thrown into the basement cells. There they waited, with only the screams and pleas of other prisoners undergoing 'heightened interrogation' to keep them company.

Segur had been badly mauled in the fighting and now he was expecting worse. He had never been so frightened in his life.

They came for him late next morning, when he was light-headed from lack of sleep and food. One on either side, dragging him along the corridor. He ached all over and his mouth tasted foul from his bleeding gums and hangover.

He was surprised and then relieved when they took him upstairs to a wood-panelled office rather than another cell. He was set down on a red-leather padded chair. A man at the desk in front of him offered him a cup of coffee.

'Sugar and milk?' said the man.

Segur gulped down the sweet, milky liquid as the man sat watching him.

When he had drunk the last of his coffee, the man spoke again.

'Heil Hitler. My name is Lieutenant Brauer.'

Segur looked at him, too frightened to speak, wondering what would come next.

'You have been a very silly boy, Gerhart Segur. Your records indicate you have a frivolous nature, suggesting a lack of total commitment to the National Socialist cause, but we have not yet made frivolity a criminal act.' He smiled, to indicate this was his little joke. 'But as this is your first offence, we are inclined to treat you leniently.'

Segur's mind was reeling. Were they just going to send him home? They weren't as bad as the tales he'd heard. Anna and Peter had been exaggerating.

He tossed over a list of names. 'Here is a list of the people we are holding, who were behaving like a bunch of savages in the Café Berta. I'd like you to think carefully and tell me if you recognise any of their names.'

Segur didn't know any of them, and said so after he had carefully read the list. He was relieved to see that Anna and Peter's names were not among them.

'Come,' said the Lieutenant. 'I have something to show you.'

He took Segur gently by the arm and steered him down the corridor, back the way they had come, and down to the basement. He barked a command to one of the uniformed guards and a door was opened. Segur thought they were going to throw him into the cell, but instead the Lieutenant said, 'Holzman. Stand to attention.'

A bundle of rags in the corner of the cell stirred and staggered to his feet. His face was so battered and bloody Segur could only guess what he really looked like.

'Good,' said the Lieutenant to no one in particular. Then he spoke to the prisoner. 'I will return to talk to you this evening.'

They went back to the office.

Segur's legs felt so weak it was a wonder he could still walk.

'You are, I hope, a sensible boy from a respectable German family.' He looked at his file. 'Wittenbergplatz? That's a good area you live in. I'm sure your parents will be mortified to know you're in trouble with us.

'Here is what I'm going to do. I'm going to send you home. You can tell your mother you were beaten up by Polack street cleaners, or something. Then you can come and see me in a week or so. If you can remember anyone else who was at the dance, anyone who wasn't on our list, then that will be very helpful.'

Segur blurted out his gratitude. 'Thank you, Lieutenant.'

'You must call me Onkel Gustav. Come back in a week. And then, after that, if you hear any more about this "swing" nonsense, or any other delinquent behaviour, then you must come and tell me.

'And tell no one about this. If you do, I will know about it. And if I hear, well, I don't need to spell it out . . .'

Segur returned as instructed. Brauer showed him the list again. He noticed how much the boy's hand shook as he held the sheet of paper.

'I don't know any of them, Lieutenant,' said Segur, with a pleading look in his eye.

Brauer believed him. He was good at this, he told himself. Knowing when someone was telling the truth or lying.

'Call me Onkel Gustav,' he said. 'You must know some of them, otherwise you would not have known the party was happening.' His voice was calm, reasonable.

'My friends told me about it,' blurted Segur.

'And did they not attend?'

There was a fatal pause. 'They didn't go,' said Segur.

Brauer smiled. 'We both know that is not the case. Several of the party escaped. Were they among them?'

Segur was staring at his feet. He was so upset he could barely speak. 'I suppose so, yes.'

Brauer's voice hardened. 'Tell me their names.'

Segur did not go back to see Lieutenant Brauer. As the months passed he began to hope that the Gestapo had forgotten about him. But one day in late June, Brauer came to visit him. He brought two policemen with him. 'A routine enquiry, Frau Segur,' they assured his mother. Segur's room was searched from top to bottom. His Duke Ellington, Benny Goodman and Count Basie 78s were stacked to one side and taken away.

'Come and see me tomorrow,' said Brauer. 'Four-thirty, sharp.'

Segur spent a restless night cursing himself for not getting rid of his forbidden music. He had paid so much for the records on the black market, he could not bear to part with them.

Brauer kept him waiting for an hour. Then he was

222

quite different this time and had dropped all pretence of smooth talking. Segur listened in terrified silence.

'You are a disappointment to me, Gerhart. I was hoping you would be able to help me, but so far you have been of little assistance. You will shortly be of military age. If we charge you with your foolish attendance with other criminal elements at Café Berta, and with possession of music liable to corrupt the spirit of National Socialism and the fighting will of the nation, then we will secure a conviction. You may find yourself sent to Plötzensee to face the hangman or the guillotine, or, if you are very lucky, placed in protective custody in an establishment we have for troublesome young people. And when you reach military age you will immediately be assigned to a punishment battalion. Here you will be given the most unappealing jobs the Eastern Front can offer. Mine clearing, disposal of unexploded shells, the most perilous offensive actions. You will be expendable. Do I make myself clear?

'However,' he let the word hang in the air for several seconds, 'if you can help me, as you originally agreed, then we will overlook these severe lapses in your behaviour.'

Segur forced himself to speak. 'What do you want me to do?'

'I want you to tell me about what your friends get up to. I want you to tell me anything, anything at all, that seems odd. I shall be the judge of whether or not this information is useful. But do start helping me, Gerhart, before my patience comes to an end.'

Segur got up to go. Brauer began to speak again. 'I would particularly like to know anything at all about

Peter Bruck. Bruck and his friend Anna Reiter. Anything at all. Remember. Time is running out.'

Segur thought about the stamp Peter had given him. He still had it in his pocket. He fetched it out and sat down again. 'There is one thing Peter said that I thought was odd. He gave me this and asked if I knew anyone who would like to buy it.'

'And why did you think it odd?' said Brauer.

'I've known him for ages now, and he's never shown the slightest interest in stamps.'

'I will look after it for you,' said Brauer. 'Try and establish a value. I will let you know. What else did he say about it?'

'He said his friend's father thought it was worth a lot of money.'

'And who is this friend and their father?'

Segur left half an hour later. Lieutenant Brauer picked up the phone. 'Herr Commandant, I have some leads I would like to follow up. A valuable stamp has come on the market. Someone trying to sell it "for a friend" . . . It's Peter Bruck . . . Yes, I have been trailing him for some time. His foster parents are very highly regarded by the Party and I need to be especially sure before I act . . . The whole business reeks of Jewish money-grubbing. We've had a couple of cases recently. They're sly, these Yids. Stamps – the perfect way to hoard their riches. Much easier to hide than jewellery, and often more valuable . . . And we have several leads on other possible accomplices – notably a Colonel Reiter and his wife. There's nothing concrete, just a lot of loose ends, but I think we should follow them up . . .'

* * *

Segur felt like he had been put through a mangle and every last drop of tittle-tattle had been squeezed out of him. That night he felt so ashamed he cried himself to sleep. He had needed to do *something* to stop Brauer sending him to a detention centre. But should he warn Peter? Then he thought of Brauer's threat. 'If you tell anyone about this, I will know about it.' He remembered the face of the beaten man in the prison cell and told himself there was nothing else he could do.

CHAPTER 30

July 21, 1943

Peter was round at the Reiters' when they heard a loud knocking at the door. Everyone froze in their steps. 'Who could it be?' said Ula.

'Let's ignore it,' said Anna.

'No,' said Otto. 'It could be anyone.'

Otto opened the door to find a scruffy, dark-haired young man of eighteen or so standing outside. His knocking had been loud enough to bring Frau Brenner out into the corridor. She stood there, arms folded, and gave Otto a curt nod. 'Your visitor is very anxious to see you,' she said as she closed her door.

'I have come for my music lesson,' the young man said.

'You must have the wrong address, there's no one here who teaches music,' said Otto.

'Please let me in for a moment,' he pleaded. He looked desperate.

Ula was standing by the door. 'Otto, let the boy in.'

The three of them stood in the hall. Anna and Peter listened from the living room.

'I think I have two Gestapo on my tail,' whispered the boy.

'That's no business of ours,' said Otto plainly. 'In fact, can you tell me why I shouldn't detain you and hand you over?'

'I have been living rough for the last month, after the

family that hid me threw me out.'

'That also is no business of ours,' said Otto. 'And why do you think we would be able to help you?'

'I heard you helped people like me,' he said.

'And who told you that?' said Otto angrily.

The boy shook his head.

Otto grabbed him by the arm and opened the door. 'Out,' was all he said, and shut the door firmly behind him.

Ula was shocked and went to open the door again. He held her back. 'Otto, how could you do such a thing?'

Otto returned to the living room. Peter and Anna looked at him in astonishment. No one knew what to say.

'How did he know about us?' Otto said eventually. 'How would he know to come here?'

It was Ula's turn to be angry. 'How could you turn him away like that?'

Otto ignored her. 'I don't think he's been living rough for a month. He certainly didn't smell like it. He didn't smell of anything. I think he's a *Greifer*. And if he knows about us then the Gestapo will know about us too.'

'What's a *Greifer*?' said Peter.

Otto shook his head in disgust. 'They're Jews who've been captured by the Gestapo. They trade their life by trapping other Jews and their helpers. I couldn't believe it when I heard about this at Bendlerstrasse, but some people will do anything to survive.'

'So where does this leave us?' said Ula.

'We'll keep our heads down, not do anything. They sent him, I'm supposing, to try to trap us. That means they don't have any hard evidence. But someone's been

227

talking, somewhere . . .'

Anna said, 'But suppose he really is a Jew on the run?'

'That's better news for us, if not for him,' said Otto. He had this way of talking about unpalatable truths that made them plain and matter of fact. That was the soldier in him. 'We'll never know. Either way, we can't just take in strangers. It's asking for trouble.'

'We didn't give ourselves away, did we?' said Ula. 'We didn't say anything to incriminate ourselves. What was that nonsense about music lessons?'

Otto shrugged again. 'Maybe he says that if he has an audience. Frau Brenner was standing right behind him. Maybe that's his way of sizing people up on the doorstep. He can't just say "I'm a Jewish fugitive." We'll have to stop the deliveries for a while. I'll talk to Schafer. See if we can get someone else to take over . . .'

Later that same evening Frau Weber was startled to hear an insistent knocking at the door. She hurried to answer and found a scruffy, dark-haired young man standing outside. 'I've come for my music lesson,' he said.

She recognised him at once as a Jew. It was a talent she had acquired in two years of helping the U-boats.

'Come in,' she said. 'Where have you been hiding?'

CHAPTER 31

July 22, 1943

Peter slept badly that night. The incident with the boy on the Reiters' doorstep had unsettled him. He was feeling particularly fragile the next morning and ill-equipped to deal with the envelope that arrived at the Kaltenbachs'. It was postmarked *General Government* and addressed to Professor Kaltenbach. He did not usually look at his post at the breakfast table, but this was too unusual to ignore. As he read it he seemed to shrink. His bustling self-importance drained away like bathwater down a plughole.

'Girls,' he announced, 'I want you to go to your rooms.' They protested. 'Go. Take your breakfast with you.'

Peter got up to go with them. Kaltenbach grabbed his sleeve and tugged him roughly back in his seat. 'You will stay here.'

When there was just Peter and Liese left in the room, Kaltenbach began to speak in a low and steady voice.

'I have just received a letter from SS-Hauptsturm-führer Fleischer, of the Race and Settlement Main Office in the General Government. He tells me he has discovered you have Jewish blood in your family.'

Peter felt a shiver pass through him. Fleischer. He must be Lothar's father. All the HJ boys had heard Fleischer boasting about him.

'Were you aware of this?'

Peter was astounded. He shook his head. He could not think of a thing to say.

'Tell me the truth,' said Kaltenbach. His voice was calm but there was a cold menace in his manner.

'I have never heard anything about it,' Peter managed to say. 'Who? Who is Jewish in my family?'

They were talking in low voices. As if the subject was so shameful it could not be discussed aloud. Kaltenbach plucked the letter from the envelope.

'Your grandmother on your mother's side, which makes you a *Mischling* of the second degree.'

'But she was a devout Catholic,' said Peter. 'It was a joke in our family, how often she went to church. She died when I was seven or eight. I can barely remember her. I remember her funeral though. She was buried in the grandest style, incense, the boys' choir, a magnificent headstone . . .'

He was babbling. The Kaltenbachs stared at him. They were making an intense effort to keep their disgust at bay.

'The Parish records show that she was born a Jew. There is no question about it,' said Kaltenbach. 'You *must* have known.'

Peter could not believe it. He thought it must be a ploy – an excuse to send him back to Poland. Then he began to wonder if it was true. After all, his mother had argued so fiercely with his father about the way the Jews had been treated when the Nazis first arrived in Poland.

'Jews are as unpopular in Poland as they are in Germany,' said Peter. 'Perhaps my parents felt it was a shameful secret?' He felt like a traitor to himself, saying these words, but he was trying to save his skin.

Kaltenbach spoke his thoughts aloud. 'We should have looked into your bloodline more carefully when we chose you. But the records then . . . achhh, they were a terrible mess in the early years of the occupation'

Then he turned his gaze to Peter. 'For two years we have been host to Jew blood. We have fed Jew blood, shared our bathroom with Jew blood,' here he seemed to shudder, 'nurtured and even cherished Jew blood . . .' he was shaking his head. He could scarcely believe it. 'Well, you're a clever race, that's for sure. Goebbels always said never to underestimate you.'

Peter was trying to stay calm. He said, 'Herr Professor, I cannot believe it. How can it be that I have been so widely praised for my Nordic appearance? How can it be that I am considered to be prime Aryan stock? You yourself, when you first met me, declared I was a first-class racial specimen. I remember that clearly.'

'You snake,' said Kaltenbach in a whisper. 'How you must have been laughing at us. Well that explains it all. No wonder we could never instil the correct spirit in you. No wonder you like that mongrel swing music. No wonder you are never first with the German greeting – this is what has been holding you back. You are *tainted* . . .'

Frau Kaltenbach had been silent until this point. 'You are a *Mischling*, Peter. I would never have believed you had Jewish ancestry.'

She paused to let this sink in. 'Now the Reich is aware of your racial heritage you will no longer be permitted to join the SS, you will no longer be permitted to join the Party, or the Civil Service, and you can forget about the *Luftwaffe*. *Mischlings* are excluded from the officer class.

231

And neither will you be permitted to see Fräulein Reiter. We will make arrangements for you to be sterilised as soon as possible.'

Peter reached for the table, white with shock. 'You mean you want to cut my balls off?' he whispered. The words were out of his mouth before he could stop them.

'Peter!' they both hissed at him.

Kaltenbach spoke sharply. 'Sit down and listen, and control your mouth. You are in quite enough trouble already. We are not savages, Peter. Second Degree Mischlings are entitled to humane treatment. You will go to hospital and the operation will be performed under anaesthetic. You will not have your testicles removed. It is a simple procedure where the tubes from the *vasa deferentia* are severed.' He put a hand on Peter's shoulders. 'You have bad blood, Peter. It is your duty not to corrupt your fellow Germans further by passing on the Jewish stain.

'Now, for the moment, we will say nothing to anyone else. Especially not the girls. I don't want this to get to them. I know how girls can gossip.'

Peter felt totally confused. He was horrified – at the prospect of being sterilised, and not being allowed to see Anna, and all the future choices in life that would now be closed to him. But at least they were not going to throw him out on the street. At least he was not going to be taken away by the Gestapo in the middle of the night, or sent back to Poland.

His day passed in a daze. What had the girls thought? How much had they overheard?

And what about Fleischer? For the moment he was away doing his preliminary army training. But when he

232

came back, the whole of Peter's HJ squad would know. Then Kaltenbach would be forced to do something.

There was a more immediate concern. How would he carry on seeing Anna? The Kaltenbachs had friends all over the district and they would soon be spotted together. He had to talk to her. As soon as he could, he slipped over to the Reiters' apartment.

She was out, but Ula was in. She greeted him with a huge smile. 'Stefan is alive,' she said, almost crying with happiness. 'We heard this morning. He's been taken prisoner. A telegram arrived from the Red Cross.'

Peter tried to look pleased, but he was too preoccupied with his own predicament. He told Ula the whole story, and when he got to the bit about being sterilised he started to cry. She put her arms around him and spoke so tenderly he felt like a little boy being comforted by the school nurse after a playground accident.

'Peter, this is all nonsense. I know enough about the Nuremberg Race Laws to tell you Professor Kaltenbach is bluffing. It would be entirely their decision to have you sterilised, and even then, I think you would have to give your consent. *Mischlings* of the second degree do not need permission to marry Germans. They are forbidden to marry Jews or other *Mischlings* of the second degree. Sometimes, second degree *Mischlings* have to undergo further racial examination to establish whether "the Jewish strain",' she lifted her eyes to the ceiling, 'is "predominant". I don't think they'll be doing that with their prize Aryan.' She ruffled his hair.

As Peter got up to go she said, 'I don't think the Kaltenbachs are going to do anything about this immediately. I think they'll want to keep quiet about it as long as they can. But it's going to come out sometime . . .'

She sighed impatiently. 'This whole "*Mischling*" business just exposes the Professor and all his Racial Science gobbledegook as the nonsense it is.'

Peter thought about that conversation a lot. Not least because it was the last time he ever saw Frau Reiter sitting at home in her kitchen.

CHAPTER 32

Otto Reiter thought little of the knock at the door that Sunday morning. On the doorstep was a man in a long leather coat and leather hat, and four uniformed policemen. It was obvious the man was plain-clothes Gestapo. They always wore those clothes. It took another second or two before Otto realised he had a machine pistol pointed at him.

'You and Frau Reiter are to come with us,' he said. 'And your daughter, too. We wish to talk to you.'

Colonel Reiter stood his ground. 'We will be quite happy to come with you. You may put away your pistol. It is absolutely unnecessary.'

The man stepped forward and punched him in the face with such force it knocked him to the ground. As Otto took a handkerchief from his pocket to staunch the blood from his mouth, he was grabbed by the other policemen.

'This is no way to treat an officer of the *Wehrmacht*,' he protested. Another of the men punched him hard in the stomach.

The police officers poured into the apartment. 'And where are your wife and daughter?' said the Gestapo man. Although Otto was in great pain he could still think straight. This was carelessness of the first degree. Surely they should have waited for them all to be home, if they had come to arrest them?

'They are both at church,' said Otto, through gritted teeth.

'Which one?'

'The Dom,' said Otto. Although Berlin's great Cathedral was the other side of the Tiergarten, and quite a walk, it was the one they usually went to. Ula enjoyed her Sunday stroll, and she loved the beautiful interior.

'And why are you not with them?' said the Gestapo man. Otto recovered some of his courage. 'We National Socialists are not encouraged to attend religious ceremonies,' he said.

The Gestapo man did not have an answer to that. It was true. But Ula and Anna were not at church. They had gone to visit the Schafers. Otto was expecting them home any minute.

'You will come with us,' said the Gestapo man. He ordered two of the policemen to stay behind and wait for Anna and Ula to return.

Otto Reiter jolted around in the back of the black van that took him to Prinz-Albrecht-Strasse. If they were treating him like this from the start, he knew that something very serious had been discovered about him or, worse, all of his family.

In his prayers Otto asked that he would die in a good cause and not just be killed by one of the bombs that were now falling on the city. So. He would die saving his wife and his daughter. He prayed now that Ula and Anna would not be arrested and taken into the cells. Only that would truly destroy him.

Luck had not completely deserted the Reiters. Ula and Anna had been returning to the apartment when they

236

saw the police draw up in their car and enter the building. Something made Ula wait and she pulled Anna to one side and they hid themselves in a doorway some distance from the apartment block. Ula's patience saved them. When Otto came out sandwiched between two policemen, and with his face bloodied, she knew to fear the worst.

Peter was alone in the Kaltenbachs' apartment when the telephone rang. Professor Kaltenbach had gone to the Institute to collect some papers, Elsbeth had gone to church and the others were visiting one of Liese's relatives. Peter had not been invited to accompany them.

When he picked up the phone, a voice said, 'Call Wulfie this afternoon.' It was Anna. Then the line went dead.

Peter was swept up in a wave of panic. Then he felt sick with fear. The sensation reminded him of that awful moment when he saw his parents' crushed and bloodied automobile. He forced himself to go into the kitchen and make a cup of coffee. Breathe deeply. Think.

What should he do? He was in a terrible state of indecision. Should he wait until he could call Anna and find out what was happening, or should he just go? Had someone betrayed them? Why didn't she tell him more when she rang?

There was a noise at the door. They had come for him already.

It was Elsbeth.

She sat down at the kitchen table. 'Seen a ghost, have you?' she said. 'You look very pale.'

Peter said nothing. He lifted the coffee cup to his

mouth but his hand was shaking so much it was all he could do not to spill it.

'For heaven's sake, what is the matter?' she said.

He didn't tell her much. Only that a good friend was on the run from the Gestapo and they might want to talk to him too.

'Vater *will* be pleased with you,' Elsbeth crowed. 'Do you want to tell me what this is about?'

There was a loud knocking at the door. Peter was too petrified to speak.

'If it's them, I'll say you are out. Go and hide in your room,' she whispered.

Even in his terror Peter felt grateful for this unexpected support, although he still did not entirely trust her.

Elsbeth went to the door, hurriedly putting her coat back on. 'One moment,' she shouted. There was a plain-clothes officer – probably Gestapo – and a policeman standing there. The Gestapo man was polite. 'Good afternoon, fräulein. We would like to talk to Peter Bruck. I understand he lives with your family.'

'I have just returned from church,' said Elsbeth. 'I don't think he's in. PETER!' she shouted. 'No . . . He went to an HJ rally in Pankow this morning. He'll be back later,' she shrugged, 'I don't know when.'

'You will understand, of course, that we will need to inspect your apartment,' said the Gestapo man.

'I will understand no such thing. My father, Professor Franz Kaltenbach, of the Kaiser Wilhelm Institute, is engaged in top-secret research. He often works from home and would not permit anyone to inspect our apartment without his being here.'

'Quite understandable, fräulein,' said the man. 'Would you mind if my colleague here waits for Peter Bruck to return?'

'Come in,' said Elsbeth, as the Gestapo man departed. 'You may sit in the hall.' She indicated to the policeman a high-backed ornamental chair, situated in the draughtiest spot. It was especially uncomfortable. 'As I said, I have no idea when he will be back.'

The man was charming. 'And where do you work in Berlin?' he asked.

'Over by Hallesches Tor,' she told him icily.

'And what do you do?'

'Nothing exciting.'

Peter was hiding on the deep window ledge behind the curtains in his room. The window recess was just high enough for him to stand upright. It was the best place he could think of, although he knew at once it was dismal. He'd heard the other man leave and watched the street below, desperately hoping that anyone leaving the apartment entrance would not look up. Some children at a window on the other side of the street waved at him. He gave them a distracted grin and a half-hearted wave back. He scarcely dared breathe.

The policeman waited and fidgeted. Whenever Elsbeth passed through the corridor, he tried to start a conversation.

'Thirsty work, waiting for people,' he said.

Elsbeth wasn't going to make him a coffee. 'I'm sure it is.'

Peter had pins and needles and shifted his weight on the window ledge. His foot caught his toy model of Hitler's staff car and it clattered to the floor.

The policeman looked at Elsbeth. 'Oh Frieda!' said Elsbeth. She looked at him and shrugged. 'We have a cat.'

The policeman began to call. 'Here Kitty! Kitty!'

'She doesn't like strangers,' said Elsbeth.

She was beginning to panic. Her father would be home sometime soon. He would know Peter was not at a rally and she guessed he would not be inclined to protect him. Elsbeth knew what she was doing was very dangerous. She could be arrested, for helping 'an enemy of the state' or some such charge. She might even find herself in Sachsenhausen, or Plötzensee. She wondered if Frau Doktor Magnussen would get sent her eyeballs in the fullness of time. And whether her father would idly come across them and her photograph during the course of his work.

An hour had passed. The policeman grew bored. She wondered if he had stayed this long so he could have the chance to talk to her. She had one more trick up her sleeve. 'Well, sir, I have to go out now,' she told him. 'You will appreciate I cannot leave a stranger in the house on his own.' This time she smiled.

Elsbeth was lucky. Before they arrived, the Gestapo man had told his accomplice to wait an hour or two at the most, if the boy was not there. They could always come back.

'Of course, fräulein,' he said, and got up to go.

They walked down the stairs together. She had to bite her lip not to show the relief she felt. As they walked out through the apartment entrance, he bowed and tipped his hat in an exaggerated display of chivalry.

'How gallant,' said Elsbeth, who was feeling frivolous, and granted him another smile. He was quite nice-

240

looking, she thought. Perhaps she could have been kinder to him. They went their separate ways, and as soon as he rounded the corner she dashed back up to the apartment.

Peter was waiting in his room. 'Thank you,' he said. 'You were very brave. I'm grateful to you.'

Elsbeth nodded. 'Why are they after you?' She sounded concerned.

Peter took his life in his hands and told her as much as he dared. 'They think I've been helping the U-boats.'

She nodded again. 'I wouldn't risk my neck helping the Jews. They wouldn't help you,' she said flatly. 'The Gestapo will be back soon. What can you do?'

Peter looked close to panic. 'I don't know.' In truth he did not want to tell her. Elsbeth was still full of Nazi poison. One minute she was helping him, the next she was spitting nonsense about the Jews.

'I've got to leave,' he said. 'Can you lend me a little money? Just a few marks, for the U-bahn?'

She fetched her purse and gave him 25 Reichmarks – it was half a week's wages. 'Take some food too,' she said. 'Hurry. Vater will be home any minute.'

Peter was so surprised at her generosity he gave her a hug. She stood there, frozen, unbending. He quickly stood back. 'Thank you. I will pay you back as soon as I am able,' he said.

He hurriedly packed a bag with a spare set of clothes and an overcoat. Then he carried away a loaf and some sausage and cheese from the larder. Quickly dressing in his *Luftschutz* uniform he was all set to leave. She was there waiting at the door. 'I'll tell them you've been called away to the Fire Observation Station, and you might have to stay there overnight . . .'

'Thank you, Elsbeth,' said Peter. 'I wish we could have been better friends.'

'Don't be sentimental,' she said, and kissed him briskly on the cheek. 'Now quickly. Get lost.'

He passed Professor Kaltenbach on the stairs. 'Guten Tag, Onkel,' he said. 'I have *Luftschutz* duties to attend to.'

Kaltenbach waved his paper. *If I ever see you again,* thought Peter, *then I'm sure to be dead soon after.*

CHAPTER 33

As soon as he felt a safe distance from the apartment, Peter went to a café to collect his thoughts. Then he walked through the Tiergarten to the Brandenburg Gate. That killed a good half-hour. As soon as he heard a clock strike noon he went at once to a public telephone and dialled the emergency number in Kreuzberg that Anna had given him. 'Hello,' he said. 'Is Wulfie there?'

He could hear the relief in her voice. 'No,' she replied. 'He's shopping in Hackescher Markt.'

He could be there in twenty minutes if he hurried.

He waited in the crowded market for ten minutes before Anna sidled up to him. Peter immediately leaned forward to kiss her.

'No, no,' said Anna. 'Just walk with me. Close by, in the same direction. Someone could be watching us. Are you sure no one followed you?' she said. She was being very businesslike. 'Good. Vati has been arrested. I'll tell you more later. Just trail behind.'

They took the S-Bahn to Jannowitzbrücke. As they waited for their train she explained the steps they'd have to take. 'If you're being followed, we need to outwit them, otherwise we'll lead them straight to where we're hiding.'

Peter nodded.

'We'll go our separate ways, then take the U-bahn to Senefelderplatz. I'll meet you in the park just up from the

243

northern exit. I'll be lurking around the bandstand.'

'I don't want to lose you, Anna,' said Peter. He was starting to feel very afraid.

'You won't,' she said. Then she was gone.

He walked to Alexanderplatz and caught the U-bahn. It was only a couple of stops. Then he waited, and waited. She turned up eventually. He felt angry with her – making him wait like this.

'Peter, don't be so bad tempered,' she chided. 'I thought someone was following me. I had to walk down to Moritzplatz to try to shake them off.'

Peter shook his head. He felt stupid now.

'Now take the U-bahn to Görlitzer Bahnhof. There's a church off to the right, on Lausitzer Platz. I'll be on the steps. Wait ten minutes before you follow me.'

She could see he was getting impatient again.

'Peter,' she warned him, 'you have got to learn that this is the only way any of us are going to stay alive for the next couple of weeks.'

She was right, of course. And Peter was surprised at how cool she was being. His own fear was making him so edgy.

It took him half an hour to get there. The stink of stale sweat in the carriages was particularly strong that day. But there she was, as she had said, on the steps of a grand red-brick church.

She nodded towards an apartment block just to the left of a café. 'We're on the fifth floor,' she said. 'Klein. Give me five minutes before you come.'

Klein – that could only be Eugen Klein. Peter had never met him, but the Reiters had talked about him. He worked as a designer at Ula's *Frauenwarte* magazine.

Peter trudged up the red lino staircase of the apartment block until he came to a heavy wooden door marked Klein. Anna had been waiting for him, peering through the spyhole. She opened the door just as he was about to knock.

'Did anyone see you?' she asked in a whisper.

Peter wanted to say 'How the hell should I know?' but he didn't. 'I don't think so. Everyone just seemed to be going about their business. I don't think anyone even noticed me coming in here.'

Ula Reiter came to greet him in the corridor. She too was talking very quietly. 'Peter! Thank heavens we found you. Come and sit down.'

Before he could ask, Ula said, 'The Gestapo have taken Otto. We saw him being dragged away. Thank God we weren't there when they came. It looks bad. They'd beaten him already, so we fear the worst.'

Peter felt sick to the pit of his stomach. 'I'm sorry, Frau Reiter,' he said.

She looked terrible. Drawn, sick with worry. She showed him into the living room. The apartment was small – the room was packed to the ceiling with overflowing bookshelves. It was like Professor Kaltenbach's study, on a grander scale. Peter moved a pile of books on the sofa and sat down.

'Why are we whispering?' said Peter.

Both of them looked at him as if he were stupid.

'We don't want any of the neighbours to know we're here,' said Anna.

'It's a tiny place,' said Frau Reiter. 'Just the one bedroom, so we can't stay for long. Just until Eugen gets our documents sorted out.'

'What documents?' asked Peter.

'We've got to go – leave Berlin as soon as possible,' said Frau Reiter. 'This is what we're going to do . . . Eugen will be back this afternoon with his camera. We need to disguise ourselves. I've been to the chemist. We're going blonde.'

She produced two packets of hair dye.

'Shouldn't I go dark?' said Peter.

She shook her head. 'No. We've thought about this. We're a family now. You and Anna are brother and sister. I'm your mother. We're all heading back to Sweden for your grandfather's funeral.'

Before he could ask another question she carried on.

'Peter and I are going to be short-sighted.' She fetched out two pairs of black-rimmed spectacles. They had plain lenses in them. 'I got them from a theatrical props shop.'

Anna continued, 'Then Eugen is going to do us some fake identity papers and travel warrants.'

'It's a good time to go,' said Frau Reiter. 'Half of Berlin is sending their children out to the countryside.' A week earlier Hamburg had been severely bombed. There were rumours of hundreds of thousands killed and a million made homeless. The German capital was sure to be a target for similar attacks.

'There'll be a lot of people for them to check,' Frau Reiter continued, 'and we can hide amongst them. We're Swedes, returning to Stockholm.'

'I don't speak a word of Swedish,' said Peter. 'I don't even know how to say hello.'

'I don't speak much either,' said Anna. 'Just a few phrases from visits to Tante Mariel. We'll just have to hope no one asks us. I'll teach you a few words later on.'

'We've worked it all out. We've been living in Berlin as your father is working for the Swedish Trade Association here.'

They spent the rest of the afternoon putting the dye on their hair and eyebrows. 'You have to be careful,' said Frau Reiter. 'Leave it in too long and you look like you've dipped your head in yellow paint.'

They all admired themselves in the bathroom mirror. 'Now your glasses too,' said Anna.

Peter was quite surprised how easily they had changed their appearance.

'It's not brilliant,' said Frau Reiter, 'but it's a start.'

It felt strange, hiding here, trying to be quiet. It was almost like a children's game, but then the awful reality of the situation would hit them. Otto in Gestapo custody. All of them fugitives.

Eugen Klein returned that evening. He was a small, dapper man with a bald head, neat beard and wire-framed glasses.

'*Frauenwarte* are all very concerned about you,' he said to Ula. 'Magda is convinced you have been killed in an air raid. Helene thinks you may be too ill to come to the telephone. She is going to your apartment this evening to see if you are all right.'

'Let's hope she doesn't come here to tell you no one's home,' said Ula.

'That's OK,' said Eugen. 'We all need to remember to whisper and no one answers the door. Simple. Anyway, you both look marvellous. Shame you can't stay dark, but they'll be looking for two women with dark hair.'

He fished out a camera from one of the shelves and

247

they set up a plain sheet against the one part of the wall that was not covered in bookshelves or picture frames. As soon as the pictures were taken Eugen said, 'I'm off to the studio. I'll be home by midnight. Help yourself to some supper.'

Peter said they could eat the food he had taken from the Kaltenbachs'. 'We don't want to clear your larder.'

As they ate, Peter raised a question he had been burning to ask. 'I wonder how they found out?'

Ula shook her head. 'It's barely worth thinking about. It could have been anyone. Maybe they've known for months. Maybe they've been following us on our deliveries. Maybe one of our helpers or one of the U-boats was arrested and had our names tortured out of them. Maybe the boy who came to our door had something to do with it . . . You could spend the rest of your life trying to untangle that particular mystery. I can't think about it. There's too much else to worry about.'

For a brief moment, Peter wondered about Segur. The last time he'd seen him, he'd given him that stamp. He wouldn't have done something like that, would he? No. Segur was his great friend. He was sure it wouldn't have been him.

They were all trying to sleep when Eugen came back. Anna on the sofa, Peter and Ula, uncomfortably, on the floor. Peter heard the door open but the others only stirred when Eugen switched on the light. Peter looked at his watch. It was half-past two.

'Look,' Eugen said. 'Train tickets, travel permits, passports, the lot. You are now Magdalena, Karin and Nils Edlund!'

They were all wide awake now. 'These look perfect!' said Ula. 'What time does the train leave?'

'There's one tomorrow morning, at ten-thirty, heading for Sassnitz. You take the ferry there to Trelleborg. You'll have to buy ferry tickets. I can't forge them.

'One final thing,' said Eugen. 'Peter, you will need a smarter overcoat. You will be mistaken for one of our foreign workers in a shabby coat like that. You can borrow mine.'

Eugen fetched a lovely herringbone wool overcoat. It was a little short for Peter. But Ula could always claim he'd just started to grow out of it.

'I couldn't,' Peter protested. 'Haven't you got something older?'

Eugen knew what he was doing. 'The three of you need to look like a family. You need to look like ordinary people that no one will give a second glance to. If Ula and Anna look smart and you look scruffy, then you will stand out. I'll swap you, though. You let me have your *Luftschutz* uniform – it will come in handy for something soon. One of our Jewish friends can make use of it.'

That seemed a fair exchange, and after all, Peter could not be carrying a Nazi uniform with him. How would he explain that?

Ula gave Eugen a huge bear hug. 'My dear friend, I shall miss you a great deal. Thank you so much.'

He gave her a sad smile. 'We shall miss you. And all the Onkel Klauses will too. But it's good that you go as soon as possible. Try to rest now, and I'll sort out a picnic for you in the morning.'

249

CHAPTER 34

August 9, 1943

Leaving the safety of the apartment was like walking naked into a school assembly. All of them felt terribly self-conscious, expecting a tap on the shoulder or a brusque demand to halt. But the world carried on, paying no heed to a mother and her two teenage children.

'Don't forget, while we're waiting,' said Ula, 'we mustn't talk. If we're questioned and we say we're Swedish, and the people behind us have been hearing us chatting away in German then we'll be in trouble. You'll just have to look morose. Children your age often look like that anyway! I will do all the talking.' She turned to Anna. 'I shall talk like your Uncle Lennart when he speaks to us in German.' They both managed a giggle at that. 'But let us hope we don't meet anyone who talks to us in Swedish.'

There were so many things that could go wrong, thought Peter. Who knew what questions they might be asked? It was one thing to think of something clever to say in the safety of your own home. Quite another to parry an awkward question from a policeman or soldier with a crowd of curious onlookers hanging on your every word. Then, a wrong answer could be the first step to the guillotine.

Lehrter Station was besieged. Queues five or six people wide and hundreds of people long snaked out from the magnificent main entrance. Almost all were women and children loaded down with bags and suitcases. They all waited in an orderly manner but they were tense and irritable. Mothers screamed at children for no good reason. Children bawled their heads off. It was a parade of human misery.

They found the back of the queue and waited. They felt very conspicuous there at the end, but soon hundreds more had arrived behind them. Sometimes the queue shuffled forward. Often it stayed still for ages. The time of departure for the train they had tickets for came and went. 'Never mind,' said Ula, 'they'll have to put us on another one. Maybe that one is running very late and it hasn't left yet?'

Anna and Peter, who had been sitting on their cases pretending to catnap, or glumly staring ahead, shook their heads. Ula realised she had spoken to them in German and blushed. But no one seemed to be paying them any attention.

The queue surged forward just after eleven o'clock in the morning. They moved out of the summer sunshine into the cool interior of the station. Peter had never been inside Lehrter Station and he was awed by its grand hall and the beautiful glazed tiles that decorated the walls. Ahead were soldiers and policemen.

As they moved closer to the checkpoints, the soldiers moved up and down, looking for someone who stood out. Jews, or foreign workers trying to escape, or young men of military age in civilian clothing. The first policeman to get that far down the line made a bee line for them.

He spoke directly to Ula. 'Why are these children

leaving the city? They are both old enough to serve in the *Luftschutz* brigades.'

Peter's heart began to thump in his chest. Ula looked affronted. She began to speak in a halting, heavily accented manner. 'Ve are now returnink to Sveden for a funeral. My husband vork here.'

The man's manner changed at once. 'I beg your pardon, madame. You will understand, I hope, if I ask to see your papers.'

She fetched their documents from her handbag. They had agreed that she should carry everything, as a mother in a foreign land probably would. Especially if her children did not speak the language.

The policeman took a long time. Peter's first instinct was to stare at him anxiously. But he knew this would make him look suspicious, so he looked away. It took every atom of willpower not to look at the man. Peter scarcely dared breathe while they waited to see what he would do next.

'Come with me, please,' he said. Peter began to get up, and Anna. Ula spoke to them quickly, in Swedish. Fortunately, the man didn't notice they had understood him. Peter could tell in Ula's eyes she was fuming at their stupidity.

Was this the time to run away? What was happening? Not being able to speak was making this situation far worse. They all walked behind the policeman. Ula said something else to them in Swedish. They nodded and said 'Ja' – that was easy at least. The word for yes was the same in both Swedish and German.

The policeman took them to a small police post at the side of the station. Then he showed them into a waiting room and left.

Peter could contain himself no longer. No one else was in the room so he whispered, 'What's happening? What are we to do?'

Ula said, 'We'll just have to see what he's doing. Look. He's left us here on our own, unguarded. If we go, we'll just make them suspicious. We'll just have to wait.'

Anna put a hand on Peter's arm and gripped it very tightly.

They waited. Peter could see one of the station's clocks. The hands moved in minuscule, quivering steps from 11.43 to 11.58. It took a lifetime.

In his private thoughts, Peter could imagine what would happen. They would all be bundled into a police van. They would be beaten black and blue. Bones would be broken. Teeth would be knocked out. He had heard far more than he ever wanted to about Gestapo interrogations. Then they would be dragged before the People's Court and sentenced to death. All three of them. How would he behave when they frogmarched him up to the guillotine? Would he whimper in fear, or would he be brave? And what would happen then? Was it really as quick as they said it was? Did your head live on a bit? Would he feel it when his head fell into the basket?

The door to the room crashed open. A railway official came in. 'Frau Edlund? Good. The next train with a connection for the Sassnitz ferry is not until four o'clock this afternoon. We will, though, ensure you have a place on it. Please accept our apologies. You may remain here while you wait. Can I get you anything?'

Peter tried not to smile. It was difficult pretending he

did not understand.

Ula looked ten years younger in an instant. 'Zhank you zo much, zir,' she replied in her Swedish-German accent. 'Coffee and cake vould be great appreziated.'

'I shall see what I can do, madame,' said the man, and gave a little bow.

As soon as he was gone, they all let loose an enormous sigh of relief. But Peter was still suspicious. 'Why are they being nice to us?'

Ula had a theory. 'On my last day at the magazine, we had a memo from the Propaganda Ministry. Sweden is to be praised to the skies. We knew what that was about. Sweden is under a lot of pressure to stop trading with us,' she whispered. 'The Americans and the Soviets are both saying they will treat the Swedes as collaborators – almost as an enemy nation – if they continue to trade with Germany. I think the Nazis are trying to be as charming as possible. They want the Swedes in Germany to go home and tell their friends how wonderful the Germans are.'

The coffee and cakes arrived and Anna and Peter remembered not to say anything to the boy who delivered them other than 'Tack', which was Swedish for 'thank you'.

The train was two hours late arriving, but before anyone else was allowed on Ula and Anna and Peter were taken to the front of the platform. When the gates were opened, they were at the head of a queue of passengers desperate to scramble aboard.

The train left shortly after seven that evening. The day had gone well. There had been no daylight bombing raid.

If the British were coming, they would not arrive until after dark.

The train crawled through the Northern suburbs – first past the dense apartment blocks and factories and marshalling yards, then kilometre after kilometre of little houses with their own gardens. Then the flat dull landscape beyond the city. Staring from the window in the crowded carriage, Peter was surprised he could still see the distant domes and spires of the city. Only when they passed Oranienburg did he lose sight of Berlin altogether. It was then the train began to pick up speed. The evening light cast long shadows from the trees and telegraph poles, making the yellow of the cornfields and the green hedgerows and trees look vivid and beautiful.

In their little compartment the other passengers jabbered among themselves. There were two women and four children – all under twelve years of age. One of the women had tried to strike up a conversation with Ula, but she had replied in very halting German. That was enough to dissuade further words.

When the slow dusk finally turned to night, Peter could stay awake no longer. With his head resting on the window, he fell into an exhausted sleep.

CHAPTER 35

August 10, 1943

Peter woke with a sour taste in his mouth and a thick head. He wanted to open the window of his stuffy compartment but everyone else still seemed to be dozing and he thought it would be mean to disturb them. It was light outside but when he wiped away the condensation on the window the view looked much the same – a milky opaque fog hung around the fields. The train had come to a stop.

Anna was snuggled next to him, her hand resting lightly on his lap, her head on his shoulder. She stirred and said, 'Guten Morgen, Peter. Have you slept at all?'

He hushed her at once and at first she looked puzzled. Then she quickly realised her mistake.

The woman at the end of the compartment stirred too – and looked over at them.

Shortly before seven the train began to move and pick up speed. The North German plain sped by and before eleven that morning they were in Neustrelitz. Here the train stopped and platform vendors called out for customers. Coffee. Sausages. Pretzels. Pumpernickel with sliced ham. Ula spoke to them in Swedish with a big smile, and cocked her head towards the platform. 'Ja' they both parroted in what they hoped was a Swedish accent.

The woman at the end of the compartment spoke to them in German. 'I could do with a coffee too, and some cake. I haven't had anything to eat since yesterday morning.'

Peter bit his tongue not to reply. Ula spoke to her in halting German: 'I get you somezing on ze platform?'

Peter wondered if this was the right thing to do. Surely it would invite more conversation? Ula left the carriage and bought them a small picnic. As she was gone, the woman looked at Anna and said, 'Ah, you look just like your mother.' Then to Peter, 'But you – you must take after your father. I can't see her in you at all.'

They both looked at her. 'No underztant?' said Anna.

The woman scoffed. 'Come on now. I heard you this morning, talking perfect German. You're just playing a silly game.' She sounded indulgent.

They both shook their heads and smiled in a vacant way. Now the woman was getting vexed. 'Well suit yourselves, you silly children.'

Ula returned with a cardboard box of food and drink, and gave the woman her coffee and cake. They exchanged a few coins. Ula spoke to Peter and Anna again in Swedish and they just nodded and said, 'Tack'.

The woman was not finished yet. She turned to Ula. 'Your children . . . they speak German, I heard them. But they won't speak to me!'

Ula did her best to look puzzled. She assured the woman they spoke almost no German at all.

'I vunder for how lonk we vill stay in ze station?' said Ula, trying to change the conversation. 'When they've been through the train,' said the woman. She nodded towards a small group of policemen on the platform who were squeezing onboard. They would almost certainly be checking everyone's papers.

Eugen Klein had done a good job on their documents. They'd certainly fooled the authorities in Berlin. But it was always an anxious moment when documents were checked. They waited only five minutes before one of the policemen came to the glass door of their compartment. 'Papers please!' he announced.

He began to chat to Ula – 'Ah, Sweden. I spent many holidays there before the war. Do you know Angermanland? We loved to camp there.'

Ula smiled and made small talk in her Swedish accent. The policeman turned to Peter and Anna. 'You lucky children. You're safe there. Not like our poor German boys and girls. Facing those air pirates day and night.'

Ula stepped in quickly. 'My children, zey only speak a tiny German.'

The woman in the compartment could not hold her tongue. 'They don't. They speak it perfectly well. I heard them this morning. Just when I woke up.'

Ula shook her head. 'No, madame. You must have been dreamink.'

That seemed to be good enough for the policeman. He bid them all good day and moved on.

The woman had dropped all pretence of friendliness now. 'I don't think you're Swedish at all. You don't talk like any Swede I've met,' she said to Ula. She turned to Peter and Anna: 'And I think you're deserters. You should be in Berlin with the *Flakhelfer* or the Fire Service.'

She turned to the other woman in the compartment. 'Do you think she sounds Swedish?'

The woman shrugged. She would not be drawn.

'Madame, you are quite wrong . . .' said Ula. But the

woman waved her away. She sat there fuming, looking at the policemen the other side of the carriage as they stood on the platform comparing papers. Then she stood up and left the compartment. She began to open the corridor window – no doubt intending to call the policemen back. But at that moment the train blew a long whistle, all set to depart, and her resolve deserted her. She flumped back in her seat and sat there, arms crossed, looking daggers at Peter and Anna. When the police boarded again, she was bound to make a fuss again.

Eventually she turned to Peter and Anna and said, 'You're very quiet, you two. Young people usually have such a lot to chat about.'

Ula spoke up. 'Madame, you are beink most unkind. These children are going to a funeral. They are very unhappy. Now pleaz, leaf uz alone.'

Peter thought he would make his own contribution. He snorted in a derisory fashion and closed his eyes to try to sleep. This was all going very badly.

Early in the afternoon, the woman's little boy told her he needed to visit the lavatory. They both got up and left the compartment, to push through the crowded corridor. When she was gone, the other woman in the compartment leaned forward conspiratorially and whispered, 'I know you're not Swedish either. You haven't got the accent quite right.'

Seeing the shock on all of their faces, she said, 'Don't worry. I don't care what you're up to! None of my business.'

Ula kept up the pretence, protesting in her poor German. The woman just winked and tapped her heart. 'Best of luck to you.'

The other woman and her boy returned and the carriage settled into a surly silence. When the train drew up at Neubrandenburg an hour later, they were deeply relieved to see her and her little boy get off.

By now the carriage was emptying, the corridors no longer packed with people. Peter could see right on to the platform and the last thing he noticed as the train drew away was the woman talking to a policeman.

When the other woman and her children left the carriage to stretch their legs, Peter said, 'Did you see that busybody talking to the police about us?'

'They won't take any notice,' said Ula.

'He was taking notes,' said Peter.

Their fellow passenger returned, but this time on her own. She smiled and announced that she and the children had found an empty carriage down the corridor. 'Best of luck to you!' she chirped again as she carried off her bags. Peter almost got up to help her with her luggage. He stopped himself and smiled blankly. No one wanted to call her bluff and actually talk to her in German.

Now they were on their own in the compartment, they began to hurriedly whisper. Ula said, 'If the police do take any notice of that woman, they will want to search the train at Stralsund, it's the next stop, or at Sassnitz. So I think we ought to play safe. If we get off at Stralsund and find a hotel, that might throw them off the scent.'

'I'm so sorry. I feel such a fool,' said Anna. She had been burning with shame all day but had not been able to say anything. 'If we'd stayed onboard, we might even have been able to catch a ferry this evening.'

Ula was hopeful. 'No matter. We're nearly there. One more night and we'll be away. I can't wait to see Mariel's face when we turn up on her doorstep.'

'Do you think they might be waiting for us at the station?' said Peter.

'No,' said Ula. 'They'll be expecting us to stay on the train. I'm sure, if anyone *is* looking for us, they'll just get onboard. Now when we get off, we need to do so separately. They'll be looking for three of us together.'

The train made slow progress to Stralsund. Shortly before they arrived, Peter went out into the corridor. He opened a window and breathed in fresh sea air. They were so close to the Baltic now. Perhaps by tomorrow evening they would be safe. The apprehension was killing him.

CHAPTER 36

Stralsund Station was busy when the train arrived at half-past five that afternoon. People were finishing work and going back to their homes on the little branch lines. Peter, Anna and Ula got off at different doors of the train and mingled with a trickle of other passengers heading for the exit. Although he kept his head down for most of the time, Peter could not resist a quick look around. He noticed two soldiers and a policeman boarding the train together and wondered at once if they were looking for them.

On the way out, Peter spotted Ula first, then Anna. As he walked down the road away from the station, he took care to keep them both in sight.

When they were halfway into the town centre, they felt confident enough to walk together. The town looked quite beautiful – all red roofs and white walls in the evening sunshine, many of the buildings magnificent structures, and with two great churches dominating the skyline. 'It's an old Hanseatic League town,' said Ula, when they were safely out of the station. 'There used to be a lot of money here.'

There still was, by the look of the prosperous, well-kept shops and buildings. Signs to the seafront appeared and they all decided, without even saying it, to walk there. 'You'd never guess we were fighting,' said Ula wistfully. It was barely 200 kilometres from Berlin, but it seemed quite unmarked by the war.

But the swastika flag still flew on the municipal buildings. And arrest would still mean torture and execution. In Berlin they took that for granted. It didn't seem right in a place like this.

Like the rest of the town, the harbour was full of remarkable old buildings. As gulls shrieked and circled overhead they stood on the quayside filling their lungs with sea air. Just across from the town, and linked by a bridge, stood Rügen Island, the final step in their journey to Sweden.

'The thing to do now, of course,' said Ula, 'would be to take you to a nice restaurant. But I don't want any more awkward questions. Especially if there are Swedish-speaking people. It's just across the water after all. So we shall find a hotel and order a meal from room service.'

'Mutti, that will be so expensive,' said Anna.

'No matter,' said Ula. 'We're nearly there. Just one more train and one more ferry. I think we can afford to use a bit of our escape fund.'

A short walk from the seafront was the Steigenberger Hotel. It was a huge modern place with hundreds of rooms. The kind of place where you could feel anonymous. Ula booked a room and they ordered a pot roast and apple pudding cake. While they waited, they washed their clothes in the bathroom and hung them up to dry.

The waiter brought their meal on a trolley with silver salvers. He made no attempt to speak to them, other than the briefest of pleasantries.

It was such a pleasure for them to talk openly. The food was excellent, and it was good to feel safe.

Ula said, 'If Otto were with us, it would be almost perfect. For now, we can only pray they are not treating him too badly.'

Anna's eyes filled with tears. 'They will kill him, won't they,' she said.

Ula knew it was true but she didn't want Anna to think she had given up hope entirely. She went to sit next to her daughter and put an arm around her. 'Strange things happen with the Gestapo,' she said. 'Sometimes people are sent to the camps rather than killed. Sometimes they even come home. We cannot give up on Otto.'

Peter chipped in. 'Your mother is right, Anna. And your father's a tough old soldier. He'll be more than a match for them.' He realised it was a stupid thing to say, even as he said it.

'Tomorrow, my dears,' said Ula, trying to sound cheerful, 'we will buy tickets to Sassnitz and by tomorrow evening we shall be safe in Trelleborg. So let us drink to that!'

Anna perked up and said, 'And let us drink to Stefan too. At least we know he's safe.'

Another day in Nazi Germany. And then they would be free.

Next morning they set off for the station in better spirits. The sun was hot on their faces and after all the travelling and sleeping in railway carriages, it had been good to start the day with a proper breakfast and a shower. Eugen Klein's passes and documents had been fine so far. Ula told them they had nothing to worry about.

When they reached the road up to the station, they

could see a long queue forming outside. 'They must have set up a checkpoint,' said Anna. 'I wonder if they do this all the time or is it just because they're looking for us?'

Ula was worried too. 'What shall we do?' she said to herself.

Peter replied. 'If we want to be really cautious, perhaps we could just come back again later?'

Anna thought that was a good idea. 'All right, then,' said Ula. 'Let's go to the seafront again and try to pass ourselves off as tourists.' Then she thought better of it. 'No. Let's go somewhere out of the way. Maybe they're looking for us in Stralsund too.'

They walked out of town and along the seashore. It was a good idea. Only a few people passed them and there were no soldiers or policemen to ask awkward questions.

When they returned to the station that afternoon, weary from carrying their bags in the hot sun, there was still a small queue outside the station. The checkpoint was still in operation.

'Perhaps I should go on my own to buy a ticket for Sassnitz, and then you two go in a little later. If they are looking for us, I'm sure they'll be looking for the three of us together,' said Ula.

CHAPTER 37

August 11, 1943

Peter watched Ula walk towards the railway station and thought how alike she and her daughter were. She was still slim and almost the same height, and both of them tied their hair up in the same way. They even walked with the same graceful stride. He could imagine a flirty tradesman or postman asking if she was Anna's elder sister. Then he thought it odd that he should be thinking things like that at a time like this. After all, they might never see her again. But he was so tired, not just from the journey, but with the constant undertow of fear, the constant need to be careful of what he said and the absolute necessity of watching his back every minute of the day. Now, the August sunshine and salty sea air reminded him of happier times, when he didn't have a care in the world. He would like to be an eight-year-old again, on holiday in Dabki, on Poland's Baltic coast, sitting on a golden beach that stretched away to infinity.

It was very difficult, being so close to freedom. They were less than a hundred kilometres from Sweden. A day's travel at the very most. Way above their heads a northbound plane trailed white vapour across the cloudless sky. It would land in Sweden in less than an hour. Wouldn't it be good, to be on that plane?

'She might be ages,' said Anna, 'so let's move and watch from further away.'

The thought of shifting his weary body back down the

street they had just walked up did not appeal to Peter, but Anna was right. 'We've got to keep our wits about us,' she said. 'It would be awful to get caught now.'

They dragged their cases away and waited. And waited. The nearby church clock struck its quarter hours and the afternoon ebbed away. Anna began to fidget. Then she screwed her face tight, trying to hold back her sobs. 'They've got her. I know it. Mutti and Vati, gone,' she said. 'How could God be so cruel?'

Peter placed an arm around her. What could he say? People were staring now.

'We just don't know what's happening,' he said. 'There might be all sorts of reasons why she's not come back.'

She shook her head. 'Shall I go and have a look?' said Peter. 'She might be in a queue, she might still be waiting as the ticket office is closed?'

Anna wiped away a tear. 'She would have come out if the office was closed,' she said very quietly. 'She would have told us. Don't go in. It's too dangerous.'

When the church clock struck six, they realised there was no point staying where they were.

'We ought to get away from here,' said Anna. 'It's a bit obvious, isn't it, us just down the road from the station, if they come looking.'

'But if we go,' said Peter, 'how can we meet up with her again, if they let her go? I can't believe we didn't talk about this – make ourselves another plan . . .'

'Well we didn't,' she snapped. 'So there's no point saying it.'

Her eyes were darting around.

'If they have arrested her, you'd think they'd come looking for us as well . . .' she said.

267

Peter nodded. That was true. No police or soldiers had come out of the station exit.

'We're stuck,' said Anna. 'No passports, no travel permits, virtually no money. What can we do?' Ula had been carrying all their documents.

They had enough between them to buy a drink and a sandwich in a café, so that's what they did.

'We'll just have to jump on a goods train that's going to Sassnitz,' said Peter.

'I do that all the time. It'll be a walk in the park,' said Anna.

Peter was stung by her sarcasm but he ignored it. Instead he reached over the table to squeeze her hand. 'I've read enough escape stories about soldiers in the Great War! They managed to slip away from worse scrapes than this. We've come this far and we've been OK. We can look after each other . . .'

He was too tired to think of anything more inspiring. He thought she might snatch her hand away, but she didn't.

They felt stronger after something to eat. Anna was trying hard to keep some hope in her heart. 'If we walk away from the south of the station,' she suggested, 'then we could try and hop on to a train that's slowing down as it approaches?'

'There's a hill too, on the way in,' said Peter. 'Trains always slow down on hills.'

Several trains did just that as they waited in long grass close to the line. But there was a flaw in their plan. 'We have to wait until it's dark,' said Anna. 'It's too dangerous if the train stops at the station and we're spotted.'

Twilight lingered for an age. Eventually night fell.

There was nothing to do to take their minds away from what was happening. Occasionally Anna would burst into tears, and that would start Peter off too. 'I can't stop thinking about what they might be doing to Mutti,' she sobbed.

Peter wished they had something, anything, else to keep them occupied. Even walking along the road would be better than this awful hanging around.

Trains came and went in both directions. The line was a busy one, with a branch to Ribnitz and Rostock off to the west. Before it went dark Peter noticed the cargo wagons had their destinations chalked on a little board at one end. That would help them make sure they caught the right train.

Soon after they heard the distant chime of 10 p.m., a goods train trundled by. They tried to run with their cases but it was difficult to match the speed of the wagons. Then Anna called over the rattling of the wheels, 'It's going to Lübeck!' That was way off to the west.

They darted back to hide in the grass. 'We'll leave the cases. Take anything we really need in our coats,' said Peter.

The next train came close to midnight. By then a chill had settled over the fields and they had cuddled up together to keep warm. This time they were lucky. The locomotive was pulling an assortment of wagons. Among them were several empty open ones. They had Sassnitz chalked on the side. The train slowed to a brisk stroll, and it was easy for Peter and Anna to run alongside and then up the small ladder that overhung the side of the wagon.

They passed through the station a minute later. The platform bridge loomed over them, but it was too late in the evening for passengers.

'If we're really lucky, we'll be straight over the water and on to Rügen Island,' said Peter. 'And then we'll be in Sassnitz by the early hours.'

A cold breeze whistled over the top of the wagon, blowing coal dust around. Peter hoped they wouldn't get too dirty. That would make them very conspicuous. He peered over the side. They were on the high bridge over the stretch of water between Rügen and the mainland.

The air became warmer as soon as the crossing was completed and they both fell asleep. Only the jolting of the wagons as the train slowed down woke them. Ahead in the sky, Peter could see the dark silhouette of a marshalling yard lighting tower.

'Thank heaven for the blackout,' he said. Still, there was a bright moon, and all around, in silvery monotone, were platforms and lifting machinery and cranes and scoops. This was no place to be a stowaway on an open wagon.

The train slowed to a crawl. Peter and Anna peered cautiously over the side. They were stopping at a platform. The locomotive came to a grinding halt and gave a couple of brief whistles to announce its arrival.

Thirty metres or so ahead stood a sentry with his back to them, his rifle slung over his shoulder. He wasn't paying anyone any attention, in fact he seemed quite restless, moving his weight from one foot to another. He started singing a song to himself, his voice carrying clear as a bell in the night air.

'If this is Sassnitz, then we need to get off here,' said

Peter, 'and find the port.'

They looked over the top again. Another sentry had joined his comrade. They could see the lamplights of other railway workers approaching. 'I think the platform will be swarming with people very soon,' said Anna.

At once they realised they were trapped. Anyone walking on the platform could peer straight into the wagon. 'We can't stay here,' said Peter. 'Besides, it's probably about to be filled with coal.'

'What shall we do?' said Anna.

'We'll have to hide under the wagon,' said Peter, 'and then try to get away just before the train starts to move again.'

'How will we know that?' said Anna. She was close to panic.

'There's usually a whistle or a hoot from the engine, isn't there?' said Peter. 'If the train is ready to go, then the workmen will have moved on to another one, or back to their hut for a coffee . . .'

'But what if the train starts to move when we're underneath it?' said Anna.

'We can't stay here,' he said. 'We'll just have to take our chances.'

After another peep over the top to check they could get out unseen, they both jumped to the ground and scuttled underneath. It was a miserable place to hide, between the gravel and wooden sleepers. The wagon axles lay just above their heads and the smell of oil and coal dust and chemicals made their noses twitch. It was just wide enough for them to lie side by side.

A couple of minutes later, they heard footsteps and voices. 'Half of them to Trelleborg,' said one. 'Half to

Rostock. We'll be all night marking these up.'

Peter and Anna lay still and silent as the voices and footsteps echoed above their heads. They felt safe enough as long as the men stayed on the platform. Across the marshalling yard they could see a patch of rough, over-grown land. From time to time a warm salty breeze wafted over. They were obviously close to the sea.

Not far behind, they heard the sound of wagons being uncoupled. 'If they come much closer,' whispered Peter, 'they're bound to spot us.' Ten minutes later they heard the chuff of a small locomotive and soon after that the sound of moving wagons. Looking down the train Peter could see they were now five or six wagons away from the end.

There was a groaning ahead of them that grew closer and closer until the axle right above their heads creaked and the wheels began to move. The locomotive was reversing towards them.

Peter looked up. Between the carriages there were dangling connecting chains. If they caught one of those on the head, it would be painful but probably no more than that, especially if the train was still moving very slowly. Being side by side was a bad mistake. They had so little room; one wrong move and a wheel would slice off a hand or a foot.

'Anna, we need to get one in front of the other. You stay here, I'll go.' She nodded and he began to wriggle forward. She saw at once he was raising his head too high and grabbed him to push him down. His jacket sleeve caught under the rim of a wheel. It pulled painfully tight for an instant, giving him a clear idea of the weight of the wheel and what it could do to flesh and bone.

Then the axle passed so close above his head he could feel it brush his hair.

'What the hell are you doing?' he pleaded. 'I nearly lost my arm.'

'And you nearly lost your head too,' she cried over the rattling and creaking.

He inched forward. One of the chains clunked against his forehead smashing the glasses he had been wearing, then bumped down his back.

The train stopped. 'Let's go,' said Peter urgently. 'Just walk away. Maybe no one will notice us?'

Anna paused. 'They might not notice you, Peter, but I'm wearing a dress.'

'I'm not going without you,' he said. 'Besides, it's dark enough. You'll just be a shape in the distance. You go. Wait for me by the tower over there with the bushes around it.'

'Peter, just . . .'

Her whispers were drowned out by the creaking of the wagons. The train was moving slowly backwards again. It was a long train but soon enough the locomotive edged nearer. Not only could they hear it chuffing towards them, but peering ahead, Peter could see steam gushing from the vents beneath the wheels and pistons, and even the glow of the firebox. Worse than that he realised the front of the engine had been fitted with a fender. If that went over them they would both be mangled horribly.

He called back. 'Anna, we're going to be crushed. We have to get out between the wheels.'

There was a three or four second gap between the wagon wheels – maybe just enough time to roll over the rail without getting sliced.

The locomotive was drawing nearer. 'You'll have to be quick,' said Peter. He thought perhaps that Anna would be too terrified to move but when he turned his head and saw her face she looked determined enough. A chain banged into the back of his neck and he flinched, his fingers instinctively grabbing the rail. He snatched them away an instant before the wheel rolled over them.

When he looked again, Anna was gone. Now it was his turn. He moved his body as close to the rail as he dared. One wagon went past, then another. He summoned up his courage, thinking, *It's now or never* . . . but the next one was the coal tender. The wheels on that were placed too close together. The locomotive itself was nearly on top of him. Peter buried his face into the gravel and waited for the awful agony to come.

CHAPTER 38

The next five or six seconds seemed to go on for ever. Screeching and grinding filled his ears, metal chains bounced along his body, he could feel burning heat on the top of his head. He wanted to scream but the sound choked in his throat. Then the noise changed. The screeching came to a crescendo and died away. The steam still chuffed and bellowed and he could feel the heat of it burning his neck and the skin on his hands. But the train had stopped. He was still alive.

Peter was right underneath the front of the coal tender. Above him were three overlapping plates connecting the driver's platform to the tender. Through gaps between them, he could see the red glow of the firebox and what must be the boots of the engine driver.

With no conscious thought he wriggled backwards down the track until he came to the gap between the tender and the first wagon. Without even pausing to look, he twisted his body out from between the wheels and began to walk towards the tower. Whatever happened he was not going to stop until he got to that tower. Anything was better than being crushed by a train. Even being shot by a sentry.

The temptation to run was overwhelming, but he knew a running figure would be noticed. The yard was full of men going about their business. And they were walking.

The further he got from the train the safer he felt. Especially when it began to move again. As soon as he reached the scrubland, he dived into the long grass and waited. When the train stopped moving and a sort of quiet settled on the night, he called out as loud as he dared: 'Anna!'

She whispered, 'Over here!' and they were together again. She hugged and kissed him, almost mad with relief.

'What now?' she said.

'It's best to move while it's still dark,' said Peter. 'Let's try to find the ferry.'

They followed their noses. The smell of the sea led them through fields along the edge of the town.

At first light Peter was horrified to notice Anna looked absolutely filthy. Her fawn coat was caked in soot. Her face was smeared with much the same.

'You look terrible,' she said to him. 'Absolutely filthy!'

'What are we going to do?' said Peter. 'We'll be spotted at once, looking like a couple of tramps.'

'And I'm starving,' said Anna.

There in the fields they came to an old bath tub filled with drinking water for cattle. It was perfect. They both stripped to their underwear and began to wash the grime from their faces and bodies. In the dewy early morning it was freezing and their teeth chattered uncontrollably. But Peter felt a strange glee, and Anna too. They began to laugh even as they shivered. It was just too ridiculous.

'What about our clothes?' said Anna. 'Don't we need to give those a wash too?'

They beat their coats with their hands. Most of the dirt came out, although the coats now looked very worn and scruffy. It was good to have something to take their minds away from Ula and what they had to do next.

'I've got a better idea,' said Peter. In the distance he could see a farmhouse. Whoever lived there had left their washing out to dry and forgotten to take it in for the night.

They ran to the farmhouse. 'Let's hope the farmer isn't up too early,' said Anna. Peter was full of admiration for her. Managing to carry on like this, after what had happened.

There were trousers, a shirt and a dress. Peter just about fitted the trousers. The dress was far too short for Anna. 'Very nice,' whispered Peter, 'but you'll cause a scandal if you wear that in the street.'

A window creaked open and they saw a shadow behind a lace curtain. They heard an old woman shouting inside the house. It was time to go.

An elderly man came out into the garden and shouted angrily as they hurried from the farm. He began to chase after them, but gave up after a few metres. When Peter turned to look, he could see him wheezing, bent over with his hands on his knees. Still, they ran until they could run no more. The trees and hedges in the fields were laden with apples and early blackberries so they ate as many as they could find for breakfast.

Anna squeezed out of the dress and quickly pulled on her grubby skirt and blouse. 'I'll just have to keep my coat buttoned,' she said. 'Let's hope it's not too hot.'

The day was looking up. They headed for the harbour with renewed hope.

The port was busy. Sweden was still one of Germany's

main trading partners and a procession of lorries full of industrial goods was backed up along the main road to the ferries. 'We need to sit this one out, I think,' said Peter. 'Wait until dark and see if we can smuggle ourselves on to the back of a lorry.'

So they sat there in the sun, hidden in the chalk hillside above the road. Anna dozed but woke with a start. 'Every time I go to sleep I have a horrible dream,' she said. After a while she sat up, but she stayed silent. Peter could tell she was trying not to think about her mother and father. 'I wish we had something to do. All this waiting, it's killing me,' she said.

By lunchtime they were thirsty and hungry, but neither wanted to risk a trip into town. They would just have to put up with it. They could see the sea sparkling before them. As they watched the ferries come and go, they knew that there, over the blue horizon, was a country where swastikas did not fly from buildings. Peter said, 'If we can get on to a ferry, we'll be there in four hours.'

Four hours. That was a morning in school, an afternoon outing to the park. It was now a matter of life or death.

Night fell with the same maddening slowness. All day the lorries had come and gone, but there was still a queue of them on the road below.

'Look, there's one with the tarpaulin come loose over the load,' said Anna. Most of the other lorries had their coverings tightly lashed.

They crept down to the road. 'How will we get in without being seen?' said Peter.

Anna shrugged. 'We'll just have to be patient.'

They waited an hour. It was agony. 'If the driver of that lorry gets out to check his load,' said Peter, 'we've lost our chance.'

'I'm more worried about the queue moving forward before we can get on,' said Anna.

Late in the evening the driver in the lorry overlooking the one with the loose tarpaulin got out and wandered back to talk to the man behind him. Anna had nodded off to sleep. Peter nudged her awake. 'Now's our chance . . .'

They crept from the shadows and hauled themselves up on to the back of the lorry. Underneath the tarpaulin were wooden cases containing bottles of chemicals. The smell caught in their parched throats and it took a terrible effort not to cough, but at least there was space to squeeze between the boxes.

They had picked their moment well. A few minutes later, they heard shouting. 'They're ready to go to the ferry!' whispered Peter. His mouth was so dry he could barely speak. The engine started and then the driver got out to check his load.

They heard him curse, then say to himself 'How did that happen?' as he looked at the loose covering. They heard his clumping boots climb up the side of the lorry. Peter felt Anna squeeze his hand tightly.

A voice shouted in the distance, 'Hurry, Dolf, we're about to set off!'

The man cursed again. The tarpaulin was pulled tight over their heads and they could hear him lashing the rope to the stays around the rim.

The lorry began to move forward. Peter and Anna

were immersed in a world of sound. It was easy enough to guess what was happening. First the lorry moved forward very slowly, stopping every few metres. That went on for ages. Then there was a conversation, dimly heard over the throb of the diesel engine. That would have been a checkpoint. The lorry moved forward – even picking up a little speed. They were jolted around and felt the weight of the boxes pressing against them. There was a rattling and juddering as the lorry mounted a ramp. Then the sound of the engine changed. They had gone from the outdoors to the inside of a metal chamber. There was more shouting as the lorry moved into position.

The engine was turned off. The driver got out and slammed the door. Eventually the deck settled down and there was another wait. 'I have to get out of here,' said Anna. 'I think I'm going to be sick. And I'm dying of thirst. We've got enough money for a drink, haven't we?'

They peered through a gap in the covering. 'It's a big ferry,' said Peter. 'It's bound to have a café or dining car . . .' Then he began to worry. 'But once we're out of here, we'll find it difficult to get back, won't we?'

Anna nodded. She was so thirsty she was finding it difficult to talk.

'Just a few more hours now,' said Peter.

Twenty minutes later they heard the low throb of the ship's engines. The whole boat shook as the ferry edged out of the quayside. The cases vibrated so much they both wondered if the glass bottles were going to break. 'I've got to get out,' said Anna. 'We don't look too shabby. We'll pass for a couple of people who have been travelling for several days. Come on, no one will look twice at us.'

The temptation was too great to resist. Peter took out his HJ dagger from his coat pocket and cut through the rope on the tarpaulin.

CHAPTER 39

Berlin
August 13, 1943

Otto Reiter lay on his bunk at Plötzensee Prison. It was just after midnight. Although he was exhausted, the bruises on his battered body and the ache from a missing tooth were keeping him awake. How much longer he would be able to stand up to his torturers, he could not predict. The coming morning or the next day, they had told him, they would start pulling out his fingernails, then his toenails. After that, they assured him, there were plenty of other techniques they could employ. It was just like the Gestapo to tell a man what lay in store for him. Let it fester in his mind. Let him fret about it.

And then what? He would be shot, or hanged or taken to the guillotine. Which was his preferred method of execution, asked his torturer. Otto Reiter had stared him in the face and showed no fear. He did not know how much longer he would be able to do that.

Otto heard the low buzz of Mosquito bombers over the city, first as a faint drone then a heavy rumble he could feel in his chest. He stood on his bed to look out of the high cell window. Searchlights were crossing the sky and he instinctively flinched as one of the planes flew right over the prison. A second later there was a loud explosion close to the perimeter wall. Bits of stone and cement peppered the windows and he flinched again as one cracked the glass above his head.

For the first time since his arrest Otto laughed. He felt an almost childlike glee at the destruction the British were wreaking on this horrible prison. He was still laughing when another bomb blew his cell and the next three or four around him to brick dust and rubble.

CHAPTER 40

Baltic Sea
August 13, 1943

Kriminalassistent Verner Schluter was not in the best humour. There were many things he would rather be doing than pretending to be a passenger on the *King Gustav* car ferry between Sassnitz and Gothenburg. He had joined the Gestapo to cleanse the Reich of Jews, not mess around on a little ship. Sassnitz was a dreary little posting. What he really wanted was to be in Berlin.

Once in a while, there were cases that interested him. Criminals. Terrorists. Jews. All on the run. Maybe making for the ferries. It was exciting work, looking for them. Catching a filthy little Jew on the last leg of their journey – when they were certain that they had actually escaped that noose around their neck – that gave him great satisfaction. Watching their faces fall as they realised they had failed.

Last week his office had been sent a telex from a Lieutenant Brauer in Berlin, warning them to look out for a woman and her daughter and a young man. Reiter, that was the name of the women, and Bruck, the boy. All of them tall, the boy blond, the females dark. The charge sheet was daunting – they could expect nothing less than the guillotine, all three of them. Maybe they would do them all on the same day – like they did those dirty traitors in Munich – the White Rose lot. From arrest to execution in less than five days. That was the way to deal with scum like that.

Wire photographs had arrived too – although the pictures were far from clear. They were a handsome bunch – all of them with classic Aryan features. The young man though, it said he was a Mischling. That was funny. He looked just like the boy in the HJ poster.

Ula Reiter nursed a small schnapps as she sat in the bar of the *King Gustav*. She had promised herself she would not touch a drop of alcohol until she arrived in Sweden. She still had to keep her wits about her. But she was nervous and persuaded herself that a little Dutch courage was what she needed. She knew, logically, that there should be no more obstacles in her path. Once she had left Sassnitz she would be safe from the Nazis. She still had the papers she needed to get into Sweden. She had her sister Mariel's phone number. She even had enough money for the train fare to Stockholm. Whatever checks she had to go through at the other end would be nothing compared to that cross-examination in Stralsund.

She would never forgive herself for leaving the children outside the station. If they had thought about what they were doing, she would have given them their papers – so at least they would have had a chance if she had been arrested. But she was exhausted, they all were, and no one was thinking straight.

They had kept her in that little room in the station until ten o'clock that night. Someone was highly suspicious. But she had stuck to her story like glue and had been highly indignant at her detention. It was a performance worthy of Garbo, she told herself.

Eventually they had let her go. Why, she could not

guess. Surely, a quick phone call to Berlin would have sealed her fate in minutes. But maybe there had been another raid and the lines were down? Either way, they did not wish to offend the Swedes any more than necessary, and that had saved her.

She came out of the station and spent the rest of the evening looking for Anna and Peter. She returned to the hotel then walked around Stralsund for another day. It had been hopeless. She could not even ask people if they had seen them. It was too risky. They should have had a plan. Somewhere to meet. But they didn't and now it was too late.

That evening she caught a train and arrived at the ferry terminal with no further hitches. She went straight on, no other questions. She felt less conspicuous on her own.

Ula Reiter was not a sentimental woman. She knew there was no point spending any more time looking for Anna and Peter. If they were captured, they might be tortured and betray her. She even hoped they would, rather than prolong their suffering. She didn't want Anna suffering to protect her. She even thought of giving herself up, to save her daughter the prospect of torture. They would all be executed anyway. But perhaps they had not been caught. Perhaps they were still trying to get to Sweden like her. There was no sense in her staying behind to be captured.

All these thoughts were running through her head when she noticed two very scruffy young people at the bar. It took her a second to recognise them. She stifled the urge to cry out. She did not even want them to see her. Not there. She would catch them when there were no other people around. It still paid to be cautious. They were not safe yet. She drained her glass and moved swiftly away.

But it was too late. Anna saw her and almost screamed with delight.

Across the bar, one of the customers flicked his newspaper to one side to see what all the noise was about. Something about the two women who were frantically embracing, and the young man who was standing to one side looking slightly embarrassed, rang a bell. The women were blonde rather than dark, and one of them was wearing unflattering glasses. But it was them all right. Kriminalassistent Verner Schluter's heart began to race.

Ula was making frantic attempts to calm Anna down. 'Mein Liebling, we mustn't make a fuss. We're not there yet. You never know who's on board and whether or not they can still take us back . . .'

Anna calmed down. 'Meet me outside, on the top deck next to the funnel,' said Ula. 'Then we can talk. You'll find it.' She left the bar.

Outside, a warm breeze blew up from the south. It really was a beautiful night and the Baltic was as smooth as a mill pond. Plain sailing. The top deck was almost deserted.

Anna and Peter found Ula easily enough and they sat down on a bench together and told their tales in urgent whispers.

'I still have the tickets,' said Ula. 'They didn't search me when they stopped me. Too keen not to offend the

Swedes for their own good, weren't they!'

'Thank heavens,' said Anna. 'Now we won't have to get back on that lorry . . .'

Ula held both their hands and said, 'In two or three hours we will be safe. We've got all the right papers. There should be no problem at the port. Now let us go and get something to eat.'

Kriminalassistent Verner Schluter had done this several times before. There was usually a fuss. Last time, when he tried to arrest a resistance terrorist, two Swedish lorry drivers had waded in. He nearly had to shoot them, and heaven knows what kind of international incident that would have caused. So he wasn't going to risk that again. Particularly not with these two handsome females. That would conjure up every gallant Swede on the ship. He would play this one very carefully.

He had heard them say they were going up to the top deck and had followed them five minutes later. There were just a couple of other people about. He sauntered up to the rail and waited for the other passengers to leave before he made his move. Schluter was just about to approach when all three of them got up from the bench by the funnel.

This was the perfect moment. He would apprehend them, and then take them to his cabin. There they would stay, under the barrel of his gun, until the ferry returned to Sassnitz.

Schluter enjoyed the look on their faces when he told them to stop and stand still. The boy even put his hands up when he saw the machine pistol, like he was in some cowboy film. Schluter told him to put his hands down.

He didn't want them drawing attention to themselves. He was sure none of them would be carrying weapons.

'You are Ula and Anna Reiter, are you not?' he said to them. 'And you . . . Peter Bruck?'

The woman spoke up. Out came a lot of nonsense about a funeral in Sweden. And them being Swedish. Schluter spoke to them rapidly in Swedish. What he said was plainly obscene and when none of them even raised their eyebrows he knew at once they were no more Swedish than Reichsführer Himmler.

He didn't even have to ask to see their papers.

Then the ship's hooter went – so loud and long a flock of seagulls took off from the superstructure around the funnel and swooped around his head as they fled from the cacophony.

Before he knew what was happening, the boy and the girl had rushed towards him. He felt himself lifted up, his back bending against the wooden rail. Then he was tumbling down. The sea smacked hard against his body and it was so cold it robbed him of his breath.

He struggled to the surface, weighed down by his leather coat, and gasped in great lungfuls of air. A wave broke over his head leaving him choking again.

By the time he had struggled out of his coat and summoned the strength to shout for help, the ship's stern was forty metres away. He called and called, as he bobbed in the fluorescent wash, but the lights of the ferry receded into the distance.

Kriminalassistent Verner Schluter used all his considerable strength and intelligence to extract himself from his predicament. Was there a weather buoy, or something else like that, close by? Were there other ships? One must be along soon? Far away on the horizon he could see the lights of settlements on the Swedish coast. He began to swim towards them, but they never seemed to get any closer.

EPILOGUE

Stockholm
September 1943

Peter woke from an afternoon sleep and went out into the garden to join Ula, her sister Mariel and Anna. They were burning leaves in the tired sunshine, and he picked up a rake from the greenhouse and began to scrape together another pile for the bonfire.

Less than a month ago Mariel had opened her front door to find them waiting, exhausted, on the steps. She simply stared in disbelief, and then rushed to hug each of them, tears streaming down her face. Later, she and her family sat in stunned silence as Ula told them about Otto.

They lived in a big house on Stora Essingen, on the waterfront overlooking the south of the city. There was more than enough room for three guests. For Peter, the light, airy rooms were the perfect remedy for his months in the Kaltenbachs' claustrophobic apartment.

'You shouldn't sleep during the day, Peter,' said Ula. 'It makes it so much more difficult to sleep through the night.'

Peter nodded. He wasn't going to disagree. But since they'd arrived here he had only been able to sleep for a few hours every night, so he caught up during the day. His dreams were too intense, too frightening: running, always running, or vague shadowy imaginings where he was trapped in a building or a train, just waiting to be caught. He knew Ula and Anna slept badly too. Otto was never far from their thoughts.

Later that afternoon they took a tram into the city centre. They walked down to the quayside, the three of them arm in arm, and looked over the sweep of the waterfront with its grand pastel mansions glowing in the sunshine. Ula said, 'All these beautiful buildings. And not a single swastika flag among them.'

For as long as Peter could remember he had been haunted by a creeping sense of dread. It had sometimes been dim and nebulous – like the fear of Hitler invading Poland – or the more immediate fear of being killed in an air raid. Or the hour by hour terror of being arrested and tortured by the Gestapo. But now there was nothing dark on the horizon. Nothing at all. Peter felt something he hadn't felt for so long. He felt free.

FACT, FICTION AND SOURCES

When writing about such an extreme and grotesque ideology as Nazism, it is easy to lapse into caricature. But instances such as the Christmas carol (p. 101), the Swastika Christmas tree decorations (p. 102), and the school text book questions (p. 59 and p. 89) are all taken from eyewitness accounts or photographs from the era. Charlotte's doll's house can be found in the National Socialist era gallery at the Deutsches Historisches Museum in Berlin.

Sometimes the exact dates of real events depicted here have been altered slightly to fit with the flow of the story. The 'human material' research into epidemic jaundice was begun in June 1943, for example, and the more grotesque aspects of Karin Magnussen's iris research were carried out, as I understand it, in 1944 rather than 1943. Also, Plötzensee Prison was bombed by the RAF on September 3rd and 4th 1943, rather than the middle of August.

The account of Piotr's examination in Chapter 2 was inspired by a passage in the autobiography of Gershon Evan (formerly Gustav Pimselstein), *Winds of Life*.

Artur Axmann's speech to the Hitler Youth in Chapter 11 is based on a speech reported in the autobiography *Other Men's Graves* by Peter Neuman (Weidenfeld and

Nicolson, London, 1958), as is the wording of the boys' oath. The speech is actually by Axmann's predecessor, Baldur von Schirach, but I've assumed Axmann would spout a similar pseudo-scientific ideology. Some of the school text book questions included here also come from Neuman's account of his childhood in Hitler's Germany.

In Chapter 14 the extract from Peter's war book comes from a translation of Walter Menningen's *Vorwärts, immer vorwärts! Vom Siegeszug unserer Infanterie im Osten* (Steiniger-Verlage, Berlin, 1942). You can read more of the story in Randall Bytwerk's fascinating German propaganda website at Calvin College, Grand Rapids, Michigan (http://www.calvin.edu/academic/cas/gpa/ kb135.htm).

The character of Ula Reiter was partially inspired by Ruth Andreas-Friedrich and Marie 'Missie' Vassiltchikov – two brave women who defied the Nazis in wartime Berlin and wrote fascinating journals about their wartime experiences.

Of the scores of books and websites I used while researching this project, the following were especially helpful:

Deadly Medicine – Creating the Master Race, eds Dieter Kuntz and Susan Bachrach, the University of North Carolina Press, 2006.

A Social History of the Third Reich by Richard Grunberger, Penguin Books, 1977.

The Racial State by Michael Burleigh and Wolfgang Wippermann, Cambridge University Press, 1991.

Berlin Then and Now by Tony Le Tissier, After the Battle, 1991.

ACKNOWLEDGEMENTS

Thank you to my editors, Ele Fountain and Isabel Ford, for their magnificent editing, and to my agent, Charlie Viney, for his support and enthusiasm, and Kate Clarke and Blacksheep for the evocative cover. And to Dorit Engelhardt for her generous suggestions, especially on the ins and outs of colloquial German, and also Anna von Hahn, Katinka Nürnberg and Stefan Roszak who ensured my stay in Berlin was a real pleasure.

Thank you also to Jenny and Josie Dowswell, Dilys Dowswell, who kindly read my first drafts, Mrs Julie Rose and the pupils of St Peter's Collegiate School, Wolverhampton, Jane Chisholm, Karin Altenberg, Anne Foster and Adam Guy.

Thanks are also due to Kaspar Nürnberg at the Aktives Museum Faschismus und Widerstand in Berlin, and to the staff of the Imperial War Museum, London, the Wiener Library, London, the Topographie Des Terrors Bibliothek, Berlin, and the Gedenkstätte Deutscher Widerstand, Berlin, for their valuable help.